PgMP® Exam
Practice Test & Study Guide
Third Edition

PgMP® Exam
Practice Test & Study Guide
Third Edition

Ginger Levin, PMP, PgMP
J. LeRoy Ward, PMP, PgMP

CRC Press
Taylor & Francis Group
Boca Raton London New York

CRC Press is an imprint of the
Taylor & Francis Group, an **informa** business
AN AUERBACH BOOK

CRC Press
Taylor & Francis Group
6000 Broken Sound Parkway NW, Suite 300
Boca Raton, FL 33487-2742

© 2012 by Taylor & Francis Group, LLC
CRC Press is an imprint of Taylor & Francis Group, an Informa business

No claim to original U.S. Government works

Printed in the United States of America on acid-free paper
Version Date: 20111216

International Standard Book Number: 978-1-4665-1362-4 (Paperback)

Visit the Taylor & Francis Web site at
http://www.taylorandfrancis.com

and the CRC Press Web site at
http://www.crcpress.com

Contents

Preface

Based on our experience in helping people to prepare for the PMP® Exam, we know that you will have questions, such as "What topics are covered on the exam?" and "What are the questions like?" Not surprisingly, some of the most sought-after study aids are practice tests, which are helpful in two ways (1) taking practice tests increases your knowledge of the kinds of questions, phrases, terminology, and sentence construction that you will encounter on the real exam; and (2) taking practice tests provides an opportunity for highly concentrated study by exposing you to a breadth of program management content generally not found in a single reference source.

We developed this specialty publication with one simple goal in mind—that is, to help you study for and pass the PgMP® certification exam. Because the Project Management Institute (PMI®) does not sell past exams for prospective certification purposes, the best option is to develop practice test questions that are as representative as possible. And that is exactly what we have done.

This guide contains study hints, a list of exam topics, and multiple-choice questions for each of the five domains covered in the PgMP® exam, according to the *Program Management Professional (PgMP®) Examination Content Outline (April 2011)*. We have prepared 20 practice questions in each of these five domains. For the Program Life Cycle domain, we have prepared 20 questions for each of the five phases in the life cycle. We have also included two 170-question representative practice tests.

As we have done in our other *PgMP® Exam Practice Test & Study Guide books*, we have included a plainly written rationale for each correct answer along with a supporting reference list. References are provided at the end of this study guide for the five domains covered in the exam: Strategic Program Management, Program Life Cycle, Benefits Management, Stakeholder Management, and Governance.

"PMP" is a certification mark of the Project Management Institute, Inc., which is registered in the United States and other nations.

"PgMP" is a certification mark of the Project Management Institute, Inc., which is registered in the United States and other nations.

"PMI" is a service trademark of the Project Management Institute, Inc., which is registered in the United States and other nations.

The questions are scenario based, as those on the PgMP® exam. While some are definition questions, they are based on a scenario.

For those who speak English as a second language (ESL), our experience in presenting program and project management courses around the world has shown that most of our ESL clients understand English well enough to pass the PgMP® exam *as long as they know the content.* Nevertheless, in an effort to avoid adding to your frustration before taking the exam, we have painstakingly reviewed each question and answer in the practice tests to ensure that we did not use words, terms, or phrases that could be confusing to people who are not fluent in English. Although the language issue may concern you, and rightfully so, the only difference between you and those who speak English as their first language is the amount of time it takes to complete the exam. If you can grasp the content expressed in this publication, then we believe that a few colloquialisms or ambiguous terms on the real exam ultimately will not determine whether you pass or fail. Your subject matter knowledge will do that.

Earning the PgMP® certification is a prestigious accomplishment, but studying for it should not be difficult if you use the tools available.

Good luck on the exam!

Dr. Ginger Levin, PMP, PgMP
Lighthouse Point, Florida

J. LeRoy Ward, PMP, PgMP
New York, New York

Acknowledgments

We want to acknowledge the efforts of our publisher, CRC Press, and especially that of Mr. John Wyzalek. Randy Burling, Joselyn Banks-Kyle, and the entire CRC team who worked tirelessly to publish this book so it would be available according to the release of the new PgMP® exam from PMI®.

Introduction

The Program Management Professional (PgMP®) Exam Practice Test & Study Guide includes five sections, each of which corresponds to one of the five domains described in the *Program Management Professional (PgMP®) Examination Content Outline* (April 2011). Each section contains study hints, a list of major topics that are encountered on the exam, and 20 multiple-choice practice questions complete with an answer sheet, an answer key that includes a rationale for each correct answer, and a bibliographic reference for further study if needed. The Program Management domain is broken into five sections corresponding to the five phases in the program life cycle as described in the *Examination Content Outline*. Given the large number of questions in this domain, we have 20 multiple-choice practice test questions for each of these five sections.

We have also included two complete practice tests, each consisting of 170 questions*, that follow the blueprint of the real PgMP® exam as described in the *Examination Content Outline*. For example:

- 15 percent of the questions relate to strategic program management
- 44 percent relate to the program life cycle as subdivided as follows:
  - 6% of the questions involve initiating
  - 11% of the questions involve planning
  - 14% of the questions involve executing
  - 10% of the questions involve controlling
  - 3% of the questions involve closing
- 11 percent relate to benefit management
- 16 percent relate to stakeholder management
- 14 percent relate to governance

To use this study guide effectively, work on one section at a time. It does not matter which section you choose first, but we recommend that you answer the

---

* Of the 170 questions on the real PgMP® certification exam, 20 are pretest questions and do not count for scoring purposes. When taking the real exam, you will not know which 20 are the unscored pretest questions, so you will need to answer each question as if it were one of the 150 to be scored. For the practice test in this publication, we provide all 170 questions as if they were real questions; there are no pretest questions in our practice exams, and the blueprint is applied to all 170 questions.

questions in the order presented, because this order reflects the *Examination Content Outline*. Start by reading the study hints, which provide useful background on the content of the PgMP® exam and identify the emphasis placed on various topics. Familiarize yourself with the major topics listed. Then, answer the practice questions that follow, recording your answers on the answer sheet provided. Finally, compare your answers to those in the answer key. The rationales provided should clarify any misconceptions. For further study and clarification, consult the bibliographic reference.

After you have finished answering the questions that follow each section, it is time to take the practice tests. We have developed scenario questions for each practice test. Note your answers on the sheets provided, compare your answers to the answer key, and use your results to determine what areas you need to study further*.

To make the most of this specialty publication, use it regularly. The tips listed below will help you to get the most out of your preparation for the PgMP® exam:

- Take and retake the practice tests. Photocopy the answer sheets so that you have a clean one to use each time you retake the practice tests.
- Consider convening a study group to compare and discuss your answers with those of your colleagues. This method of study is a powerful one. You will learn more from your colleagues than you ever thought possible.
- Make sure that you have a solid understanding of the exam topics provided in each section.
- Consult our bibliography, or other sources that you have found useful, for further independent study.
- Most importantly, create a study plan and stick to it. Your chances of success increase dramatically when you set a goal and dedicate yourself to meeting it.

To further enhance your study, the two practice tests are available on-line at http://www.ittoday.info/pgmp/examhome.html. Either in this book or on the web, the practice tests are an essential study tool created with one goal in mind: helping you to pass your exam and become PgMP® certified.

---

* PMI® grades the PgMP® exam by assigning each question a degree-of-difficulty factor (which is not know to you) and a certain number of points that will be awarded if it is answered correctly. When you answer a question correctly, the value of that correct answer may, and probably will, be different from the value of other questions because of this "factor." To pass the real PgMP® Certification Exam, a candidate must earn a total score equal to or higher than the "cut score" of 325. We do not have a degree-of-difficulty number for the questions in our practice tests. However, we have written every question as if it had the higher degree of difficulty. We believe that if you can correctly answer at least 90 percent of the questions on these practice tests, then you should be prepared to pass the real PgMP® Certification Exam.

About the Authors

Dr. Ginger Levin is a senior consultant and educator in portfolio, program and project management with more than 40 years' experience in the public and private sectors. Her specialty areas include program management, business development, maturity assessments, metrics, organizational change, knowledge management, and the project management office. She is active in providing training to others as they study for their PgMPs®. She is an Adjunct Professor for the University of Wisconsin-Platteville in its master's degree program in project management and at SKEMA, France and RMIT University in Melbourne, Australia in their doctoral programs in project management. Before her consulting and teaching career, she was President of GLH, Incorporated, a woman-owned small business in the Washigton, DC area for 15 years, specializing in project management. Earlier, she had a career in the U.S. Government, working for six agencies in positions of increasing responsibility for 14 years.

Dr. Levin is the author of *Interpersonal Skills for Portfolio, Program, and Project Managers* and the coauthor of *Program Management Complexity: A Competency Model, Implementing Program Management: Templates and Forms Aligned with the Standard for Program Management*—Second Edition (2008); *Project Portfolio Management; Metrics for Project Management; Essential People Skills for Project Managers; Achieving Project Management Success Using Virtual Teams; The Advanced Project Management Office: A Comprehensive Look at Function and Implementation; People Skills for Project Managers; Business Development Capability Maturity Model;* and ESI International's *PMP® Challenge!* She was a major contributor to ESI's *PMP® Study Guide.*

Dr. Levin is a member of the Project Management Institute (PMI®) and a frequent speaker at PMI® Congresses and Chapters and the International Project Management Association. She is certified by PMI® as a Project Management Professional (PMP®), and a Program Management Professional (PgMP®), and she was the second person in the world to earn the PgMP® designation. She is also certified as an Organizational Project Management Maturity Model (OPM3®) Professional.

"*OPM3*" is a trademark of the Project Management Institute, Inc., which is registered in the United States and other nations.

Dr. Levin holds a doctorate in public administration from The George Washington University, where she also received the Outstanding Dissertation Award for her research on large organizations. She also holds a master of science in business administration from The George Washington University and a bachelor of business administration from Wake Forest University.

J. LeRoy Ward, ESI Executive Vice President, Product Strategy and Management, is responsible for ESI's worldwide product offerings and international partnerships. His 17-year career with four U.S. federal agencies has served to complement Mr. Ward's delivery of project management programs to clients around the world.

Mr. Ward has authored numerous articles and publications, including *Project Management Terms: A Working Glossary*; with Ginger Levin, *Program Management Complexity: A Competency Model, PgMP® Exam Practice Test and Study Guide, PMP® Exam Challenge!* and, with Carl Pritchard, *The Portable PMP® Prep: Conversations on Passing the PMP® Exam*, a nine-disc audio CD set.

A dynamic and popular speaker, Mr. Ward frequently presents on program and project management and related topics at professional association meetings and conferences worldwide. Since 1991, he has worked to provide the most comprehensive guidance to project management professionals, helping them to pass the PMP® Exam.

Mr. Ward holds bachelor of science and master of science degrees from Southern Connecticut State University and a master of science degree in technology management, with distinction, from The American University. He is a member of numerous professional associations, including the International Project Management Association, the American Society of Training and Development, and the Project Management Institute (PMI®). He is certified by PMI® as a Project Management Professional (PMP® No. 431) and as a Program Management Professional (PgMP®), and he was one of the first to earn the PgMP® designation.

List of Acronyms

AC: actual cost

ANCI: Annual net cash inflows

BAC: budget at completion

CEO: chief executive officer

CFO: chief financial officer

CIO: chief information officer

CMMI: Capability maturity model integration

COBOL: Common Oriented Business Language

CPI: cost performance index

CV: cost variance

EMEA: Europe, Middle East and Africa

EPMO: enterprise program management office

ESL: English as a second language

ETC: estimate to complete

EV: earned value

GAAP: Generally Accepted Accounting Principles

HVAC: heating, ventilating, and air conditioning

IP: intellectual property

IRR: internal rate of return

ISO: International Organization for Standardization

IT: information technology

KPI: key performance indicator

M&A: mergers and acquisitions

NPV: net present value

OBS: organizational breakdown structure

***OPM3*®:** Organizational Project Management Maturity Model

PDA: Personal Digital Assistant

PERT: Program Evaluation and Review Technique

PgMP®: Program Management Professional

PMBOK*® *Guide: *A Guide to the Project Management Body of Knowledge*

PMI®: Project Management Institute

PMIS: program management information system

PMO: program management office

PMP®: Project Management Professional

PPM: project portfolio management

PV: planned value

PWBS: program work breakdown structure

R&M: reliability and maintainability

RACI: responsible, accountable, consulted, informed

RFI: Request for Information

RFP: Request for Proposal

RFQ: Request for Quotation

ROI: return on investment

SMART: specific, measurable, actual, reliable and time-based

SME: subject matter expert

SPC: statistical process control

SPI: schedule performance index

SV: schedule variance

SWOT: strengths-weaknesses-opportunities-threats

VOC: Voice of the customer

WBS: work breakdown structure

Strategic Program Management

Study Hints

The Strategic Program Management* questions on the PgMP® certification exam, which constitute 15% of the exam or 25 questions.

These questions do not relate to any of the domains or process groups within the *Standard for Program Management—Second Edition*; however, this area is referred to often within processes to ensure that the program initially supports and continues to support the organization's overall strategic goals and objectives.

Before the program is chartered, this area is important to make sure the program should be pursued in the organization. Therefore, time and attention are needed to perform an initial assessment of the program by defining its objectives and requirements to make sure they are in alignment with the organization's goals and objective. A high-level roadmap or timeline for the program also should be part of its business case before the program is officially approved. The program's business case should show a mission statement to describe why the program is important. Also, it requires justification for the funds that will be required. Exam questions will emphasize key parts of the program's business case.

Before the program is approved, the sponsor must identify key stakeholders who will be involved in and/or affected by the program and consult with them to make sure the program is one that supports organizational objectives, is feasible, is in line with the organization's priorities as stated in its portfolio, and is aligned with the organization's strategic plan. Exam questions will focus on key stakeholders and how to best ensure their support for the program.

Specific benefits for the program also should be part of the business case and are part of this domain even though benefits management is another domain in the exam. Benefits are the outcomes of the program and in identifying them,

---

* Please note that Strategic Program Management is not one of the Program Management Process Groups described in *The Standard for Program Management*, 2nd edition (hereafter referred to as *The Standard*); however, it is one of the five domains in the *Examination Content Outline* (2011) that makes up the exam. Nonetheless, a wealth of information from *The Standard* appears in the questions in this part of the exam.

a cost-benefit analysis, market analysis, and other research should be conducted. By doing so, a high-level scope statement can be prepared along with a high-level benefits realization plan. It is important to keep in mind that programs are established because through a program greater benefits can be delivered than if the projects in the program were managed in a standalone fashion. A benefit means an improvement to the running of the organization, and benefits can be either tangible ones, which can be quantified, or intangible ones, which are qualitative and more difficult to measure. Both types of benefits should be documented and included in the program's business case.

As well, there are more constraints when managing a program than a project, and these constraints such as regulations, standards, sustainability, cultural considerations, geographical considerations, politics, and ethical concerns must be considered before a program is approved. Questions will focus on the impact of the various constraints that will affect the program to help decision makers decide whether or not to approve it.

Strategic program management also involves evaluating integration opportunities, which means considering resource requirements, facilities, finances, assets, processes, and systems in the various program activities, including the non-project work, so they are aligned and integrated across the organization.

Once the program is approved, then the initiation process begins.

This area covers a substantial volume of material, especially since it is not discussed as a separate chapter within the *Standard for Program Management*. However, in the Standard, many of the items in this domain are in the Pre-Program Preparations Phase. You should study the contents regarding this phase in the Standard but recognize now it contain a far broader treatment.

Following is a list of the major topics in the Strategic Program Management domain. Use this list to focus your study efforts on the areas that are most likely to appear on the exam.

Major Topics

Project, program, and portfolio definitions
Program management definition
Relationships between—

- Program management and portfolio management
- Program management and project management

Program factors

- Organizational process assets
- Enterprise environmental factors
- Enterprise external factors

Program management as part of organizational planning

- Aligning with organizational goals and objectives
- Ensuring the best mix of project investments
- Ensuring the best use of resources

Initial program assessment

- Defining objectives
- Identifying requirements
- Identifying risks
- Establishing a high-level roadmap
- Defining a program vision statement
- Defining a program mission statement
- Assessing business/organizational objectives
- Performing scenario analysis
- Performing strategic planning and analysis

Pre-Program preparations phase

- Phase objectives
- Key activities
- Strategic benefits of the program
- Plan to initiate the program
- Objectives and alignment with organizational goals
- High-level business case
- Program checkpoints
- Organizational change management
- Approval for program initiation

- Identification of the program sponsor
- Stakeholders at this stage

Benefits management and strategic program management

- Benefits identification
- Research methods to identify benefits
- Market analyses
- High-level cost/benefit analysis
- Initiation benefit realization plan

Program selection and approval

- Available resource requirements
- Fit with the organization's strategic goals
- Benefits analysis (tangible and intangible benefits)
- Program risks
- Financial analysis indicators
- Organizational environment
- Program dependencies
- Cost-benefit analysis
- Integration opportunities
- Milestone schedule
- Stakeholder alignment
- Vision and mission
- Program deliverability
- Feasibility

Constraints and program objectives

- Regulatory and legal
- Social impacts
- Sustainability
- Cultural considerations
- Political climate
- Ethical
- Intellectual property laws and issues

Existing organizational work
Existing components
Financial environment

- Type of program
- Funding models

- Funding goals
- Funding process
- Financial analysis
- Funding methods
- Financial benefits
- Financial integration opportunities
- Funding authorization

Practice Questions

INSTRUCTIONS: Note the most suitable answer for each multiple-choice question in the appropriate space on the answer sheet.

1. Assume you are working for an organization, ABC, which has about 500 people in it. Recently, your executives attended a one-day training program that presented an overview of portfolio, program, and project management. When the CEO, CFO, and CIO returned from this session, you were tasked to provide a list of all of the projects under way in the organization for their review. You had received your PgMP®, based on your work in a previous organization (XYX), and also your PMP®. Two other people in ABC have PMPs®, but you are the only person certified as a program manager. When you reviewed all the projects before giving the list to the executive team, you recommended to them that some of the multiple projects under way be managed as a program. This is because—

   a. Deliverables are independent
   b. A collective capability is delivered
   c. Resource constraints affect projects
   d. Risk planning activities are comparable

2. You met with the members of the Executive team in your company ABC. They were impressed with your knowledge of program management, and since they had attended the one-day seminar, they told you they wanted to make sure every project under way, and also every program they set up, supported the organization's strategic goals. You explained in your previous company, XYZ, that programs were set up because they could link projects in various ways, one of which is when—

   a. Changes in organizational direction affect project work and relationships to other projects
   b. Independent benefits among the projects are detailed in the benefits measurement plan
   c. Different clients, suppliers, and technologies are included in the project
   d. Discrete pacing of the projects affects the program

3. When you worked previously in company XYZ, considered to be one of the first organizations to set itself up as one that is project based and also considered projects and programs to be strategic assets to the organization, you pointed out to the executives in your current company, ABC, as they are beginning this initiative now to manage multiple, related projects as a program that in terms of the relationship between ABC's organization, and the program, programs are part of the—

    a. Mobilization process
    b. Strategic objectives
    c. Strategic options
    d. Portfolio

4. However, as ABC moves to set up programs, this means it will be a major culture change in the organization as the people are more used to working on projects. The Executive Team learned at its one-day seminar that each program must have a defined list of its expected outcomes and resulting benefits, and a focus on benefit management is necessary for effective program management. Benefit management will be a new change for ABC as no one has identified benefits from projects in the past. Since each program has this emphasis on outcomes to be expected and benefits to be realized, it is best accomplished through—

    a. The Program Governance Board
    b. The program sponsor
    c. Portfolio management
    d. The customer

5. You are one of many project managers working on the new plasma screen development program. Your project has not yet started, but the program manager is anxious to have it begin because the program is running behind schedule. But before you can receive the go-ahead to start, it is necessary to—

    a. Create a schedule
    b. Define the expected benefits in the business case
    c. Consult with key stakeholders to understand their requirements
    d. Conduct a kickoff meeting to gather lessons learned from previous projects

6. Assume you are the program sponsor for this new program on the new plasma screen development to replace all existing LCD screens and enhance plasma's screens so they can be viewed in 4-D. Before you received approval for this program, you performed an initial program assessment. You wanted to define your program's objectives, requirements, and risks. Focusing on requirements, you decided one way to proceed in order to make sure your stakeholders were involved in this process from the start and also to gain their support for this program was to—

   a. Use focus groups
   b. Consult with experts for suggestions based on work on previous programs
   c. Conduct a customer acceptance review
   d. Define a high-level program roadmap

7. Assume you are working in a Fortune 500 company. Recently, your company hired an outside *OPM3® Certified Professional* to conduct an Organizational Project Management Maturity Assessment of its program management practices in terms of the standardize, measure, control, and continuous improvement areas. As the company has been working in program management for some time and has a defined methodology in place that is regularly followed, you were not surprised that it scored extremely high in terms of the number of Best Practices from this assessment. As part of your company's program management methodology, there is a formal selection process in place. This is characteristic of an organization that—

   a. Has a program governance structure
   b. Has a program management office (PMO)
   c. Has a project and program management career path
   d. Is more mature in program management

8. As you work to prepare the business case for the new plasma screen program, you recognize it is essential to identify potential benefits that will accrue from establishing this program. You have assembled a team of stakeholders and plan to interview them for their opinions on the possible benefits, both tangible and intangible. Your goal is to present to your selection committee in your business case specific, measurable benefits that you believe can be delivered and controlled. You also want the people who will be involved in your program to recognize these benefits and their importance. Therefore, it is important that you make sure that once approval is received that—

   a. You meet regularly with stakeholders to keep them informed about the progress of your program
   b. Your benefit realization plan is integrated with your program management plan
   c. Every member of your team participates in the development of the benefits realization plan and signs off on it
   d. All the intangible benefits you identified are now quantified

9. You are preparing the business case to obtain organizational leadership approval for a new program to implement a company-wide customer relationship management system to better manage sales activities and leads. You have been meeting with many people as you work to prepare this business case, and already you have heard a lot of the more than 600 salespeople in your company object to it. They are becoming negative stakeholders even before your program begins because they view your proposed program as one in which will radically change how they are doing business. But, you believe, as do some other executives, that such a new program is a change that is critical to your company's future success. Your business plan therefore should clearly address—

   a. The technical feasibility of the project
   b. The strategic nature of the program to the company
   c. How generally accepted methods of change management will be used
   d. How the return on investment will be calculated to demonstrate success

10. Assume you are working for the Motor Carrier Safety Administration in your government, responsible for the regulation of motor carriers in your country. You are a senior executive in this Administration, and you are getting ready for a meeting with the Administrator of the Agency and the other senior executives to review new programs and projects for the next budget cycle to be part of the overall portfolio. You have suggested that a program be established to consolidate various projects that require overhaul of existing regulations to ensure there is greater competition in the industry and also improved safety to the public. The public is a major stakeholder in this program and will be the major beneficiary if this program is selected. As you work on this business case for the upcoming meeting, recognizing the importance of the public as the key stakeholder, you need to evaluate a number of key constraints to ensure alignment of all stakeholders and program deliverability. This means you need to consider—

    a. Resource assumptions
    b. Cost/benefit analysis
    c. Sustainability
    d. Readiness

11. Realizing that before you meet with the Agency Administrator and the other members of the senior staff that funding is limited especially with your President's mandate to reduce spending at the federal government level by 50%, that you need to estimate the high-level financial benefits of your regulatory overhaul program to ensure it receives approval from your Agency Administrator and the other senior leaders. You also know it is extremely rare to obtain complete funding for any program from the beginning, but your Agency will manage the program. You must consider a variety of funding models as you prepare this analysis such as—

    a. Whether funds can be obtained from the Department of Transportation, to which your agency reports
    b. Trends in resource availability including the use of contractors to do this work
    c. Net present value
    d. Internal rate of return

12. You are a member of your organization's Product Portfolio Committee. The head of your enterprise program management office (EPMO) recommends that a program be undertaken to develop a series of products for the next-generation automobile to be run using helium. In deciding whether or not to approve this program, of the following, which one is the most important for your committee to consider—

    a. Proposed schedule
    b. Benefits
    c. Feasibility studies
    d. Key resources

13. You are a member of your organization's Product Portfolio Committee. The head of your enterprise program management office (EPMO) recommends that a program be undertaken to develop a series of products for the next-generation automobile to be run using helium. In deciding whether to approve this program, the second most important consideration of your committee is the—

    a. Proposed schedule
    b. Benefits
    c. Feasibility studies
    d. Key resources

14. You are a functional manager in your organization, the head of the Department of Engineering, and a member of the Selection Committee for new programs. At the committee meetings, you review potential programs. One key factor that you consider as to whether to approve the program is the—

    a. Who will be the program manager?
    b. What is the preliminary budget estimate?
    c. What is the source of program funding?
    d. What are the next steps to get the program started?

15. As a result of all of your hard work and diligence to get your program started, and based on the business case that you developed, you have received approval form your Portfolio Review Board, which consists of your organization's senior leaders, to proceed. The Board authorized you to initiate your program. However, you now need to—

    a. Define program alignment with the strategic plan
    b. Define your program mission statement
    c. Establish a high-level road map
    d. Identify and evaluate integration opportunities and needs

16. You are on the program planning team to develop a program for the next generation of drugs to combat joint disease. The executive sponsor has asked that you prepare market research and feasibility analysis to help determine the viability of the program. As part of the business case, this research is necessary to—

    a. Justify the program
    b. Proceed with benefit analysis and planning
    c. Issue the program charter
    d. Establish the governance board

17. Assume you are a member of your agency's Program Selection Committee, and the Committee has just met to determine which programs and projects it should pursue. Your program to develop the next generation Air Force radar system was approved. Since you now have the authorization to proceed, your committee then has to—

    a. Develop a program budget
    b. Identify and receive the key resources needed for planning
    c. Establish the rules for subcontractor selection
    d. Identify the feasibility studies that need to be conducted

18. As you worked to obtain approval for this Air Force radar program, you realized the necessity of benefits management as part of program management. You realize it is challenging to determine benefits, especially to somehow quantify the qualitative benefits, and you also decided to contact some key stakeholders as you were preparing your business case to define a preliminary benefits realization plan as part of it. Before you obtained official approval, benefits management begins with—

    a. Benefits planning
    b. Benefits identification
    c. Benefits analysis
    d. Benefits management development

19. You are a member of your insurance company's Program Selection Committee. You are considering a number of programs to pursue. Each has identified benefits that support your company's overall strategic plan, but you need to select the one with the shortest payback period. Program A is estimated to cost $100,000 to implement and have annual net cash inflows of $25,000; Program B is estimated to cost $75,000 with inflows of $20,000; Program C is estimated to cost $225,000 with inflows of $80,000; and Program D is estimated to cost $275,000 with inflows of $90,000. You recommend that your company select—

Program a NPV at	Program B NPV at	Program C NPV at	Program D NPV at
5% = $2,399	5% = $2,105	5% = $6,400	5% = $4,065
10% = $3,112	10% = $1,254	10% = $3,275	10% = $1,852
15% = $1,402	15% = $1,001	15% = $1,679	15% = $925

NPV = Net Present Value

    a. Program A
    b. Program B
    c. Program C
    d. Program D

20. You are a member of your manufacturing company's Program Selection Committee. You are considering a number of possible programs to pursue. Each has identified benefits that support your company's overall strategic plan. Data are available on four possible programs, but you can select only one because of resource limitations.

Program A IRR	Program B IRR	Program C IRR	Program D IRR
42%	40%	36%	33%

IRR = Internal Rate of Return

Based on this information, you recommend that your company select—

a. Program A
b. Program B
c. Program C
d. Program D

Answer Sheet

1.	a	b	c	d

2.	a	b	c	d

3.	a	b	c	d

4.	a	b	c	d

5.	a	b	c	d

6.	a	b	c	d

7.	a	b	c	d

8.	a	b	c	d

9.	a	b	c	d

10.	a	b	c	d

11.	a	b	c	d

12.	a	b	c	d

13.	a	b	c	d

14.	a	b	c	d

15.	a	b	c	d

16.	a	b	c	d

17.	a	b	c	d

18.	a	b	c	d

19.	a	b	c	d

20.	a	b	c	d

Answer Key

1. b. A collective capability is delivered

   The outcomes of the individual projects included in a program combine to deliver a collective capability to the organization.

   Project Management Institute. *The Standard for Program Management,* 2008, 6

2. a. Changes in organizational direction affect project work and relationships to other projects

   Projects and programs must support the organization's vision, mission, and values. A change in organizational direction may link projects within a program, because it affects ongoing work and relationships among projects.

   PMI®, *The Standard for Program Management,* 2008, 6

3. d. Portfolio

   Organizations address the need for change by creating strategic business initiatives, which are executed in the form of projects or programs that constitute the organization's portfolio. Programs and projects are part of the organization's portfolio, which is composed of a set of current initiatives.

   PMI®, *The Standard for Program Management,* 2008, 6–7 and 10

4. c. Portfolio management

   The program receives extensive inputs, especially in the early phases, from portfolio management. These inputs may include strategic goals and benefits, funding allocations, requirements, timelines constraints, and assumptions.

   PMI®, *The Standard for Program Management,* 2008, 9

5. b. Define the expected benefits in the business case

   Each project has certain benefits associated with it. The expected benefits are defined in the project business case before the project is initiated.

   PMI®, *The Standard for Program Management,* 2008, 257

6. a. Use focus groups

   Focus groups are used in requirements analysis to assemble a group of people and ask questions about their attitudes to the product, service, and concepts. Requirements analysis techniques are required in strategic program management as an initial assessment of requirements helps ensure from the start that the program is aligned with the organization's strategic plan, objectives, priorities, vision, and mission statements

   PMI®, *The Standard for Program Management*, 2008, 108, and 111

   PMI. *Program Management Professional* (PgMP)® *Examination Content Outline*, April 2011 6

7. d. Is more mature in program management

   In organizations that are mature in program management, there typically exists a mechanism to select programs for execution. Signs of maturity can include a governance structure, a career path for program management, and a program management office (PMO).

   PMI®, *The Standard for Program Management*, 2008, 23

   PMI. *Program Management Professional* (PgMP)® *Examination Content Outline*, April 2011 6–7

   David Williams and Tim Parr, *Enterprise Program Management Delivering Value*. New York: Palgrave Macmillan, 2006, 171

8. b. Your benefit realization plan is integrated with the program management plan

   A benefits plan that is not integrated with the program management plan is a common pitfall; they must be aligned, and a dynamic process with benefit reporting should be incorporated with program reporting. This integrated program management plan then provides visibility and ownership at the sponsor level and at the delivery level

   PMI®, *The Standard for Program Management*, 2008, 23, 31, and 109

9. b. The strategic nature of the program to the company

   During the Pre-Program Preparations phase and in Strategic Program Management, programs are initiated to achieve the organization's strategic objectives.

   PMI®, *The Standard for Program Management*, 2008, 23

10. c. Sustainability

    There are a number of constraints in strategic program management. Sustainability is critical as the benefits from the program should be ones that remain over time. Other constraints include regulatory and legal, social impacts, cultural considerations, the political climate, and ethical concerns.

    PMI®, *The Standard for Program Management*, 2008, 31–32

    PMI. *Program Management Professional* (PgMP)® *Examination Content Outline*, April 2011 6

11. a. Whether funds can be obtained from the Department of Transportation, to which your agency reports

    Funding models range from those being funded within a single organization, those managed within a single organization but funded separately, or those entirely funded and managed from outside the parent organization.

    PMI®, *The Standard for Program Management*, 2008, 210

    PMI. *Program Management Professional* (PgMP)® *Examination Content Outline*, April 2011 6

12. b. Benefits

    Program selection criteria and materials may range from vague and informal to detailed, specific, and formal. Strategic objectives and expected benefits are the key selection criteria.

    PMI®, *The Standard for Program Management*, 2008, 23

13. d. Key resources

    In considering whether to select or approve a program, it is essential to consider whether or not the key resources are available especially with resource capacity issues so critical in organizations.

    PMI®, *The Standard for Program Management*, 2008, 23

14. b. What is the preliminary budget estimate?

    Each program proposed for selection should include a preliminary budget estimate. As part of the high-level business plan, the estimate should be as detailed as possible at this stage. Although it is a conceptual estimate, it is a key factor in program selection in strategic program management.

    PMI®, *The Standard for Program Management*, 2008, 24

    PMI. *Program Management Professional* (PgMP)® *Examination Content Outline*, April 2011 6

15. d. Identify and evaluate integration opportunities and needs

In Strategic Program Management, it is essential to identify and evaluation integration opportunities and needs such as human capital and human resource requirements. It is also important to identify skill sets, facilities, finance, assets, processes, and systems within the program activities and operational activities in order to align and integrate program benefits within and across the organization.

PMI®, *The Standard for Program Management*, 2008, 22–23

PMI. *Program Management Professional* (PgMP)® *Examination Content Outline*, April 2011 6–7

16. b. Justify the program

Programs must be justified using a valid business case that identifies the needs to be satisfied and the benefits to be gained as a result of committing resources to its attainment. This is one of the tasks in Strategic Program Management.

PMI®, *The Standard for Program Management*, 2008, 22

PMI. *Program Management Professional* (PgMP)® *Examination Content Outline*, April 2011 6–7

17. b. Identify and receive commitment of key resources needed for planning

Once the organizational leadership has approved the program, it then is necessary to identify and evaluate integration opportunities and needs. This identification includes human capital and human resource requirements as resources will be needed in initiating the program and for planning it. The people who will plan the program will not necessarily end up on the core program team.

PMI®, *The Standard for Program Management*, 2008, 23

PMI. *Program Management Professional* (PgMP)® *Examination Content Outline*, April 2011 6

18. b Benefits identification

Benefits management directs business change. As a program manager, you identify and qualify the business benefits before you implement the program.

PMI®, *The Standard for Program Management*, 2008, 20

David Williams and Tim Parr, *Enterprise Program Management Delivering Value*, New York: Palgrave Macmillan, 2006, 169

19. c. Program C

     In using net present value (NPV) as a selection criterion, a dollar one year from now is worth less than a dollar today. The more the future is discounted (higher discount rate), the less the NPV of the program. If the NPV is high, then the program is rated high. In this situation, you would select Program C.

     PMI. *Program Management Professional* (PgMP)® *Examination Content Outline*, April 2011 6–7

     Dragan Z. Milosevic. *Project Management ToolBox: Tools and Techniques for the Practicing Project Manager*. Hoboken, NJ: John Wiley & Sons, Inc., 2003, 42–44

20. a. Program A.

     The Internal Rate of Return (IRR) is the discount rate where the NPV for the cash flow is zero. There is no closed-form formula for it. IRR is computed iteratively, and "hone's in" on the exact discount rate that produces a NPV of zero. Most spreadsheet software can calculate it. Given the data in this question, Program A is superior to the others. While the IRR discounts future values, it does not consider the size of a program.

     PMI. *Program Management Professional* (PgMP)® *Examination Content Outline*, April 2011 6–7

     Dragan Z. Milosevic. *Project Management ToolBox: Tools and Techniques for the Practicing Project Manager*. Hoboken, NJ: John Wiley & Sons, Inc., 2003, 44–45

Initiating the Program

Study Hints

PMI in the *PgMP® Examination Content Outline* has established a Program Life Cycle consisting of:

- Initiating
- Planning
- Executing
- Controlling
- Closing

In this life cycle, Initiating represents 6% of the questions or 10 questions on the exam.

We have elected to provide 20 questions for you for practice in the book, and the sample 170-question exams will contain 10 questions.

The questions on the exam concentrate on additional methods to gain greater support and approval for the program. They focus on the need to ensure that the program's values and objectives are aligned with those of the organization as documented in the program mandate. The primary output is the program charter, which often contains the vision statement and is used to authorize the program and commence planning. Other key outputs are the program road map and the program financial framework.

You should be familiar with the two processes in the Initiating Process Group, Initiate Program and Establish Program Financial Framework, which are in Figure 3-2 of *The Standard* (p. 43). For each of these processes, think about their purpose, its inputs, its tools and techniques, and its outputs. Program funding and resources are required to support the activities involved in Initiating the Program.

Questions may address the roles and responsibilities of the program manager and the core team as well as possible program organizational structures. The program sponsor and the program manager are identified as outputs of the

Initiate Program process. You should be familiar with results from this phase of the life cycle.

Other questions may address a high-level program scope statement that then sets the stage for a more detailed scope statement in the planning phase of the life cycle. As well, questions may involve developing a high-level milestone plan by using the goals and objectives of the program to ensure the program is aligned with stakeholder expectations, especially those of the sponsor. A program resource accountability matrix is another potential area for questions during this phase as roles and responsibilities are identified for the program's core team. The importance of a program kick-off meeting with stakeholders is another area of emphasis.

Following is a list of the major topics covered in Initiating the Program. Use this list to focus your study efforts on the areas that are most likely to appear on the exam.

Major Topics

Initiating Process Group

- ■ Initiate Program
- ■ Establish Program Financial Framework

Key roles

- ■ Assignment of executive sponsor
- ■ Assignment of program manager
- ■ Identification of potential members of the sponsoring group, governance board, or program board
- ■ Identification of key decision makers/stakeholders

Program charter

- ■ Input from stakeholders
- ■ Initiate and design program benefits
- ■ Justification
- ■ Vision
- ■ Strategic fit
- ■ Outcome
- ■ Scope
- ■ Benefit strategy
- ■ Assumptions and constraints
- ■ Risks and issues
- ■ Time line
- ■ Resources needed
- ■ Program governance
- ■ Initial high-level road map
- ■ Measurement criteria for the program and its projects

Stakeholder analysis and negotiating techniques
High-level milestone plan/program road map

- ■ Program goals and objectives
- ■ Historical information
- ■ Preliminary program work breakdown structure
- ■ Align program with stakeholder expectations

Common inputs to and outputs of processes

- ■ Assumptions
- ■ Constraints

- Historical information
- Organizational process assets
- Lessons learned
- Supporting details
- Information requests
- Program management plan updates
- Program status and performance reports

Program financial framework

- Purpose
- Funding source
- Funding goals
- Payment schedules
- Funding methods

Updates to the business case
Resource accountability matrix

- Core team
- Differentiate between program and project resources

Program kickoff meeting with stakeholders

Practice Questions

INSTRUCTIONS: Note the most suitable answer for each multiple-choice question in the appropriate space on the answer sheet.

1. Although your program is part of a portfolio with four other programs and 14 separate projects, it has no direct relationship or interdependencies with any of these other initiatives. However, the success of your program will depend on which two areas for which all these other initiatives are competing?

   a. Physical space and technology assets for team members
   b. Funding and executive sponsorship
   c. Funding and available resources
   d. Available resources and technology assets

2. You have recently joined a corporation that is a leader in the development of products for the automotive industry. You are pleased to be selected as a program manager, because you know that this company has established a culture of management by programs. The company operates within a program management structure, and each program manager is responsible for products in certain years. You are responsible for new products to be developed over the next five years. This means that—

   a. Your core team will remain intact until your products are released
   b. In performing a stakeholder analysis, you need to consider the other program managers
   c. The way the organization is structured means that there is no need to compete for resources
   d. The Program Office will support all the program managers in the company

3. Assume that in your automotive company, you will be appointed as the program manager for the 2016 new line of hybrid cars that only will use gasoline if the vehicle has traveled more than 300 miles. This program is a major change for your company as it has not entered the hybrid market until this past year, and the new line of vehicles is to have an average of 75 miles per gallon. The current hybrid gets 30 miles per gallon. You are going to produce at a minimum five different vehicles: a coupe, a sedan, a luxury SUV, a minivan, and an inexpensive SUV. Finally, your program charter was approved, and you were officially named as the program manager. You were fortunate to work with your sponsor in developing the charter and you also—

   a. Used input from all stakeholders
   b. Relied extensively on historical information
   c. Convened a panel to assist in its preparation using the Delphi technique
   d. Sent a draft of the charter to the proposed members of the Governance Board for their input

4. You are responsible for a program to develop the next-generation cellular phone. The program includes a number of key products and is set up according to the "father-son" model. Because programs are responsible for delivering benefits, you want to ensure that the targeted benefits are measurable. In your benefits management life cycle, you should identify such benefit metrics during the—

a. Benefits identification phase
b. Benefits analysis and planning phase
c. Benefits planning phase
d. Benefits transition phase

5. You are responsible for a program to develop the next-generation cellular phone. The program includes a number of key products and is set up according to the "father-son" model. Because programs are responsible for delivering benefits, you want to ensure that the targeted benefits are measurable. You now are working in the Program Initiation phase; one purpose is to—

a. Establish and staff the infrastructure that the program will use
b. Set up the program control framework for planning, monitoring, and controlling the program
c. Build a high-level road map that provides direction on how the program will be managed
d. Complete the program team staffing

6. You have recently been assigned as the program manager on a global drug development project. You have read and thoroughly understand the program's business case and overall objectives. However, you are curious as to the key program outcomes that are required to achieve the program vision. These outcomes are stated in the—

a. Program mandate
b. Preliminary project scope statement
c. Technical and economic feasibility study
d. Program charter

7. Assume you now have obtained approval of your charter for your program in your automotive company for the development of the new line of hybrid vehicles. This program will be extremely complex given its development of the five vehicles and also the goals and objectives to be met. You realize as well that you are going to have a number of issues and risks to resolve. However, you are pleased you are the program manager and that the charter now has been issued. Your next step is to—

    a. Perform a more detailed analysis of the identified risks in the charter to help in deciding how best to respond to them should they occur

    b. Determine the key benefits to be realized by the program

    c. Describe the program outcomes required to achieve the program's vision

    d. Conduct a program kick off meeting with key stakeholders

8. You are the program manager responsible for building a dam that will provide flood control and generate electricity for millions of residents. The dam will have five turbines generating electricity. The program sponsor, the local provincial government, has only enough money to install three turbines. The income generated from those three turbines will then be used to fund the remaining two turbines. As part of your planning, you estimate that in month 26, Turbine No. 4 will be fully operational, and in month 38, Turbine No. 5 will come online. You and the team document this in the—

    a. Benefits realization plan

    b. Staffing management plan

    c. Benefits analysis phase

    d. Constraints and assumptions plan

9. You are a program manager working for a conference planning company. Your program has been launched as a component of your company's portfolio. Your organization has been in existence for 10 years; therefore, as you prepare your program charter and road map, you should consider the—

    a. Organizational structure

    b. Program management information system

    c. Authority tolerance levels

    d. Program budget baseline

10. Your company, a major dairy cooperative, has embraced portfolio management. In the past, some projects continued indefinitely, even after their sponsors had left the company, and no one could remember why they had been initiated. Now all programs and projects are part of the portfolio, which is where investment decisions are made. In response to a growing consumer demand for organic foods, the company is attempting to capitalize on this demand by entering the organic foods market. You are appointed as program manager. Your program is the result of—

    a. A suggestion by a functional manager in the company
    b. The need to remain competitive with others in the field
    c. A strategic directive
    d. A recommendation from your major customer

11. You have been appointed program manager for a Motor Carrier Safety Administration program to develop new regulations that avoid the need for highway weigh stations yet ensure that weight restrictions are followed. You must complete the program in two years, and the agency must approve the regulations in one year. You have not started the planning process. At this time, your first step is to—

    a. Secure program funding
    b. Assign project managers to each project in the program
    c. Plan the program's TO-BE state
    d. Manage each of your stakeholders

12. You work for a company that produces and distributes catalogs focused on luxury items such as jewelry, home furnishings, clothing, and accessories. In addition to the major undertaking of catalog production, several projects are under way to make the catalogs available online; ease of ordering and faster delivery time are key objectives. Many people in the company support the catalog production initiatives as well as some of the Web-based initiatives. The company should—

    a. Aggressively pursue the Web and discontinue its print production of the catalogs
    b. Set up a program structure for the Web projects and the ongoing catalog production
    c. Appoint a project manager to report directly to the CEO to coordinate activities
    d. Implement critical chain scheduling to avoid potential bottlenecks in resource allocati

13. Your city is in the early stages of determining whether or not it should construct a new shopping mall. Already, there is a major shopping mall at the northern part of the city, but its location is inconvenient for many residents of the city given the extensive traffic. In the southern part of the city, there is a small mall that lacks large department stores. The city is considering a program to develop a mall in the center of the city, and if it is approved, you will be the program manager. You believe approval is basically guaranteed, and you are looking forward to this challenge. Your funding will largely come from—

    a. Retained earnings
    b. Bonds
    c. Equity partners
    d. Payment from future lease income

14. As the portfolio manager for an aerospace and defense contractor, you recommend that programs be initiated when your company decides to bid on contracts. Given the business development process and the need to focus on capture management, the pre-proposal phase may last several years, especially on major government defense projects. As you work to initiate the program, which of the following is critical—

    a. Statement of Work
    b. Contract program work breakdown structure (PWBS)
    c. Program financial framework
    d. Program road map

15. You are working in your city to have a new shopping mall that is centrally located. Your charter is under development, and if it is approved, you will be the program manager. You have not managed a program as complex as this one as in the past, you worked on smaller programs or projects. This program is to have at least seven different projects, and they have been identified so far in the charter. In addition, you realize you may need to add some projects as the program gets under way. Therefore, you plan to include in your charter—

    a. A description of the other projects you believe you should add
    b. The need for a Program Management Office to support this program
    c. Methods you plan to use to procure external resources
    d. A high-level milestone plan

16. Assume you are working for an international training company. It has decided to add several new lines of courses because it tracks its courses now to the Project Management Institute's publications and standards. You will be the program manager for these new courses, and you plan to have a team of people from your international organization located in different countries to support you as you will want to translate each course into at least four other languages and pilot test them in other parts of the world. After your program is initiated, you then will work to authorize the various projects within it. Furthermore, it is important to have a high-level plan for the program's components. This plan is—

    a. Used to start initiating the program
    b. Stated in the Authorize Projects process
    c. Stated as part of the program charter
    d. Set forth in the preliminary program scope statement

17. While fax machines are basically considered to be outdated, a number of people still rely on them for methods to send information, especially if they lack access to scanners and lack high-speed Internet connections. Your company is considering a new line of fax machines as it has specialized in them and wants to make sure fax remains as a way to distribute information. This new line of fax machines would make it easy to send information from one's computer or a tablet to the fax machine and not have to rely on printed documents. The new program would also enable transmission of printed materials but at a far faster speed with immediate confirmation that the recipient received it. As you determine funding methods for your program, you should first consider—

    a. Performing a program financial analysis
    b. Various funding methods
    c. Payment schedules
    d. Program funding source

18. As you prepare your program charter for your new program for your international training company, you have a vision of continuing as the industry leader, and you are anticipating the various other credentials the Project Management Institute may offer in the future. You and several others in your company regularly attend and participate in the various Congresses that are held and are active in a number of the PMI Communities of Practice. However, this is an internal initiative, and funding is a key concern, especially given the economic downturn in your country and the fact that many people do not sign up for the existing courses until the last minute. You are now at the end of the Program Initiation phase of the life cycle. This means which of the following people should be identified by this time?

    a. Program manager and executive sponsor
    b. Program manager and core program team members
    c. Program manager and program management office (PMO) director
    d. Program manager and program control officer

19. Your government agency has been considering adding a new program to its existing portfolio of the development of national parks in your country. You have heard about this possible program through a friend, who is on the agency's Portfolio Review Board. Once you learned about this possible program, you went to others on the Review Board and requested to be the program manager for it. This park is to be located in a state that now does not have a national park, and it is expected to add jobs as it is developed and later maintained plus increase visitors to this state through its development, further increasing revenue. You are pleased you were selected as the program manager, and since then you have been working to develop the program's charter. One reason you were selected early is that during the Initiate Program Process you can—

    a. Authorize the program
    b. Provide expert judgment
    c. Prepare the strategic directive
    d. Guide the initiation process

20. You are one of the core team members developing the program charter for the next generation of medical imaging technology. There is significant market opportunity, but the competition is strong, and the wrong technical approach could set the company back several years. To ensure that the program charter is viable, a best practice is to—

    a. Conduct a SWOT analysis
    b. Conduct an assumptions analysis
    c. Use the nominal group technique
    d. Use an influence diagram

Answer Sheet

1.	a	b	c	d
2.	a	b	c	d
3.	a	b	c	d
4.	a	b	c	d
5.	a	b	c	d
6.	a	b	c	d
7.	a	b	c	d
8.	a	b	c	d
9.	a	b	c	d
10.	a	b	c	d

11.	a	b	c	d
12.	a	b	c	d
13.	a	b	c	d
14.	a	b	c	d
15.	a	b	c	d
16.	a	b	c	d
17.	a	b	c	d
18.	a	b	c	d
19.	a	b	c	d
20.	a	b	c	d

Answer Key

1. c. Funding and available resources

   Programs are often unrelated to other initiatives within a common portfolio; however, all initiatives typically compete for funding and other resources, both of which are finite in most organizations.

   PMI®, *The Standard for Program Management*, 2008, 9

2. b. In performing a stakeholder analysis, you need to consider the other program managers

   Other program managers in an organization should be included in the stakeholder analysis, because they may be competing for limited resources within the organization, or the goals of the various programs may conflict.

   PMI®, *The Standard for Program Management*, 2008, 235

3. a. Used input from all stakeholders

   Stakeholder involvement in the development of the charter helps to gain their support for it and their commitment to the program.

   PMI. *Program Management Professional* (PgMP)® *Examination Content Outline*, April 2011 8

   PMI®, *The Standard for Program Management*, 2008, 24

4. b. Benefits analysis and planning phase

   Benefit metrics are required to keep the expected benefits in line with the original business plan. They are determined during the benefits analysis and planning phase of the program benefits management life cycle or in the Program Initiation phase of the program life cycle. The program architecture is developed to map how the projects in the program will contribute to achieving the required benefits. Metrics are established to assist in this process.

   PMI®, *The Standard for Program Management*, 2008, 20

5. c. Build a high-level road map that provides direction on how the program will be managed

   In the Program Initiation phase, the team continues to develop the foundation for the program by preparing a detailed road map, which describes how the program will be managed and links the program activities to the expected benefits.

   PMI®, *The Standard for Program Management*, 2008, 78

6. d. Program charter

   The program charter provides the basis for program setup. Among other things, the charter defines the vision (or the end state) of the program, describes how the program will benefit the organization, and describes the key program outcomes that are required to achieve the vision.

   PMI®, *The Standard for Program Management*, 2008, 24–25

7. d. Conduct a program kick off meeting with key stakeholders

   A kick-off meeting with the program team is a recommended best practice once the team has been established. However, one is also recommended with the key stakeholders in the initiating phase and is especially important after the charter has been approved to familiarize the organization with the program and continue to obtain stakeholder buy in to it.

   PMI. *Program Management Professional* (PgMP)® *Examination Content Outline*, April 2011 8

   PMI®, *The Standard for Program Management*, 2008, 24

8. a. Benefits realization plan

   Benefits realization planning is part of program initiation as well as in program planning. It includes benefits delivery scheduling and intended interdependencies among the benefits, alignment with the organization's strategic goals, metrics and measurements, benefits delivery responsibility, and benefits realization.

   PMI®, *The Standard for Program Management*, 2008, 31

9. a. Organizational structure

   In programs where the parent organization is established, knowledge of the present structure is important as an input to the Initiate Program process to assess the organization's capacity to apply resources and start the program.

   PMI®, *The Standard for Program Management*, 2008, 76

10. c. A strategic directive

    The strategic directive formally expresses the organization's concept, vision, and mission for the program, the intended benefits, and the program benefits. It is an input to the Initiate Program process.

    PMI®, *The Standard for Program Management*, 2008, 6 and 76

11. a. Secure program funding

    Even though cost and budget estimating are not completed during the Initiate Program process, program funding is required to support the program through the initiation and planning phases.

    PMI®, *The Standard for Program Management*, 2008, 42

12. b. Set up a program structure for the Web projects and the ongoing catalog production

    This program could be set up to include project work for the Web initiatives as well as work on the ongoing activities to focus on benefits delivery from this work.

    PMI®, *The Standard for Program Management*, 2008, 74–75

13. d. Payment from future lease income

    During the Establish Program Financial Framework process, on large capital programs such as shopping malls and commercial space, funding is generally provided by bank loans or future lease income.

    PMI®, *The Standard for Program Management*, 2008, 210

14. d. Program road map

    When programs are initiated as a result of a decision to bid on a contract, an output from the Initiate Program process is the program road map, which shows the chronological representation of the program's intended duration. It is a valuable tool to show the high-level overall scope and execution of the program and serves to bridge program activities and expected benefits.

    PMI®, *The Standard for Program Management*, 2008, 78

15. d. A high-level milestone plan

    This plan uses the goals and objectives of the program along with applicable historical information and other available resources such as a work breakdown structure, scope statements, and a benefit realization plan in order to align the program with the stakeholders, including sponsors. This milestone plan could be considered a more detailed high-level road map for the program as it moves forward.

    PMI. *Program Management Professional* (PgMP)® *Examination Content Outline*, April 2011 8

    PMI®, *The Standard for Program Management*, 2008, 24–25

16. c. Stated as part of the program charter

The charter is the primary output of the Initiate Program process. Among other items, it includes a discussion of program components to describe how the projects and other components are configured to deliver the program's benefits This often includes a high-level program plan for the components.

PMI®, *The Standard for Program Management*, 2008, 24

17. d. The program funding source

The program funding source is an input to the Establish Program Financial Framework process. Programs have a variety of potential funding sources, and they depend on the type, size, and complexity; geography, and whether it is internally funded or requires outside funding sources.

PMI®, *The Standard for Program Management*, 2008, 211

18. a. Program manager and executive sponsor

The program manager and executive sponsor are identified at the end of the Program Initiation phase in the program life cycle. Also identified are potential members of the sponsoring group, governance board, or program board.

PMI®, *The Standard for Program Management*, 2008, 25

19. d. Guide the initiation process

One output of the Initiate Program process is the formal appointment of the program manager. He or she should be assigned as soon as possible to guide the initiation process and to ensure that the charter and the business case contain the parameters needed to manage the program.

PMI®, *The Standard for Program Management*, 2008, 78

20 a. Conduct a SWOT analysis

A SWOT (strengths, weaknesses, opportunities, and threats) analysis is a recommended approach to take in developing a viable program charter. It can be used in the Initiate Program process as an aid to developing a comprehensive feasibility study.

PMI®, *The Standard for Program Management*, 2008, 77

Planning the Program

Study Hints

The Planning the Program questions on the PgMP® certification exam, which constitute 11 percent of the exam, or 19 questions, focus on many critical areas in program management and emphasize the importance of detailed and comprehensive program planning. In fact, *The Standard for Program Management* describes 22 processes in the Planning Process Group. Many of these processes are similar to those described in the fourth edition of *A Guide to the Project Management Body of Knowledge (PMBOK® Guide)* (2008); however, the focus in program management is on planning at the program level and not at the individual project level. Several new processes have been defined for program management that are not covered in project management, including Plan and Establish Program Governance Structure, Develop Program Infrastructure, Develop Program Architecture, Define Program Goals and Objectives, Plan for Audits, Plan Program Stakeholder Management, and Develop Program Financial Plan. Note that Stakeholder Management, including Communication Management, and Governance are covered in separate sections of this book and will not be covered in depth in this section.

Similar to the *PMBOK® Guide*'s work breakdown structure (WBS), which is essential for project planning, the PgMP® includes the preparation of a program WBS (PWBS). This PWBS does not replace the WBS for each of the projects in the program, but it does provide an overview of the program and shows how the projects and non-project work fit into the overall program structure. You should be familiar with these 22 processes and the concepts in their corresponding inputs, tools and techniques, and outputs. Study Figure 3-5 in *The Standard* (p. 45).

During the planning process, the Program Setup phase is completed, and the phase-gate decision is made to move into formal program execution. The detailed program management plan is prepared. You should be familiar with its contents and importance, as it defines the means by which the program is initiated. The emphasis is to ensure that the program's mission, vision, and values support those of the organization. The planning processes are iterative, and because of the length of the program and the multiple projects in it, plans need to be revisited and updated when components are initiated or closed, during the organization's fiscal year and budget planning cycle, when unplanned events occur, and based on outputs of some other processes.

Following is a list of the major topics covered in Planning the Program. Use this list to focus your study efforts on the areas that are most likely to appear on the exam.

Major Topics

Planning Process Group

- Develop Program Management Plan
- Plan Program Scope
- Define Program Goals and Objectives
- Plan Program Quality
- Plan Program Risk Management
- Identify Program Risks
- Analyze Program Risks
- Plan Program Risk Responses
- Develop Program Infrastructure
- Develop Program Requirements
- Develop Program Architecture
- Develop Program WBS
- Develop Program Schedule
- Develop Program Financial Plan
- Estimate Program Costs
- Plan Program Procurements
- Budget Program Costs

Program work breakdown structure (PWBS)

- Purpose and use
- Preparation
  - Decomposition techniques
  - Guidelines for a common PWBS methodology
  - Requirements documents
- Program packages
- WBS matrix

Program management plan and schedule

- Determine purpose and contents
- Best practice library
- Link to strategic plan
- Program management information system
- Subsidiary plans

Program scope statement

- Contents and use
- Link to business strategy

Program infrastructure

- Program management information system
- Capacity planning
- Program resource plan
- Core team assignments
- Opportunities for team motivation
- Monitoring and escalation mechanism
- Program quality and scope management system

Transition planning

- Purpose and plan contents
- Stakeholder involvement
- Responsibility of the receiving organization
- Transition events
- Exit criteria

Risk management planning

- Contents of the program risk management plan
- Program risk register
- Probability and impact assessment
- Expected monetary value and decision tree

Program financial plan and metrics

- Program cost estimates
- Program budget baseline
- Key performance indicators

Practice Questions

INSTRUCTIONS: Note the most suitable answer for each multiple-choice question in the appropriate space on the answer sheet.

1. As you work to develop a new washer and dryer that will not require any electricity and also will decrease your monthly water bill by 50% assuming you use the washer at least once per week, you have a complex program to manage. Thus far, even though you are still in the early phases of your program, you have six separate projects in it. Now, you are developing the schedule for your program. To do so, you need a detailed review of the overall schedule at each level of the six projects. This example shows that—

   a. Processes between programs and projects are distinct
   b. It is the program manager's job to actively manage and oversee each of the program's constituent projects
   c. Each project within a program has numerous interdependencies that require active management
   d. Both a top-down and a bottom-up approach are useful for program planning

2. You are Company A's program manager for the development of an online banking system for your community bank, for which your company will receive $20 million. Because the bank would like to implement this system quickly, it has also contracted with Company B. You must implement your system completely in six months to ensure that you beat Company B's schedule. At this point, you have an expense estimate of $2.5 million. You will lose $10 million if you cannot deliver the product in six months, but if you can complete it sooner, you will earn an additional $25 million, for a total of $45 million. Your risk management officer performs a risk analysis and tells you that there is a 70 percent chance that the project will be completed ahead of schedule. Your company has completed similar projects in the past; judging by these experiences, there is a 30 percent chance that your final expenses will increase by $10 million. What is the expected value of your program if it is completed ahead of schedule?

   a. $29 million
   b. $32 million
   c. $42.5 million
   d. $45 million

3. Working as Company A's program manager for the development of an on line banking system for your community bank, you have been asked to provide a list of deliverables and the success criteria for the program and its products, services, and results that must be included in the procurement documentation that is provided to potential suppliers. This list is derived from an analysis of the—

   a. Benefits realization plan
   b. Project work breakdown structure (WBS)
   c. Contract WBS
   d. Program scope statement

4. You are managing a program to establish a new distribution center. The facility's location was selected because labor costs were low, but it is in a remote area. Now gasoline prices have increased 30 percent and are forecasted to rise another 20 percent in the next six months. In planning for the procurement of transportation services, you need to—

   a. Prepare a competitive analysis of service providers
   b. Recommend to your sponsor that the program be terminated and the distribution center be moved to a more urban area
   c. Prepare a contract management plan
   d. Encourage bidders by providing simplified legal requirements in the form of standard terms and conditions

5. As program manager, you find yourself repeatedly changing and refining the program management plan as a result of a number of factors, such as changing external conditions, market factors, stakeholder requirements, and currency fluctuations. A member of the program governance board stops you in the corridor and asks what is wrong with the program. You remind this person that program planning is—

   a. An inexact science, and so long as the program is within acceptable variance levels, everything is fine
   b. An iterative process, and as issues arise and are addressed, the plan will naturally fluctuate
   c. Basically a process of elimination, and as work is accomplished, future work is progressively elaborated
   d. Only done at predefined intervals to reduce administrative expenses

6. You are Company A's program manager for the development of an online banking system for your community bank, for which your company will receive $20 million. However, the bank is so interested in implementing this system quickly that it also contracts with Company B. You must implement your system completely in six months to ensure that you beat Company B's schedule. At this point, you have an expense estimate of $2.5 million. You will lose $10 million if you cannot deliver the product in six months, but if you can complete it sooner, you will earn an additional $25 million. Your risk management officer performs a risk analysis and tells you that there is a 30 percent chance that the bank will change its requirements and a 70 percent chance that the project will be completed on time or ahead of schedule. Your company has completed similar projects in the past, and on the basis of these experiences, you know that there is a 30 percent chance that your final expenses will increase by $10 million. If no risks occur, the value of your program will be—

   a. $2.5 million
   b. $17.5 million
   c. $29 million
   d. $42.5 million

7. You are conducting a program kickoff meeting for a new accounting system that will affect more than 500 accounting professionals in 10 locations. The preliminary schedule shows that in month 13, the transition of the system to the users will begin. The Director of Accounting is quite concerned about the impact of the new system on the employees. To ensure a smooth transition, you, as program manager, need to ensure that the director that the program has—

   a. A sufficient number of people to operate the new system
   b. Enough money in the budget to ensure that the employees receive the appropriate training
   c. The necessary lead time to get people ready
   d. An understanding of the steps needed to move from a development state to an operational state

8. Your firm's senior program manager is overwhelmed with stakeholder problems and has asked you to join the team as the program's resource manager. More than 20 people have already joined, and 15 more are expected over the course of the next month. The senior program manager believes that no additional members will be required. However, in casual observation you detect some problems. A handful of people seem to be working extraordinarily hard, whereas others do not seem to have enough to do. As a program resource manager, your first priority must be to—

   a. Identify the compensation package for each team member that will drive the best performance

   b. Determine the people, equipment, materials, and other resources that are needed and obtain them

   c. Identify those skills that are critical to the program but are not possessed by current team members

   d. Ensure that program resources are allocated across projects to ensure that they are not overcommitted

9. Assume you are working on a program to review and then update as needed all the regulations in your National Highway Transportation Safety Administration especially since people now are using small helicopters for their travel of distances less than 50 miles in your country. Many of the regulations in your Agency were put in place when the Agency was established over 40 years ago, and therefore, a detailed review is needed. Some internal and external audits have made recommendations concerning some of the regulations, which were never implemented. You therefore have a major program to manage and are preparing your program work breakdown structure. You believe a bottom-up approach to preparing it is desirable because—

   a. The top two levels of each project's work breakdown structure (WBS) can be included in the PWBS

   b. Project-related artifacts are then part of the PWBS

   c. The management and control responsibilities of the project team are determined

   d. Earned value reporting is simplified

10. Assume you are working on a program to review and then update as needed all the regulations in your National Highway Transportation Safety Administration especially since people now are using small helicopters for their travel of distances less than 50 miles in your country. Many of the regulations in your Agency were put in place when the Agency was established over 40 years ago, and therefore, a detailed review is needed. Some internal and external audits have made recommendations concerning some of the regulations, which were never implemented. You therefore have a major program to manage. You have prepared your program scope statement, your PWBS, and your program architecture so you have your technical baseline set. Now, it is time to develop the schedule for this program. An essential element as you develop it is—

    a. Determining the timing of program packages
    b. Estimating required resources for each activity
    c. Focusing on resource leveling across the constituent projects
    d. Adjusting leads and lags

11. You are the program manager on a multiyear, multimillion-dollar transportation program for the provincial government. Funding for your program is allocated on a fiscal year basis, yet your program transcends multiple years. This situation will affect how your costs are—

    a. Estimated
    b. Obligated
    c. Committed
    d. Budgeted

12. You are the program manager on a multiyear, multimillion-dollar transportation program for the provincial government. Funding for your program is allocated on a fiscal year basis, yet your program transcends multiple years. Because of the challenges in cost estimating and the lack of additional funding to support your program, each of your project managers adds a contingency reserve. As program manager, you should—

    a. Add an additional reserve to cover the non-project work activity of the program
    b. Establish a set amount for the contingency reserve
    c. Use scenario analysis in the Estimate Program Costs process
    d. Ask the project managers to ignore the pessimistic estimate as they prepare estimates for their projects

13. You are the program manager for a series of new condominium developments in City A. Each of these condo developments is a separate project, as the county has different zoning requirements in its various cities. Your company has developed similar condos for a neighboring city, City B. The City B program manager tells you that many different sellers can support the various subcontracts. With respect to awarding subcontracts, the fastest approach is to—

    a. Ask each seller to prepare a detailed proposal so that you can evaluate its technical and managerial approaches
    b. Limit the evaluation criteria to purchase price
    c. Review each potential subcontractor's financial capacity as a key evaluation criterion, along with life-cycle cost
    d. Base your evaluation criteria primarily on an understanding of need and technical capability

14. You are the program manager for a new program in your company that will provide global support services for supply chain integration. This program will support your multi-national corporation, and you have a total of nine countries involved in it; three are in Asia Pacific, one is in Europe, Middle East and Africa (EMEA), two are in Latin America, and three are in the United States. Your corporate headquarters are in London. You plan to outsource a large portion of proprietary development work to a country located in Canada. A key evaluation criterion in selecting the vendor is to assess—

    a. Its technical capability
    b. References to see how successful it has been on other contracts of a similar nature
    c. The level of compatibility between your company's culture and processes and the vendor's
    d. The provisions the vendor has in place to protect intellectual property

15. As the company's risk expert, you have been requested by the program governance board to perform a risk assessment on the Apex program, which includes more than 25 projects. The focus of your assessment should be on—

    a. Analyzing response mechanisms for individual components
    b. Ensuring that each project has a risk mitigation plan
    c. Interproject risks
    d. Stakeholder risk tolerance and thresholds

16. As the organization's troubled program recovery specialist, you have been called in to take over a program that has had difficulties from the start. An initial assessment reveals that the project-level requirements have not been completed. This needs to be accomplished before any work can be initiated. One way to reduce the time needed for the requirements-gathering cycle is to—

    a. Use as many business analysts as you can find in the organization
    b. Require each project manager to function as a business analyst until such time as the requirements have been gathered
    c. Outsource all the requirements activity so each project manager can devote his or her time to the more important parts of the project
    d. Apply the use of normalized templates, forms, and guidelines to make the process consistent across all projects

17. You are the program manager for a new program in your company that will provide global support services for supply chain integration. This program will support your multi-national corporation, and you have a total of nine countries involved in it; three are in Asia Pacific, one is in EMEA, two are in Latin America, and three are in the United States. Your corporate headquarters are in London. You plan to outsource a large portion of proprietary development work to a country located in Canada. As you move to evaluate vendor proposals, you want to make sure you are doing so objectively. This means you need to define the processes, procedures, and evaluation criteria in sufficient detail in the—

    a. Procurement management plan
    b. Request for information
    c. Contracts management plan
    d. Contract statement of work

18. You are the executive sponsor of a program that provides global support services for supply chain integration. The program is experiencing quality problems in the individual projects. After meeting with the program manager to discuss the issues, you suggest that one way to improve quality is to—

    a. Identify alternatives on scope definition methods through inputs from subject matter experts
    b. Apply a common approach to the creation of the work breakdown structure across projects for consistency in scheduling, resourcing, and cost control
    c. Align acceptance criteria for the deliverables across phases and projects with the program objectives
    d. Use a "gates" go/no-go system at different checkpoints in the program

19. You and your team have prepared the program work breakdown structure (PWBS) shown below in Figure 3.1. Assume that this program involves the development of products, each of which follows the same sequence.

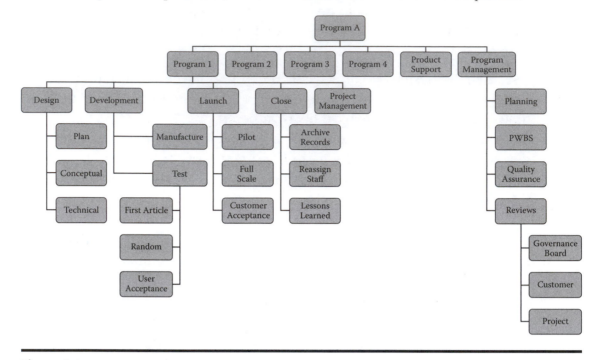

Figure 3.1

In this PWBS, a program package is

a. Project 1
b. Design
c. Program Management
d. Plan

20. You are the program manager on a program that is using multiple suppliers. In fact, more than 75 percent of the program's work effort is being done by third-party suppliers. Given your past experience in working with contractors, you know that performance problems will probably surface. To prepare for such problems, you decide at the start of the program to—

a. Prepare a contract management plan
b. Establish a contracts change control system
c. Establish an alternative disputes resolution process to handle conflict
d. Use only those contractors that are not on the qualified seller list

Answer Sheet

1.	a	b	c	d
2.	a	b	c	d
3.	a	b	c	d
4.	a	b	c	d
5.	a	b	c	d
6.	a	b	c	d
7.	a	b	c	d
8.	a	b	c	d
9.	a	b	c	d
10.	a	b	c	d

11.	a	b	c	d
12.	a	b	c	d
13.	a	b	c	d
14.	a	b	c	d
15.	a	b	c	d
16.	a	b	c	d
17.	a	b	c	d
18.	a	b	c	d
19.	a	b	c	d
20.	a	b	c	d

Answer Key

1. d. Both a top-down and a bottom-up approach are useful for program planning

   Program managers coordinate efforts among projects, but they are not involved in actively managing the individual projects. However, the processes between programs and projects are iterative. Planning requires a top-down and a bottom-up approach to obtain relevant information at various levels and to ensure buy-in from program stakeholders.

   PMI®, *The Standard for Program Management*, 2008, 46

2. b. $32 million

   You will earn the difference between $20 million plus 70 percent of the additional $25 million and $2.5 million in expenses plus 30 percent of the additional $10 million in expenses, or—

   $$[\$20m + (0.7 \times \$25m)] - [\$2.5m + (0.3 \times \$10m)] =$$

   $$(\$20m + \$17.5m) - (\$2.5m + \$3m) =$$

   $$\$37.5m - \$5.5m = \$32m$$

   NOTE: Remember that expected value is calculated as probability multiplied by the monetary value of the risk.

   PMI®, *The Standard for Program Management*, 2008, 172–174

   PMI®, *A Guide to the Project Management Body of Knowledge* (PMBOK® Guide), 2008, 298–299

3. d. Program scope statement

   The program scope statement is the basis for future program decisions, and it defines and articulates the scope of the program. It also contains a list of the program's deliverables and success criteria; these factors require consideration, because they may need to be included in procurement documentation.

   PMI®, *The Standard for Program Management*, 2008, 108 and 187

4. a. Prepare a competitive analysis of service providers

   In the Plan Program Procurement process, a competitive analysis of service providers is a tool and technique to identify those suppliers that provide specific products and services.

   PMI®, *The Standard for Program Management*, 2008, 189

5. b. An iterative process, and as issues arise and are addressed, the plan will naturally fluctuate

As competing priorities, assumptions, and constraints are worked and resolved to address critical factors, such as business goals, deliverables, benefits, time, and cost, the plan will change over time.

PMI®, *The Standard for Program Management*, 2008, 46

6. b. $17.5 million

Decision-tree analysis is used to show the situation and the implications of each of the available choices. It also provides the expected monetary value for the various alternatives. If no risks occur, the value of your program would be calculated as follows:

$$\$20m - \$2.5m = \$17.5m$$

PMI®, *The Standard for Program Management*, 2008, 172–174

7. d. An understanding of the steps needed to move from a development state to an operational state

Transition planning, which is an output of the Develop Program Management Plan process, involves identifying all the steps that are necessary to transition the program to an operational state.

PMI®, *The Standard for Program Management*, 2008, 83

PMI®, *A Guide to the Project Management Body of Knowledge (PMBOK® Guide)*, 2008, 298–299

8. c. Identify those skills that are critical to the program but are not possessed by current team members

During the Develop Program Infrastructure process, a program resource plan is prepared. The first step is to identify the skills that are critical to the program but are not possessed by existing team members. This ensures that these key resources can be obtained and will be available when required.

PMI®, The Standard for Program Management, 2008, 86

9. a. The top two levels of each project's work breakdown structure (WBS) can be included in the PWBS

The PWBS typically extends to the first one or two levels of each project's WBS. The bottom-up approach can show these levels as the PWBS is developed.

PMI®, *The Standard for Program Management*, 2008, 114

10. a. Determining the timing of program packages

   During schedule development at the program level, the timing of the program packages and the non-program activities must be determined. This enables the scheduler to forecast the completion date of the program and of each milestone within the program or the key deliverables for each project.

   PMI®, *The Standard for Program Management*, 2008, 127–128

11. d. Budgeted

   Cost budgeting is based, in part, on how any financial constraints impose boundaries on the budget. Fiscal year budgetary planning cycles impose such boundaries, causing the program team to possibly use different techniques over the life cycle.

   PMI®, *The Standard for Program Management*, 2008, 215 and 222

12. b. Establish a set amount for the contingency reserve

   Your project managers need a common approach for contingency reserves. As program manager, you should standardize this approach so that the cost estimates are not overstated. The contingency reserve amount determination is an input to the Estimate Program Costs process.

   PMI®, *The Standard for Program Management*, 2008, 219

13. b. Limit the evaluation criteria to purchase price

   In the Plan Program Procurements process, the program manager and team will decide the best approach for identifying suppliers. Additionally, they will determine the best types of contracts to be used, the most appropriate payment terms, and other key factors. In a program in which the procurement item is available from a number of acceptable sellers, evaluation criteria can be limited to purchase price. In this context, purchase price is the cost of the item plus any ancillary expenses.

   PMI®, *The Standard for Program Management*, 2008, 190–191, 195–196

14. d. The provisions the vendor has in place to protect intellectual property

   Protecting intellectual property is of paramount concern for any company when outsourcing, and, in particular, when outsourcing to a company in a foreign nation, especially considering the differences in legal systems and standards of protection.

   PMI®, *The Standard for Program Management*, 2008, 196

15. c. Interproject risks

    Program-level risk analysis concentrates on how projects relate to each other and the threats and opportunities found there and not on the individual risks at the project level. These impact assessments of interdependencies are a tool and technique in the Analyze Program Risks process.

    PMI®, *The Standard for Program Management*, 2008, 174

16. d. Apply the use of normalized templates, forms, and guidelines to make the process consistent across all projects

    Having a standard set of tools and templates reduces the time involved in requirements gathering because teams can get started right away without first having to design their own methods for gathering requirements.

    PMI®, *The Standard for Program Management*, 2008, 110–111

17. a. Procurement management plan

    The procurement management plan includes descriptions of all activities and deliverables that are required to define, integrate, and coordinate procurement activities at a program level. Among other things, it discusses proposals and the processes, procedures, and evaluation criteria to objectively evaluate them.

    PMI®, *The Standard for Program Management*, 2008, 190–191

18. c. Align acceptance criteria for the deliverables across phases and projects with the program objectives

    Acceptance criteria, by definition, constitute a level of quality deemed important by the program. If defined properly, such criteria will ensure that the deliverables produced will improve the quality aspects of the program.

    PMI®, *The Standard for Program Management*, 2008, 109

19. d. Plan

    The PWBS is a deliverable-oriented hierarchical description of the total scope of the program. A program package is the lowest level of the PWBS. Selections a., b., and c. are either not in the PWBS or are not at the lowest level of the PWBS.

    PMI®, *The Standard for Program Management*, 2008, 114

20. a. Prepare a contract management plan

    The contract management plan, which is an output of the Plan Program Procurements process, covers contract administration activities throughout the life of the contract and includes documentation, delivery, and performance requirements that the buyer and seller are obligated to meet.

    PMI®, *The Standard for Program Management*, 2008, 191

Executing the Program

Study Hints

The Executing the Program questions on the PgMP® certification exam, which constitute 14 percent of the exam, or 24 questions, focus on phase four in the program life cycle: Delivery of Program Benefits or in the Executing phase in the life cycle from the *Examination Content Outline*. Because the program has passed the third phase-gate review, the program infrastructure has been set up, and the program management plan has been prepared. During this phase of the program life cycle, component projects of the program are initiated, component interfaces are managed, and the development of program benefits is managed. This phase of the program life cycle links to the benefits realization phase of the program benefits management life cycle

The Executing Process Group includes eight processes that ensure that benefits management, stakeholder management, and program governance follow established policies and procedures. The purpose of these processes is to produce the program deliverables and intended benefits. The Executing Process Group ensures that stakeholders receive required information in a timely manner; therefore, the program's communication channels must be administered. Because resources are typically difficult to obtain, questions may cover trade-offs and adaptations in the use of program resources throughout the program life cycle. The emphasis is on the provision of resources at the program level. Because this process group includes information distribution, questions may focus on the need for continuous interaction with the program's stakeholders to ensure that their information requirements are met, along with engaging program stakeholders to ensure that they contribute to the outcome of the program. This group also includes the Conduct Program Procurements process, which focuses on selecting suppliers and issuing contracts. Study Figure 3-28 in *The Standard* (p. 56) and familiarize yourself with the Executing processes.

Please recognize that since stakeholder management is a separate domain on the exam, questions involving information distribution and interactions with stakeholders primarily are covered in this domain in this book. Similarly most benefit delivery questions are covered in the benefit management domain in this book, and relevant governance questions are in the governance domain section.

Following is a list of the major topics covered in Executing the Program. Use this list to focus your study efforts on the areas that are most likely to appear in the exam.

Major Topics

Executing Process Group

- Direct and Manage Program Execution
- Manage Program Resources
- Manage Program Architecture
- Manage Component Interfaces
- Engage Program Stakeholders
- Distribute Information
- Conduct Program Procurements
- Approve Component Initiation

Component projects

- Initiation requests
- Initiation criteria
- Transition requests
- Manage interrelationships
- Component payment schedule
- Component cost estimates
- Component charters
- Closure requests

Executing program management plans

- Integrating processes
- Focusing on project and program work packages in progress
- Providing cumulative deliverables and other work results
- Facilitating and resolving inter-project issues, risks, and constraints
- Managing relationships across program components
- Ensuring a consistent program architecture
- Conducting program procurement activities
- Contract types
  - Evaluation criteria
  - Contract negotiation
- Using tools in the planning phase
- Auditing results

Establishing consistency for decision making

- Uniform standards
- Resources
- Infrastructure

- Tools
- Processes
- Evaluate status

Leading the team

- Training
- Coaching
- Mentoring
- Recognition
- Performance reviews

Capturing lessons learned

Practice Questions

INSTRUCTIONS: Note the most suitable answer for each multiple-choice question in the appropriate space on the answer sheet.

1. As the program manager for the annual construction program for a large government agency, you prepared the program management plan and scope statement that were approved by all stakeholders. Nine months later, a small group of influential stakeholders wants to increase the program's scope by including all maintenance and operations of the buildings. You should—

   a. Require that the stakeholders demonstrate the return on investment to the organization for increasing the scope of the program
   b. Reject the proposal because maintenance and operations do not fall under program management
   c. Respond favorably because programs have a wide scope that may need to change to meet the organization's benefits expectations
   d. Inform the stakeholders that they need to make the business case to the program sponsor for approval

2. As program manager for a global payroll application, you have project teams in Bangalore, Singapore, London, and Washington, D.C. Currently, each team is following its own time-reporting process, which seems to be working well. From the perspective of global program management, you should—

   a. Define and apply a mandatory common time-reporting process
   b. Allow each location to use its own process in consideration of its unique cultural norms and local holiday schedule
   c. Define a common time-reporting process that each location has the option to use
   d. Do nothing because the current approach appears to be working well and there are other more important issues on which to focus

3. An audit of your program has just been completed. The audit report claimed that a new process that had been implemented was receiving strong resistance from the users, thus indicating that a change impact review had not been conducted early enough in the program to detect potential barriers to adoption. Ensuring that such a review is conducted is clearly the responsibility of the—

   a. Program manager
   b. Program sponsor
   c. Program office
   d. Benefits manager

4. You are meeting with the team member who is responsible for the project management information system (PMIS) for your program. Because the data that will be captured are of a scientific and medical nature, the PMIS will generate more than eight terabytes (8,000 gigabytes) of data. Given the critical importance of the PMIS, you and the PMIS team member agree that the first order of business is to—

   a. Consolidate existing data to maximize storage capability
   b. Integrate all financial data
   c. Produce timely and valid inter-project information
   d. Define the program data naming conventions

5. Many organizations that practice portfolio management for programs and projects use enterprise resource planning software. Your large program to implement a culture that focuses first on a standardized approach to portfolio management in which every proposed project or program must be justified with a business case and formally approved by a Portfolio Review Board before it can be initiated is using enterprise resource planning software. It is also beneficial at the individual program and project levels. Since you are using it on your program, your best course of action is to—

   a. Use your program management office (PMO) for support with this software
   b. Handle it through the portfolio management office
   c. Have a core team member work with it throughout the program
   d. Set it up so that a program control framework is also established

6. Your program management plan for your program for new pharmaceutical product to assist people with insomnia without any adverse side effects has been approved. Already, you have three projects in this program, and you have selected the project managers. You also have a core team of four people who report directly to you, and they have been selected and helped in the planning phase. Now, you are ready to assign team members to the various projects in your program. One factor that you should consider in the assignment process is to—

   a. Align pay/compensation to industry norms
   b. Align personnel aspirations to available roles
   c. Assign to the project managers those persons who will be the best performers
   d. Assign team members with similar personalities to the same projects to reduce the risk of team conflict

7. Your company is small and has only 90 people. Its annual sales are about 5 million US and have been at this amount for the last three years. Recently, the CEO and the other two senior executives met and prepared a long-term strategic plan for the next three years. The company provides services primarily in the government market and has a high win rate, but a low capture ratio, which has made it difficult for the company to grow. The executives want to focus on improving the capture ratio. You are the program manager to help lead your organization into one that has annual sales in the 15–20 million range in the next two years. Because the organization is a small one, it makes sense that as the program manager, you manage which of the following plans in an integrated fashion?

   a. Scope, schedule, and cost
   b. Resource, staffing, and cost
   c. Procurement, resource, and staffing
   d. Cost, quality, and schedule

8. With the last Space Shuttle mission completed, you have been selected by the Administrator of the National Aeronautics and Space Administration (NASA) to plan and execute the next new program at its Cape Canaveral campus. This is a highly classified program, which will take the United States into space throughout the galaxy into the 2030s. You have determined the program requirements and now are preparing your program architecture in order to—

   a. Ensure that the architecture is consistent across deliverables
   b. Maintain the integrity of program delivery
   c. Produce cumulative benefits
   d. Establish the organizational structure in which work will be done

9. With the last Space Shuttle mission completed, you have been selected by the Administrator of the National Aeronautics and Space Administration (NASA) to plan and execute the next new program at its Cape Canaveral campus. This is a highly classified program, which will take the United States into space throughout the galaxy into the 2030s. Your program now has seven projects in it. You have a PMO as well, which will support your program, and a core team of five people who also report to you. However, you are working now to manage the resources of your program, and you need to consider as you do so the—

   a. Component status reports
   b. Program schedule
   c. Scope management plan
   d. Compensation plan

10. You are managing a program to develop a new source of energy that can be used in the northern and southern hemispheres when solar power is not available. Working with your core program team and your governance board, you have identified a number of component projects. However, your company has several key projects under way, and resources will be difficult to acquire for this new program. In determining whether to use internal or external resources, one key consideration is—

    a. The cost of external resources
    b. Your ability to negotiate with functional managers for the needed staff
    c. The availability of external resources
    d. The impact on the morale if external resources are used

11. You are supported on your program by a variety of contractors who need to work closely together to deliver program benefits. Two of the contractors are blaming each other for missed deadlines. It appears that a critical milestone was missed by Contractor A, the output of which was needed by Contractor B. However, Contractor A alleges that Contractor B provided the wrong specifications. In this situation, your first step should be to—

    a. Seek liquidated damages from both contractors because of the missed dates
    b. Alert your attorney to the possibility of litigation and its associated expense
    c. Review the termination clause in each contract to see what your options are
    d. Ensure there are unambiguous contract management procedures

12. You are managing a program to develop a new product to protect all workers from germs in the workplace so everyone is assured that the workplace is clean. They will not have to worry in the future if a co-worker has a transmittable disease. However, you have just learned that there was a failure to adhere to a major scope element in the work breakdown structure (WBS) of one of the key projects. This problem means that—

    a. Changes to the program architecture may be needed
    b. Rebaselining may be required
    c. A change request has been approved
    d. New metrics are required

13. You are working on an emergency response program for your city and have realized that you lack the needed resources to support your program. Over the years, your organization's Procurement and Contracts Department has compiled a qualified seller list. This list will be extremely helpful to you when you—

    a. Prepare your program procurement management plan
    b. Issue requests for proposals (RFPs) or requests for quotations (RFQs)
    c. Plan contract evaluation criteria
    d. Advertise in the local newspaper for your procurement requirements

14. As you work on this emergency response program for your city, you recognize you will need a number of different types of supplies and services to support your program and its component projects. Many different techniques can be used to evaluate proposals that are submitted. All use—

    a. Predefined weightings
    b. Expert judgment
    c. Screening systems
    d. Weighting systems

15. You were fortunate as the program manager for the new source of energy to be used in the northern and southern hemispheres when solar power is not available to be able to determine the criteria to use to select your core team and your project managers. This was especially important since your company has a severe shortage of resources available. Now that your team is in place, you need to focus on—

    a. Reviewing the project manager's performance
    b. Setting up a team-based reward and recognition system
    c. Establishing a 360 degree rating system that you will use for your own performance evaluation
    d. Meeting with the Human Resource Department regularly for guidance

16. As the program manager for the development of a next-generation personal digital assistant (PDA) that can be used on computers, airplanes, trains, and phones, you have identified seven candidate projects to comprise your program. You also have identified seven capable project managers to manage these projects who have the requisite knowledge, skills, and competencies to do the required work against an aggressive schedule and demanding stakeholders. Before each project can officially begin, it is important that—

    a. The program's business case be reviewed
    b. All subsidiary plans of the program have been completed and approved by every stakeholder
    c. A specific approach to monitor overall program performance has been determined
    d. Each project has a defined charter

17. Assume you are the program manager for your pharmaceutical company for a new product designed to cure sleep apnea. As part of your program potential patients will not need to first go to a hospital to diagnose whether they have this condition and stay the night. You of course must get regulatory approval and conduct numerous clinical trials before your new product is ready so your program will last at least five years. You hope to be the first to market with this product even though your business development manager has said that a competitor is also working in this area. Based on your previous work on long programs, you know it is hard to sustain morale among your team, and many often then volunteer to work on projects that may be in trouble just to see results. Therefore, this time, you are—

    a. Setting up a process where your resources are dedicated to your team and cannot be used on other projects
    b. Setting up a master schedule that has some early milestones, which you know you can meet
    c. Asking each team member to sign a commitment statement to your program as they join your team
    d. Having weekly performance reviews with your project managers, who in turn will have similar performance reviews with their team members

18. Assume you are the program manager for your pharmaceutical company for a new product designed to cure sleep apnea. As part of your program potential patients will not need to first go to a hospital to diagnose whether they have this condition and stay the night. You of course must get regulatory approval and conduct numerous clinical trials before your new product is ready so your program will last at least five years. You hope to be the first to market with this product even though your business development manager has said that a competitor is also working in this area. You have decided to use standard Key Performance Indicators for your program and have adopted the Balanced Scorecard approach a well. You want to do so in order to—

    a. Minimize the information that is to be reported
    b. Make sure that information is available in a format that has a template so a lot of time is not spent on the reporting process
    c. Set up the reports to be provided on a weekly basis to all stakeholders
    d. Evaluate the program status while maintaining current program information

19. Working on a major program to upgrade the software used in your country's airspace system to make it far easier for the air traffic controllers to use and also to avoid incidents of their falling asleep at times when there is limited activity or having tremendous stress when there is a lot of activity, you are facing many challenges in your role as a program manager. You have seven projects on your program and expect to add others. One project is about to close. You need to make sure before it does close that—

    a. Deliverables are complete, and scope is compliant with the functional overview
    b. Deliverables have exceeded the original requirements, and there is universal agreement upon all stakeholders about the project's success
    c. The detailed administrative procedures for program closure have been followed, which are managed by your Program Management Office
    d. The program manager and team have been reassigned to other projects now that this project is complete

20. Program management is new to your company. You are managing the first program as you have taken program management training and have a track record of successfully managing complex and multiple projects. You know, however, that program management is different from project management in many ways. Your team is new to program management, and no one on the team has been exposed to it. Some team members have questioned the new approach, and others have asked why the organization has decided to manage projects as programs rather than as standalone projects. The project managers on your program are concerned they may lack visibility in this concept, limiting their opportunities for advancement and benefits. This shows that you must—

a. Persuade them that program management is desirable and becoming a program manager then can be the next step in their career
b. Set up a training session for your project managers and team members to explain the benefits of program management
c. Establish an open-door policy and invite anyone who has concerns to meet individually with you or to call you without any fears that in doing so their performance may be criticized
d. Establish a policy of "no surprises" and provide your team with the same status information that the executives receive

Answer Sheet

1.	a	b	c	d		11.	a	b	c	d
2.	a	b	c	d		12.	a	b	c	d
3.	a	b	c	d		13.	a	b	c	d
4.	a	b	c	d		14.	a	b	c	d
5.	a	b	c	d		15.	a	b	c	d
6.	a	b	c	d		16.	a	b	c	d
7.	a	b	c	d		17.	a	b	c	d
8.	a	b	c	d		18.	a	b	c	d
9.	a	b	c	d		19.	a	b	c	d
10.	a	b	c	d		20.	a	b	c	d

Answer Key

1. c. Respond favorably because programs have a wide scope that may need to change to meet the organization's benefits expectations

    A key difference between a program and a project is that the program has a wide scope that may require changes to meet the organization's benefits expectations, especially programs that are ongoing on an annual basis. Change can come from both inside and outside the program, and program managers should be prepared to manage it and exploit it.

    PMI®, *The Standard for Program Management*, 2008, 11

2. a. Define and apply a mandatory common time-reporting process

    In executing a program, it is important for each team member to record his or her time in accordance with a well-defined, common standard. Cultural norms and country holiday schedules have little to do with the number of hours or days someone works on a program.

    PMI®, *(PgMP®) Examination Content Outline*, 2011, 10

3. a. Program manager

    The program manager must set clear goals, assess readiness, plan for the change, monitor the change, and address those who are not fully embracing the change.

    PMI®, *The Standard for Program Management*, 2008, 11–12

4. d. Define the program data naming conventions

    To avoid confusion and the proliferation of numerous naming conventions across projects, the program should have a standard naming convention for all data, and the application of such conventions should be consistent across all projects. This will increase efficiency and productivity across the program team.

    PMI®, *(PgMP®) Examination Content Outline*, 2011, 10

5. a. Use your program management office (PMO) for support with this software

    Programs tend to have a supporting infrastructure that includes specific processes and procedures as well as physical facilities. The infrastructure may include program-specific tools such as enterprise resource planning software.

    PMI®, *The Standard for Program Management*, 2008, 11–12

6. b. Align personnel aspirations to available roles

Team members tend to be more motivated when they are working on projects or in roles in which they have strong interest. Therefore, a program manager should always consider someone's personal interest or desires when making assignments.

PMI®, *(PgMP®) Examination Content Outline, 2011*, 10

7. d. Cost, quality, and schedule

During the Executing processes, it is common practice to manage the cost, quality, and schedule plans as an integrated plan and to provide status information and requested changes through the Monitoring and Controlling processes.

PMI®, *The Standard for Program Management*, 2008, 55

8. a. Ensure that the architecture is consistent across deliverables

Program architecture is the structure of the products that are produced by the component projects of a program and the technical relationships that exist between and among these products.

PMI®, *The Standard for Program Management*, 2008, 57

9. a. Component status reports

Component status reports are a key input, because they can be used to identify project execution problems that stem from resource allocation issues. Resources should be allocated to meet key program needs.

PMI®, *The Standard for Program Management*, 2008, 57 and 92

10. a. The cost of external resources

You consider a number of factors regarding the use of internal or external staff. This decision is based on the length of time the particular skill set is needed, the availability of internal resources, the cost of external resources, and the timing of the need.

PMI®, *The Standard for Program Management*, 2008, 91–92

11. d. Ensure there are unambiguous contract management procedures

Contract management procedures are a tool and technique in the Conduct Program Procurements process. Successful buyer-seller relationships depend on such factors as trust and good working relationships, both of which are best addressed at the program level. Conflict is best addressed early and usually privately in a spirit of collaboration.

PMI®, *The Standard for Program Management*, 2008, 196

12. a   Changes to the program architecture may be needed

The Manage Program Architecture process ensures that well-structured relationships among the program elements adhere to the governing rules as defined in the architecture. This is an example in which changes to the architecture may be necessary.

PMI®, *The Standard for Program Management*, 2008, 117

13. b. Issue requests for proposals (RFPs) or requests for quotations (RFQs)

Qualified seller lists are used when RFPs, RFQs, or requests for information (RFIs) are issued. They can save time in the overall program procurement management process, because they list only known sellers who can provide needed products and services.

PMI®, *The Standard for Program Management*, 2008, 195

14. b. Expert judgment

Proposal evaluation systems are a tool and technique in the Conduct Program Procurements process. Although a number of different approaches can be used, all use expert judgment and evaluation criteria.

PMI®, *The Standard for Program Management*, 2008, 195

15. a. Reviewing the project manager's performance

Once project managers are assigned to a program, a specific system is needed to evaluate their performance such as an individual performance plan or a management-by-objectives plan. The program manager should work with the project managers to set up performance goals and evaluation criteria and then should review performance and provide feedback to them in terms of meeting project and program goals

PMI, PgMP® *Examination Content Outline*, 2011, 10

16. d. Each project has a defined charter.

In order to formally initiate projects in a program, they require a charter that defines why the project is needed and how it supports the program's charter and overall program benefits. Among other things, this charter also should show the project manager's authority to assign resources to the project that will then achieve program objectives

PMI, PgMP® *Examination Content Outline*, 2011, 10

17. b. Setting up a master schedule that has some early milestones, which you know you can meet

    It is easy for team members to lose motivation especially on large programs. One approach is to celebrate success among your team and maximize their contribution to achieving program goals. If the master schedule has early milestones set up that are ones that can be met, this then provides an opportunity to celebrate success and build a winning team.

    PMI, PgMP® *Examination Content Outline*, 2011, 10

18. d. Evaluate the program status while maintaining current program information

    Key Performance Indicators are a best practice in program management especially to show how the program remains in alignment with strategic goals and objectives, and the Balanced Scorecard is helpful in setting performance targets. The purpose is to be able in executing to evaluate the program's status in order to monitor and control the program while maintaining current program information.

    PMI, PgMP® *Examination Content Outline*, 2011, 10

19. a. Deliverables are complete, and scope is compliant with the functional overview

    Before the request to close a project is approved, the program manager must ensure the project's deliverables are complete. The scope should be compliant with the functional overview so requirements are met as well as the success criteria in the scope statement.

    PMI, PgMP® *Examination Content Outline*, 2011, 10

20. b. Set up a training session for your project managers and team members to explain the benefits of program management

    Program management is used because through it more benefits can be achieved than if the projects were managed in a standalone fashion. There is a far greater emphasis therefore on strategic alignment, benefits realization, stakeholder management, and governance than in project management. As a program manager, one must lead by training among other things in order to improve team engagement and achieve commitment to the program's goals.

    PMI, PgMP® *Examination Content Outline*, 2011, 10

Controlling the Program

Study Hints

The Controlling the Program questions on the PgMP® certification exam, which constitute 10 percent of the exam, or 17 questions, continue to focus on phase four of the program life cycle, on the benefits realization phase of the benefits management life cycle, and more specifically on monitoring and controlling the program and its components. The expected benefits need to be in line with the original plan, the level of risk must remain acceptable, and accepted best practices must be followed. The questions in this area address the importance of communicating with the program governance board and other stakeholders regarding benefits delivery and expected future benefits from the program, thus underscoring the importance of this process group.

The Monitoring and Controlling Process Group consists of 12 processes, as shown in Figure 3-37 in *The Standard* (p. 60). The emphasis of this process group is on collecting and consolidating data from the various program packages in the PWBS. You should expect to answer questions on earned value and should be familiar with the various earned value terms and formulas. You should also expect to answer some questions about program trends and the need to communicate these trends to the program's stakeholders. Stakeholders are emphasized in the Manage Program Stakeholder Expectations process, covered in the stakeholder domain in this book. Other work involves governance oversight and managing benefits, covered in the respective domains in this book.

Because monitoring and controlling involves preventive and corrective actions, some questions include scenarios in which the program manager and the core program team must decide on the best course of action. Questions may involve configuration management and the Monitor and Control Program Changes process. Remember that change requests are outputs of many of the process groups, and as such, approved change requests are inputs to many process groups. Because the program manager is responsible for managing program issues, the use of an issue register is required, and its contents may be reviewed by the governance board. Activities in the Manage Program Issues process are conducted in parallel with activities in the Monitor and Control Program Risks process, where the risk register is used. Many of these processes will occur throughout the program's life cycle, from initiation to closure. Furthermore, it is essential to focus on monitoring and controlling the program's scope, schedule, and budget, and if contracts are to be awarded, to focus on administering program procurements.

Following is a list of the major topics covered in Controlling the Program. Use this list to focus your study efforts on the areas that are most likely to appear on the exam.

Major Topics

Monitoring and Controlling Process Group

- Monitor and Control Program Performance
- Monitor and Control Program Scope
- Monitor and Control Program Schedule
- Monitor and Control Program Financials
- Manage Program Stakeholder Expectations
- Monitor and Control Program Risks
- Administer Program Procurements
- Manage Program Issues
- Monitor and Control Program Changes
- Report Program Performance
- Provide Governance Oversight
- Manage Program Benefits

Preventive and corrective actions
Proactive and reactive cost control
Managing and controlling changes

- Change requests
- Coordinating changes
- Change control board
- Change request log
- Impact analysis
- Approved change requests
- Variance analysis

Meetings and reviews

- Presentations
- Status review meetings
- Lessons learned reviews

Program management controls

- Standards
- Policies and procedures
- Program plans
- Performance reports
- Forecasts
- Program performance analysis
- Issue analysis

- Program metrics
- Impact assessments
- Time and cost reporting systems
- Inspections
- Reviews
- Oversight
- Audits
- Contracts
- Documentation
- Regulations

Earned value

- Schedule and cost variance
- Schedule performance index and cost performance index
- Estimate at completion
- Estimate to complete
- Budget at completion

Trend analysis
Issue register
Monitoring and controlling risks

- Contingency reviews
- Risk register
- Risk-review meetings and audits
- Monitoring the environment

Administer program procurements

- Change control systems
- Engaging and managing suppliers
- Payment systems
- Budget management systems

Practice Questions

INSTRUCTIONS: Note the most suitable answer for each multiple-choice question in the appropriate space on the answer sheet.

1. As a program manager on the next generation nuclear submarine, you have six projects so far in your program, and this is only year one. You know additional projects and non-project work will be added as the program continues since it is scheduled to last for at least seven years. One of your responsibilities is to ensure that common activities among projects are coordinated to maximize the use of resources and achieve results that would not be possible if the projects were managed in a standalone fashion. This is done in the

   a. Program Execution phase
   b. Benefit Realization phase
   c. Monitoring phase
   d. Monitor and Control Program Performance process

2. As a program manager on the next generation nuclear submarine, you have six projects so far in your program, and this is only year one. You know additional projects and non-project work will be added as the program continues since it is scheduled to last for at least seven years. You know from your work on programs, that change is inevitable on both on the overall program and its projects. As a program manager for this nuclear submarine program, you use a change management system as part of the program management information system (PMIS). You do this during as part of your work in—

   a. Integrating overall change control
   b. Working to deliver incremental benefits
   c. Executing the projects
   d. Monitoring and controlling program performance

3. Your program, which designs, develops, and manufactures a class of farm equipment that can be used above the Arctic Circle, has been requested to consolidate data and status for a key stakeholder. Part of your work involves maintaining a spare parts inventory and fulfilling spares requests for clients. In consolidating your report, you—

   a. Do not include the spares data because they are really not part of the defined program and do not fit the definition of a project
   b. Include the spares data, even though they are non-project work, because they are part of the program
   c. Include the spares data because you can reasonably define fulfilling a spares order as a project
   d. Ask the stakeholder who requested the report whether he or she wants to see the spares data

4. You have been asked to assume the management of a program to rebuild the water desalinization plant for Haddad, Saudi Arabia. Much of the equipment on the job is being leased. The program has been under way for more than five years. You decided to conduct an audit of the hundreds of lease agreements, and you found that you are making payments on leases for equipment that is not being used. Your next step is to—

   a. Set up a system to alert your team to this problem on future leased resources
   b. Use a resource register
   c. Recommend corrective actions
   d. Inform your governance board because it is focused on the program's financial status

5. Your program to produce the first polycarbonate city car is making progress. The prototype vehicle is performing well and, in certain instances, exceeding the original specifications. The client is concerned that the cost to manufacture the car will cause the car to be priced at a level that the average consumer cannot, or will not, pay. The client has asked you to see whether you can reduce the cost of manufacturing the vehicle yet still meet the specifications. In response to this request, you should—

   a. Establish a cost change management system
   b. Rebaseline your schedule
   c. Take corrective actions
   d. Implement lean Six Sigma manufacturing processes

6. You have been asked to assume the management of a program to rebuild the water desalinization plant for Haddad, Saudi Arabia. Much of the equipment on the job is being leased. For each program in your company, key deliverables are noted in the program schedule. You are using earned value on your program. The schedule performance index indicates that you will not meet your proposed schedule, and you are only about 20 percent complete to date. You need to—

    a. Issue a revised schedule to your program team
    b. Update the program master schedule
    c. Update your schedule management plan
    d. Inform your stakeholders

7. As program manager for development of a next-generation catalytic converter, you have a core team of six people. So far, you are in the first year of your program, scheduled to last four years, and you have three projects as part of your program. The project manager of the first project to design the converter has raised an issue to you as he feels it has far reaching consequences. You decide to use an issue register. After each issue is identified, your core program team records it in this register. The next step is to—

    a. Subject the issue to analysis by a reviewing authority
    b. Appoint a member of the program team to resolve the issue
    c. Ask the person who raised the issue to propose a resolution
    d. Refer the issue to the head of the program management office (PMO) for analysis and tracking

8. Assume you are managing a program for the judicial branch of your government, and you are reporting to the Chief Information Officer of the Administrative System of the Courts. The program is the number one priority on the Court's list of ongoing programs and projects in the portfolio. The purpose of your program is to manage a legacy system conversion program, and thus far, your team has identified a number of issues for your resolution. Many of them involve COBOL programming, so you have assigned them to a COBOL subject matter expert on your core team. This person owns all the COBOL issues, which means that he or she—

    a. Is responsible for all COBOL-related project work
    b. Has the authority and means to resolve COBOL issues
    c. Has been appointed so that no COBOL issues will require resolution at a higher level
    d. Can modify program scope if needed to resolve issues

9. However, before you joined the judicial branch of the government, you worked in the executive branch in the Federal Trade Commission. You were one of the first people in the Commission to attain the PMP® and as you then moved into program management work, you attained your PgMP®. As you have managed programs in this Commission, you found that one of the major purposes of the Manage Program Issues process is to identify, track, and close issues so that stakeholder expectations are aligned with program activities and results. This alignment can be accomplished by several methods, including—

   a. Adjusting enterprise environmental factors
   b. Leveraging opportunities
   c. Adjusting program priorities
   d. Performing program scope analysis

10. One of the issues on your program is difficult to resolve because it concerns serious personality conflicts. Although it was raised by Project Manager A, it affects Projects B and C. Each of the three project managers has a different solution, and there is a stalemate. You cannot resolve this issue on your own and still maintain a good relationship with all three, so you escalate it to your executive sponsor for resolution at the next governance board meeting. This unresolved issue is—

   a. Put in a "parking lot" on the issues register until it is resolved
   b. Handled as a result of the Manage Program Issues process
   c. Sent to the enterprise program management office (EPMO) to see whether it has been encountered and resolved on similar projects
   d. Best analyzed by a neutral party who will make a recommendation to the executive sponsor

11. You realized in your work on the next generation nuclear submarine that since it will last seven years, you will probably have scope changes. You want to prepare for them and be able to exploit them as much as possible. However, because most scope changes have associated costs, every proposed change requires analysis to determine whether it should be implemented. After the analysis, the program manager makes a decision. The next step is to—

   a. Communicate the decision to the stakeholders involved
   b. Update the scope register
   c. Revise the work breakdown structure (WBS)
   d. Revise the program management information system (PMIS)

12. Now, a scope change request is approved for your program. It involves increasing the functionality for end users in a new operating system for Bluetooth®-ready mobile phones and computers and is estimated to require an additional $1 million. Your program governance board recommended to the executive sponsor that this scope change be approved to maintain a competitive advantage. Your next step is to update the—

    a. Scope management plan
    b. Budget baseline
    c. Program work breakdown structure (PWBS)
    d. Scope statement

13. You are the legacy system conversion program manager in your company. You need to update the company's business development/sales tracking system, which was developed in C++. Your governance board recognizes the importance of including this project in your program and asks you to prepare a cost estimate for this new project. The board approves your estimate. You now should—

    a. Update the program budget baseline
    b. Revise the cost management plan
    c. Prepare a resource management plan
    d. Identify staffing needs

14. Because of their size, complexity, and duration, programs tend to be more important than projects in most organizations, and program managers tend to interact more with senior management, often through the governance board or steering committee that oversees the program. Throughout the program, it is especially important to monitor and control program changes. A useful tool and technique is—

    a. Change request log
    b. Impact analysis
    c. Change register
    d. Program metrics

15. You are the program manager on a mergers and acquisition (M&A) team that is responsible for integrating your company with the one it has recently acquired. The company you acquired has a history of failure in such mergers; your company is now its fourth owner, and unfortunately, things are not going well. In a meeting with your executive sponsor after the last governance review meeting, he suggested that you set up—

    a. Biweekly reviews
    b. A different governance structure
    c. Benchmarking studies
    d. An audit plan

16. In a program performance meeting, you asked the project manager of Project A what the status was. She responded by saying that the total project budget of $600,000 was evenly allocated over the project's six-month life. She has just completed the second month of the project and has finished 50 percent of the work. What earned value method information is available thus far?

    a. Earned value
    b. Planned value
    c. Actual costs
    d. Earned value and planned value

17. Every program is planned on the basis of a set of hypotheses, scenarios, or assumptions. As a newly appointed program manager, you ask one of your core program team members to explore the validity of these assumptions and to do so periodically as a way to identify risks. This is important as part of the—

    a. Risk response analysis
    b. Risk monitoring function
    c. Issue management activities
    d. Risk analysis options

18. You are a program manager on an international program that relies on contractors for approximately 75 percent of its work. Some of the contracts apply to a specific project, but five contracts span six of the projects. You have one basic ordering agreement, which enables you to obtain temporary resources as required for this complex program. In terms of the Administer Program Procurements process, you should review the—

    a. Program reports
    b. Procurement register
    c. Contract management plan
    d. Change requests

19. Your program is beginning to miss key milestones because of delays by your customer, with whom you have a contract. Your goal is to ensure that corrections are made as quickly as possible, so you decide to conduct a contract performance review earlier than planned. During this review, you and the customer realized that there was a deficiency in the contract. Your next step is to—

    a. Prepare a change request
    b. Document the causes for the delay and bring it to your attorney's attention
    c. Prepare an assignment of claims form
    d. Document the delay and discuss it with the steering committee

20. You are preparing for a meeting of your program's governance board. On your program, you are using earned value for monitoring, control, and forecasting. The planned value is $30,587, and the earned value is $26,365. You are working on a customer-imposed schedule for the completion of the program. Looking at the schedule variance (SV), you conclude that—

  a. The SV is −$4,222, and the program is behind schedule
  b. The SV is 1.16, and it appears that the schedule will be met
  c. The program is behind schedule, and the tasks on the critical path are affected
  d. The budget at completion is $46,475, but the delays are insignificant

Answer Sheet

1.	a	b	c	d
2.	a	b	c	d
3.	a	b	c	d
4.	a	b	c	d
5.	a	b	c	d
6.	a	b	c	d
7.	a	b	c	d
8.	a	b	c	d
9.	a	b	c	d
10.	a	b	c	d

11.	a	b	c	d
12.	a	b	c	d
13.	a	b	c	d
14.	a	b	c	d
15.	a	b	c	d
16.	a	b	c	d
17.	a	b	c	d
18.	a	b	c	d
19.	a	b	c	d
20.	a	b	c	d

Answer Key

1. b. Benefits Realization phase

   Phase three in the benefits life cycle is benefit realization. Here, components are monitored, the benefit register is maintained, and benefits are reported

   PMI®, *The Standard for Program Management*, 2008, 20

2. d. Monitoring and controlling program performance

   The program management information system is a tool and technique used in the Monitor and Control Program Performance process. Among other things, it includes a change management system.

   PMI®, *The Standard for Program Management*, 2008, 82 and 94

3. b. Include the spares data, even though they are non-project work, because they are part of the program

   At the program level, monitoring and controlling involves obtaining and consolidating data on status and progress from individual projects or program packages (that is, non-project tasks).

   PMI®, *The Standard for Program Management*, 2008, 59

4. c. Recommend corrective actions

   To avoid penalties or ongoing lease payments, leased resources should be tracked to ensure that they are returned when the lease expires or when they are no longer needed. Based on the audit findings, it is now necessary to request changes or recommend corrective action requests.

   PMI®, *The Standard for Program Management*, 2008, 202

5. c. Take corrective actions

   As an output of the Monitor and Control Program Financials process, corrective actions are taken in response to unanticipated changes or to any problems that affect the program's objectives.

   PMI®, *The Standard for Program Management*, 2008, 226

6. b. Update the program master schedule

   Updates to the program's master schedule are an output of the Monitor and Control Program Schedule process and are required as a result of delivery performance of the program against the agreed schedule.

   PMI®, *The Standard for Program Management*, 2008, 134

7. a. Subject the issue to analysis by a reviewing authority

   After an issue is identified, it should be recorded in the issue register. The next step is to subject it to analysis by a reviewing authority or board. Issue reviews should be conducted regularly.

   PMI®, *The Standard for Program Management*, 2008, 96

8. b. Has the authority and means to resolve COBOL issues

   The issue owner should have the authority and means to resolve and close COBOL issues. If an issue cannot be resolved, then it should be escalated progressively higher until resolution is achieved.

   PMI®, *The Standard for Program Management*, 2008, 96

9. d. Performing program scope analysis

   It is important that the program manager ensure that stakeholder activities are aligned with the program's activities and deliverables. Issues may be sent to the core team member responsible for program risk management, program governance, or program scope management. When issues are sent to the core team member responsible for program scope management, then it is important to determine the effect that such issues have on the program's scope.

   PMI®, *The Standard for Program Management*, 2008, 96

10. b. Handled as a result of the Manage Program Issues process

    Ideally, issues should be resolved by the program manager or the component project managers. If resolution is not possible, then an issue is escalated progressively higher on the authority scale until resolution is achieved. Escalated issues are an output of the Issue Management and Control process.

    PMI®, *The Standard for Program Management*, 2008, 95

11. a. Communicate the decision to the stakeholders involved

    It is important to tell the person who requested the scope change and the affected stakeholders whether it will be implemented. Approved change requests are an output of the Manage and Control Scope process, and communications are the primary tool for managing stakeholders expectations.

    PMI®, *The Standard for Program Management*, 2008, 123 and 241

12. b. Budget baseline

The program budget baseline is an input to the Monitor and Control Program Financials process. When a change request with significant cost implications is approved, a program budget baseline update should be prepared as an output of the Monitor and Control Program Financials process.

PMI®, *The Standard for Program Management*, 2008, 225–226

13. a. Update the program budget baseline

As an output of the Monitor and Control Program Financials process, updates to the program budget baseline are needed when there are significant cost impacts. These updates are communicated to program stakeholders as appropriate.

PMI®, *The Standard for Program Management*, 2008, 226

14. b. Impact analysis

Impact analysis is a tool and technique in the Monitor and Control Program Changes process, which explores the effect of the proposed changes on the program. It assesses the accuracy of any assumptions and identifies the potential risks and benefits that possible changes may have on the component projects.

PMI®, *The Standard for Program Management*, 2008, 268

15. a. Biweekly reviews

Review meetings, which are regularly scheduled and include well-planned agendas and documented records of decisions made, enhance the effectiveness of the governance process. They are a tool and technique used by governance boards

PMI®, *The Standard for Program Management*, 2008, 262

16. d. Earned value and planned value

For the earned value (EV) of the project, note that half the work has been completed, for an EV of $300,000. The planned value (PV) through month two is $200,000. Remember that the estimate was $600,000 spread evenly over six months (or $100,000/month).

PMI®, *The Standard for Program Management*, 2008, 133

Pritchard, Carl L., *The Project Management Drill Book: A Self-Study Guide.* Arlington, VA: ESI International, 2003, Chapter 1

17. b. Risk monitoring function

Risk monitoring includes evaluation of whether program assumptions remain valid. This function is ongoing throughout the life of the program as part of the Monitor and Control Program Risks process.

PMI®, The Standard for Program Management, 2008, 180

18. c. Contract management plan

The contract management plan is used to administer contracts for significant purchases and acquisitions. It covers contract administration activities throughout the life of the contract and is used effectively to manage a variety of suppliers. It is a tool and technique of the Administer Program Procurements process.

PMI®, *The Standard for Program Management*, 2008, 191, 201

19. a. Prepare a change request

A contract performance review is a tool and technique in the Administer Program Procurements process. Change requests or recommended corrective action requests should be raised when the performance problems are the result of a deficiency in a contract.

PMI®, *The Standard for Program Management*, 2008, 202

20. a. The SV is –$4,222, and the program is behind schedule

Schedule variance (SV) is calculated by subtracting the planned value (PV) from the earned value (EV); that is, $SV = EV - PV$. At this point, the SV is –$4,222. The program is behind schedule; however, without additional information, the effect on the critical path is not known.

PMI®, *The Standard for Program Management*, 2008, 133

PMI®, *PMBOK® Guide*, 2008, 182

Closing the Program

Study Hints

The Closing the Program questions on the PgMP® certification exam, which constitute three percent of the exam, or five questions, emphasize the last phase in the program life cycle, Program Closure. This phase formalizes the acceptance of products, services, or results that brings the program or one of its projects to completion. The program's work is complete, and benefits from the program are accruing and will continue to do so in the future. A number of key activities are included in this phase, and you should be familiar with these activities as they are listed on p. 30 of *The Standard*.

This phase tracks to the benefits transition phase in the program benefits management life cycle. At this time, the benefits from the project and non-project activities are consolidated, and the ongoing responsibility to sustain the benefits is transferred in accordance with the program transition plan. Many associated ongoing activities are involved with ensuring and sustaining benefits, and these activities differ in each organization.

The Closing the Program questions will address the Closing Process Group, which consists of three processes—Close Program, Approve Component Transition, and Close Program Procurements—as shown in Figure 3-50 of *The Standard* (p. 67). You should recognize that administrative closure is ongoing and should not wait until the program is complete. Each project within the program is closed at different times, as are the associated contracts. If a project is terminated for any reason, it may be closed earlier than scheduled or anticipated. Lessons learned are collected throughout the program life cycle. Closure activities, therefore, occur throughout the program and not just at completion of the program.

Following is a list of the major topics covered in Closing the Program. Use this list to focus your study efforts on the areas most likely to appear on the exam.

Major Topics

Closing Process Group

- ■ Close Program
  - – Release resources
  - – Final reports
  - – Knowledge transition
- ■ Approve Component Transition
  - – Component transition decision
  - – Benefits realization report updates
  - – Lessons learned
  - – Program management plan updates
- ■ Close Program Procurements
  - – Close contracts
  - – Procurement performance reports
- ■ Close budget allocation

Program Closure phase

- ■ Complete program performance analysis report
- ■ Benefits review
- ■ Conduct a post-review meeting
- ■ Disband the organization
- ■ Dismantle the infrastructure
- ■ Provide customer support
- ■ Document current state if an early transition
- ■ Meet contractual obligations
- ■ Deliver required payments
- ■ Obtain formal acceptance from stakeholders
- ■ Perform supplier reviews
- ■ Reconcile the budget
- ■ Document lessons learned and best practices
- ■ Provide feedback and recommendations
- ■ Store and index documents
- ■ Manage required transitions

Benefits transition phase

- ■ Execute the transition
- ■ Consolidate coordinated benefits
- ■ Transfer ongoing responsibility

Intellectual property requirements
Communication of program results

Practice Questions

INSTRUCTIONS: Note the most suitable answer for each multiple-choice question in the appropriate space on the answer sheet.

1. You have been managing a major software program for six years under contract to a Fortune 500 company. You have been helping this company move to Cloud computing. Finally, you completed the last project in this program, and it is time to officially close the program. Although you have completed your program, your customer requires telephone and e-mail support in case an issue arises or a defect is detected. Such assurance is—

    a. An activity to be done as part of closing the program
    b. Outside the scope of the program
    c. An ongoing activity that is part of the program
    d. A standard best practice

2. You are managing a program for the first time in your telecom company. It is to convert all the existing phone lines in your city to ones that are underground to prevent outages during hurricanes and tornadoes, which are common to your region of the country. You realize that since you have seven projects in this program that various projects will close at different times during the life cycle of your program. These closing activities are—

    a. Limited to the project's life cycle
    b. Covered as you close the program
    c. Followed by a certificate of program completion
    d. Limited to closure of each project

3. As the closing manager for a program that has been under way for five years in your company, you must ensure that all deliverables were completed and that program objectives and measurable program success criteria were met. You meet with the former program manager, the governance board, key stakeholders, and members of the core program team. To further confirm that all the work has been completed, you review the—

    a. Program work breakdown structure (PWBS)
    b. Issue register
    c. Benefits register
    d. Program management plan

4. You are a program manager, and one of your component projects is complete. You work with the project manager to ensure that all closure activities are finished. The project manager has numerous tasks to complete; at the program level, you need to—

    a. Review relevant contract documentation
    b. Confirm that the project's benefits have been delivered
    c. Assess the project's budget
    d. Confirm that project closure has occurred

5. You are in the closing phase of managing a major program in your company. Your program included 11 separate contracts and was a significant endeavor for your organization. You and your team are commended for your work, and your governance board recommends that the enterprise program management office (EPMO) review procurement performance reports to focus on which one of the following organizational process assets?

    a. Those contracts that were terminated for convenience or default
    b. The procurement management plan
    c. The contract management plan for each of the 11 contracts
    d. The procurement process

6. You are managing a program to deliver a new tractor that will use 75 percent less fuel. This tractor will be manufactured using lean manufacturing techniques and will be offered for 30 percent less than the price of your competitors' equipment. The Marketing Department forecasts a major demand for this product, and the Sales Department is advertising it extensively at trade shows. You decide that you need a product support group. It should be set up—

    a. When the program is initiated
    b. When the product is in the test stage
    c. At the beginning of the project that produces the actual product
    d. When the product is deployed to customers

7. You establish a program support function to provide ongoing product support for the heating, ventilating, and air-conditioning (HVAC) program for the new class of amphibious warfare vehicles. This group is developing and implementing repair and return facilities and process requirements. You emphasize to the manager and team the importance of reliability and maintainability (R&M); however, R&M can only assist in ensuring—

    a. Successful, on-time product delivery
    b. A policy of zero defects
    c. That attention is paid to benefits sustainment
    d. That all documented benefits are realized as planned

8. Finally, it is time to close your HVAC program. You now have completed the new class of amphibious warfare vehicles, and you need to now execute the transition plan to the operations group in your company. You also need to reassign personnel, close the infrastructure, collect and document your lessons learned, meet with your governance board, and archive all documentation. When you are executing your transition plan you focus on—

   a. Ensuring the program has satisfied all requirements
   b. Managing the redeployment of all project resources
   c. Conducting reviews of your suppliers
   d. Collecting performance reviews of project team members

9. You work with numerous subcontractors and suppliers on your program. Your company considers two of the subcontractors to be valued partners; however, three of the subcontractors have not worked on any previous programs or projects for your company. Furthermore, one supplier and two subcontractors have worked with competitors, and one subcontractor uses a competitor as a supplier. To protect proprietary information, it is important that each supplier and subcontractor—

   a. Works independently and reports any conflicts of interest to your company's ethics officer
   b. Has a different member of your core team as contract administrator
   c. Signs a nondisclosure agreement
   d. Signs a "noncompete" agreement

10. You are the Business Change Manager on a mobile workforce initiative to decrease the costs associated with office space. As a result of this initiative, 2,000 employees now work in their homes, thereby saving the company millions per year in lease fees. Now that the culture change has been complete, you are working to close this program. You realize program closure activities are distinct from those of other phases of program management because closure activities—

   a. Do not require involvement with sellers or suppliers
   b. Occur at the end of the program life cycle
   c. Are handled by someone who is appointed as the closing manager
   d. Occur throughout the program

11. You are the project manager overseeing one of the largest components of a new product development program. A key supplier is working with you, but things are not going well. The work is much more complex than anyone thought, and the original contract specifications have long been obsolete. The supplier has not been able to make much progress, and it is difficult to determine whether the supplier is to blame. You decide that your best option in this case is to terminate the contract for convenience. This means you need to—

    a. Document actual work performed
    b. Update your qualified supplier list
    c. Perform a supplier performance review
    d. Pay the supplier the full price agreed upon as it is difficult to determine whether the supplier is to blame

12. You are appointed closing manager for Program A. The original program manager and other staff members have been reassigned. Your activities are focused on sustaining benefits and ensuring that all closure activities are complete. While you have many responsibilities, you do not need to—

    a. Archive the program records
    b. Update personnel records of the program staff
    c. Provide customer support according to contractual terms and conditions
    d. Manage the required transition to operations

13. Lessons learned can be reported in various ways. For consistency and quality, each program should adopt a standard approach. In the closing phase of the program, the program manager should—

    a. Address the advantages and disadvantages of the methods used to gather and report on lessons learned
    b. Ensure that each team member contributed a requisite number of lessons learned
    c. Survey the customer and the team for overall program satisfaction
    d. Report these lessons learned to the chief knowledge officer

14. You have been appointed closing manager for a program that has been under way for eight years. You have met with the program manager to talk about lessons learned. You have also met with the core program team members and reviewed the lessons learned that were documented by each of the six projects in this program. Your next step is to—

    a. Select the key lessons learned and archive them
    b. Archive all the lessons learned
    c. Index each project's records
    d. Assign metadata tags to the records so they can be easily located using a content management system

15. As program manager, you follow a detailed closure process that was developed by the enterprise program management office (EPMO). You have customized this procedure somewhat to fit the unique requirements of your program. Project C is now in its closing phase. This means it is your responsibility to—

    a. Conduct a performance review with the project team members
    b. Reallocate resources to other program components
    c. Perform a final performance review
    d. Update personnel records

16. You are a program manager for an aerospace company that is developing the C888 aircraft. Each of the component projects is scheduled to end at a different time. You establish a product support team that you will manage as part of your program responsibilities by providing upgrades during the product life cycle. Such upgrades are often used in which one of the following management approaches?

    a. Project management
    b. Earned value management
    c. Program management
    d. Operational management

17. You are managing the development of a series of heating, ventilation, and air-conditioning (HVAC) products. Each product is being managed as a separate project. Because the products will be completed at different times, you have a product support group. Your team has also established a configuration management system as a subsystem of the overall program management information system (PMIS). Changes have been requested to the product that was delivered in Project A. These changes affect the product from Project B, which is in production. You focus on—

    a. Responding to customer complaints regarding the product already delivered from Project A
    b. Ensuring that support is properly scheduled for Projects A and B
    c. Ensuring that a policy of zero defects is implemented as part of the quality assurance and control activities
    d. Conducting a thorough audit and extensive testing of future products before they are delivered

18. Each project in your program, Program B, is developing a specific product. Together your program will have eight separate products once it is complete. You establish a product support group to provide ongoing support for all the products in your program. A critical success factor is to ensure that—

   a. Staff members are physically collocated with the project team
   b. Support is available on a 24/7 basis
   c. Support is properly scheduled when changes are made
   d. Staff members are trained in project management and product support requirements

19. You are the program manager responsible for product development for your company's Class C vehicles. You have six projects in this program. After five years, the program is finally in the closing stage. You had more than 40 contracts on the program, so you need to pay attention to—

   a. Payment approval requests
   b. The payment control system
   c. Checklists
   d. Budget allocation reconciliation

20. A critical part of program management is managing the intellectual property that is created. One of your senior engineers left the company three weeks before your program was complete. A key scientist departed a year early. For program success you need to ensure that—

   a. Lessons learned are documented
   b. Program staff are not able to join competing firms at any time
   c. The organization conducts exit interviews with anyone who leaves the program
   d. Knowledge assets are transferred into the organization's knowledge repository

Answer Sheet

1.	a	b	c	d
2.	a	b	c	d
3.	a	b	c	d
4.	a	b	c	d
5.	a	b	c	d
6.	a	b	c	d
7.	a	b	c	d
8.	a	b	c	d
9.	a	b	c	d
10.	a	b	c	d

11.	a	b	c	d
12.	a	b	c	d
13.	a	b	c	d
14.	a	b	c	d
15.	a	b	c	d
16.	a	b	c	d
17.	a	b	c	d
18.	a	b	c	d
19.	a	b	c	d
20.	a	b	c	d

Answer Key

1. a. An activity to be done as part of closing the program

   The activities in the Closing Process Group lead to transition of artifacts, benefits monitoring, and ongoing operations to other groups. One key activity, which is generally defined by contract, is to provide customer support to an operational support function to ensure that guidance and maintenance are available in case any issues arise or any defects are detected after release.

   PMI®, *The Standard for Program Management*, 2008, 66

2. b. Covered as you close the program

   The Close Program process involves both project and non-project activity. As each project closes, the process is performed to capture information and records, archive them, communicate the closure, and obtain sign-off from the appropriate parties. Closure activity occurs throughout the program.

   PMI®, *The Standard for Program Management*, 2008, 98

3. d. Program management plan

   The program management plan is an input to the Close Program process and consists of a number of subsidiary plans, each of which needs to be reviewed to ensure that all requirements have been met, all final updates have been made, and all outstanding or active components have been brought to an orderly close.

   PMI®, *The Standard for Program Management*, 2008, 99

4. b. Confirm that the project's benefits have been delivered

   Program component closure focuses on closure issues at the program level. It involves ensuring that closure has taken place at the project level, but it is not a substitute for normal project closure activities. The benefits realization report should indicate that the projects have provided the benefits enumerated in the benefits realization plan.

   PMI®, *The Standard for Program Management*, 2008, 270

5. d. The procurement process

As an output of the Close Program Procurements process, procurement performance reports, which include the results of contract performance reviews, are reviewed. Updates to the organization's process assets are important because they can help or improve the program procurement process for future use.

PMI®, *The Standard for Program Management*, 2008, 206

6. c. At the beginning of the project that produces the actual product

A critical success factor for benefits assurance and sustainment is to make product support available at the beginning of the project that will actually produce the product. This allows the project that creates the product to define and provide life-cycle information for product support and benefits sustainment.

PMI®, *The Standard for Program Management*, 2008, 32

7. a. That attention is paid to benefit sustainment

The benefits, products, or services ultimately delivered by a program need to be sustained after the program is complete and when they are in operation or used.

PMI®, *The Standard for Program Management*, 2008, 31

8. a. Ensuring that the program has satisfied all requirements

The program transition plan outlines the steps to move the program from a development state to an operational state pending approval that the program has satisfied all requirements and is ready to turn over to a client or to an operational group.

PMI®, *The Standard for Program Management*, 2008, 83

9. c. Sign a nondisclosure agreement

Intellectual property must be captured and documented for future use. Nondisclosure agreements protect intellectual property that is developed during a program. The Closing Process Group includes an approach to ensure that all intellectual property must be captured for future use to ensure legal protection of this important asset.

PMI®, *The Standard for Program Management*, 2008, 66

10. a. Occur throughout the program

    Program closure activities do not occur only at the end of a program; rather, they occur throughout the program, each time a project is completed. These activities are important to ensure that valuable information is not lost.

    PMI®, *The Standard for Program Management*, 2008, 67

11. c. Document actual work performed

    Early termination of a contract is a special case of contract closure and can result from a mutual agreement of the parties or from the default of one of the parties. In this case of termination for convenience, the program manager needs to ensure that the contract record indicates actual work performed, the work not performed, and the circumstances of termination. Contract closure also includes updating the contract records according to the contract closure procedure, which is a tool and technique of the Close Program Procurements process.

    PMI®, *The Standard for Program Management*, 2008, 205

12. b. Update personnel records of the program staff

    In this situation, the original program manager conducts a performance evaluation with the program team members and updates the personnel records as well as any skills databases.

    PMI®, *The Standard for Program Management*, 2008, 30

13. a. Address the advantages and disadvantages of the methods used to gather and report on lessons learned

    Different approaches to collecting lessons learned have different advantages and disadvantages. The program manager should describe the approach that was used and document its advantages and disadvantages to identify organizational knowledge management practices for future programs.

    PMI®, *PgMP® Examination Content Outline*, 2011, 11

14. b. Archive all the lessons learned

    Although only selected lessons learned may be incorporated into the program's final report, all lessons learned and program-related documents should be archived so that they can be considered and used in future programs.

    PMI®, *The Standard for Program Management*, 2008, 30 and 100

15. b. Reallocate resources to other program components

At the program level, resources that become available from one project may be reallocated to other components that are active in the program or are soon to be activated as a component transition decision is made.

PMI®, *The Standard for Program Management*, 2008, 269–270

16. a. Project management

Benefits sustainment may follow a structured approach, but it typically does not require true program management principles to operate the end product. However, upgrades to a product often use project management to design, develop, and implement such changes.

PMI®, *The Standard for Program Management*, 2008, 31

17. b. Ensuring that support is properly scheduled for Projects A and B

After a product is deployed, any support must be scheduled to avoid interruption to the customers' use of the item to the greatest extent practicable.

PMI®, *The Standard for Program Management*, 2008, 32

18. c. Support is properly scheduled when changes are made

Ongoing benefits assurance and sustainment encompass a number of critical success factors. One factor is ensuring that support is properly scheduled when changes are made to a deployed product so that customers can support the updated product.

PMI®, *The Standard for Program Management*, 2008, 32

19. d. Budget allocation reconciliation

Budget allocation reconciliation is a tool and technique in the Close Program Procurements process. Variations are typical in categorization, allocation, and summarization between program and program component plans, contracts, and organizational charts of account. These variations make it difficult to directly relate expenditures between different program and organization components.

PMI®, *The Standard for Program Management*, 2008, 205

20. a. Lessons learned are documented

Lessons learned should be identified and documented throughout the program management processes. They should then flow to the Program Closure phase for final analysis and archival.

PMI®, *The Standard for Program Management*, 2008, 39

Benefits Management

Study Hints

Benefits management is the third domain in program management. These questions constitute 11%, or 19 questions, on the PgMP® exam. Since programs are established in order to obtain greater benefits than if the projects and other work that comprise them were managed in a standalone fashion, it is essential to focus on benefits management from the time the program was set forward in its business case, as a candidate to be in the organization's portfolio, until the program is officially closed, and the realized benefits then are transferred to others.

This area, therefore, focuses on the importance of the benefits realization plan and the criteria that are used to determine whether the benefits in the plan actually are met. This plan requires detailed and ongoing communications with stakeholders, especially if there are changes to the plan during the life of the program. Any changes, especially when benefits are realized as described in the plan or if they need to be modified, must be communicated to stakeholders, especially to the governance board and to the sponsor.

Additionally, a benefits transition plan is needed and a benefits sustainment approach. This means that once the program ends, its benefits then are transitioned to customers, end users, or to a product or an operations support group. These stakeholders require involvement in the program and a detailed understanding of the benefits of the program so they are able to sustain them once a project in the program is complete as well as the entire program.

Metrics then must be monitored to make sure the benefits are realized as stated in the plan and are communicated to stakeholders often in terms of a benefits realization report. Some benefits will be tangible and easily quantifiable, while others will be intangible and difficult to quantify but may be of equal or greater importance depending on the specific program. These benefits also must be continually reviewed to make sure the program remains in alignment with the organization's overall strategic objectives.

As risks (both threats and opportunities) and issues arise, or as new projects are added, and others are completed, the benefits realization plan requires review and update to see if changes are required.

Benefits management, therefore, is ongoing throughout the life of the program, and its life cycle also requires review. The benefits processes in *The Standard for Program Management—Second Edition* (2008) also must be studied and their concepts understood. Key inputs and outputs regarding the benefits realization plan should be reviewed.

Major Topics

The Importance of Benefits Management to Program Management

- Delivering and managing benefits
- Responsibility for benefit delivery
- Benefit-related risks
- Governance determines that benefits are delivered, and value is realized
  - Gate reviews
  - Periodic heath checks
- Plan Program Quality Process
  - Quality standards and oversights for benefit achievement
- Benefits sustainment
  - Support is available
  - Demands are understood so resources are available
  - Ongoing support adds value
  - Ongoing benchmarking of support activities
  - Support representatives are part of the program activities
  - Support is properly scheduled
- Support personnel have the training they require

Benefits Life Cycle

- Benefits identification
- Benefits analysis and planning
- Benefits realization
- Benefits transition

Benefits Realization Plan

- Include benefits in the program management plan
- A subsidiary plan to the program management plan
- Output of Define Program Goals and Objectives Process
  - Identifies business benefits
  - Documents how the benefits will be realized
  - Uses interviews, brainstorming, and review sessions
  - Shows changes to processes and systems
  - Describes how transition to new arrangements will occur
  - Ensures planned outcomes are realized before the program is closed
- Input to Report Program Performance Process
- Input to Plan and Establish Governance Structure Process
  - Value delivered when benefits are used
  - Plan identifies when and how the benefits will be realized
  - Examples of benefit realization measures
- Link the benefits to expenditures

Benefits Realization Report

- Output of Report Program Performance
  - Notes benefits may be realized before the program is complete
  - Quantify the incremental benefits
- Consider benefit dimensions
- Measure components against the benefit realization plan
- Output of Manage Program Benefits Process
  - Link to the Program Governance Plan
  - Benefits realization plan versus actual
  - Ensure benefits were realized in a timely way
  - Monitor the plan regularly
  - Evaluate the plan each time a component closes
- Ensure all benefits are realized before closure
- Use Governance to evaluate benefits
- Analyzed by the program team and reported to executives

Manage Program Benefits Process

- Shows governance is being followed
- Ensures a defined set of reports or metrics on benefits
- Facilitates effective reviews and show they have value
- Uses benefit realization analysis techniques

Program Transition Plan

- Describes how benefits will be transitioned and sustained

Practice Questions

1. Assume you are leading a consortium of four other firms. This is the second time your consortium has worked for this specific client, and it seems that the interpersonal relationships between the people on your team and the client's team are positive, and there is trust between the two groups. You hope for future business with this consortium and this client once your program is complete. Your success is measured primarily according to—

    a. Payback period
    b. Sustainment of benefits
    c. Products delivered according to specification
    d. Products delivered on time and without the need for existing funding

2. As you lead this consortium, XYZ, in its program work for company DEF, you have a large team and a large number of stakeholders. Since the consortium is of interest to the senior executives of all four firms, you and your core team seem to be in constant meetings and briefings with the executives and submitting reports to them, not to mention the meetings and briefings with the points of contact in company DEF. You also have a Governance Board overseeing your work with representatives from the four firms. The person who is ultimately responsible for delivering the program benefits is—

    a. Program director
    b. Your Chief Executive Officer, since your firm leads the consortium
    c. The head of the Governance Board
    d. Program sponsor

3. Working on the next generation of computing since Cloud computing, as the program manager for the G6 program, you believe you have a major innovative, new development product. You are developing this new product for a client, firm MNO, and now you are at a point in your program where one of the projects in this G6 program is complete. You are delivering it to the MNO client representative, who wants to measure now how this benefit has helped MNO. Measuring benefits should focus on—

    a. The degree to which the benefit has been adopted and used by its intended recipients
    b. The level of customer satisfaction achieved, as measured by specific surveys
    c. Improvement in the performance of business operations from the AS-IS state
    d. The morale of the individual employees who are responsible for executing the new process or operation

4. In your work on the G6 program, which was set up with eight separate projects, since each project in it has inter-relationships with other projects especially in terms of the benefits to be delivered, you decided one best practice to follow was to track the benefits described in your benefit realization plan in a benefit register and make this register visible not only to your entire team but also to your client, firm MNO. You felt such a benefit register would help track the benefits accrued by the eight projects, thus enabling your organization, Corporation G99, to realize and sustain all the benefits of its investment in your G6 program. In terms of the program benefit management life cycle, this register ends when—

   a. Benefits are delivered incrementally
   b. Benefits are transferred to product support
   c. Benefits planning is completed
   d. The program is terminated

5. In your business case for a new product in which people would have personal helicopters to take them to and from work and other places that would be inexpensive to purchase and also maintain, you realized a best practice was to set up a vision for this new program as already you had three projects in it. Your vision refers to the end state of the program and how it will benefit the organization. As a program manager working on this personal helicopter program, when you manage the transition from the AS-IS to the TO-BE state, you are working in the—

   a. Benefits analysis and planning phase
   b. Monitoring the Incremental Benefits phase
   c. Benefits realization phase
   d. Program Setup phase

6. Working on your personal helicopter program for company BCD, one of your first tasks as the program manager was to build on the benefits in the business case and prepare a benefits realization plan. You have kept this plan up to date as you first had three projects in your program and now have eight. Now, you are measuring how each benefit is realized, which means you are working in the—

   a. Program Setup phase
   b. Executing phase
   c. Benefits Measurement phase
   d. Delivery of Program Benefits phase

7. Finally, your program, G6, which has taken the concept of Cloud computing to the next level, and your eight separate projects as well as some ongoing work, is complete. Your client, MNO, is extremely satisfied with the work you and your team members have done. They also have been impressed with the quality of the work done by your three program contractors and have recommended you and your team to work with another company. Your executive team is extremely pleased. As program G6 is closed, now benefit management is focusing on a number of key initiatives, including—

   a. Reporting planned versus actual benefits at the current point in time
   b. Ensuring that the benefits delivered are in line with the original business case
   c. Ensuring stakeholder agreement on the factors contributing to the benefits
   d. Prioritizing the value of each of the program components to prove return on investment (ROI)

8. However, on program G6, when you and your core team performed its program analysis review in the closing phase to help prepare your final performance report on this program, you reported to your Governance Board that you believe one of the key benefits that caused program G6 to be set up in the first place was only achieved to a partial extent; you did meet client MNO's requirements, but you and your team recognize more could have been done. And, to complicate the issue even further, even though your client, MNO, is pleased, your program is significantly over budget and behind schedule. Personally, you and your team are not in jeopardy of losing your jobs because MNO is pleased and has recommended you to another organization. However, your next step is to—

   a. Document in the final program report the reasons for the deviation
   b. Review the program- and project-level requirements to see whether they were accurately captured
   c. Recommend to the stakeholders and others that the program be officially closed, and a new project be initiated to deal with the issue
   d. Document the reasons for the deviation and record them in the lessons learned archives so that other program managers will not make the same mistakes

9. You are the Business Change Manager on a mobile workforce initiative to decrease the costs associated with office space. As a result of this initiative, 2,000 employees now work in their homes, thereby saving the company millions per year in lease fees. To ensure that all the benefits have been achieved and that change has successfully occurred, as the program is closing, you need to—

   a. Calculate the annual lease savings and provide a report to the executive sponsor
   b. Provide state-of-the-art technology to the "home employees" so that they remain productive
   c. Ensure as part of the transition plan that the program team members are provided advice and counsel for appropriate redeployment to other projects or programs
   d. Work with Human Resources to ensure that each employee's home office is set up with the proper equipment and facilities to avoid future litigation resulting from inadequate or unsafe working conditions

10. You have been appointed program manager for Program XYZ. You have assembled your team and have begun work on your benefits realization plan. The person who wrote the plan delivered it to you. After you read it, you told the team member that the plan was missing a key component. It did not describe—

    a. How the potential impact of any planned program change affects the benefits outcome
    b. A method to identify interdependencies of benefits within program components
    c. A way to link the outputs to the planned program outcomes
    d. An assessment of the value and organizational impact of the program

11. Assume you are the program manager for the next generation of parachutes for your Department of the Army. Each of the new parachutes must have a reliability rating of 99.99%, and certain types of parachutes will be deployed in certain conditions given climate and terrain. In total, your program has five projects; all work is to be done in three years. As you regularly report on the status of the benefits of this program, you must measure the benefits that have accrued to date and communicate the information to your program sponsor and the program governance board. The metrics and procedures you are using for this reporting are stated in—

    a. Program charter
    b. Benefits realization plan
    c. Program management plan
    d. Key performance indicators

12. Assume your government is in serious financial difficulty and may even default on some government issued funds. Spending has been out of control; in fact, many question whether the numbers reported are accurate. However, you are managing a program to cut the spending of the National Park Service in your Department of Interior by 50%. You and your team have seven projects in your program. It has been extremely difficult as you had to evaluate each park, the work done in the Regional Offices, and the work done by the Headquarters staff to determine how to equitably reduce the spending. Finally, you have completed this program and have made the spending cuts, which were approved by the Secretary of the Interior. Now that the program is closed, benefits management focuses on a number of key initiatives including—

  a. Forecasting the ongoing value of the benefits
  b. Ensuring that the benefits delivered are in line with the business case
  c. Ensuring stakeholder agreement on the factors contributing to the benefits
  d. Prioritizing the value of each of the program components

13. Working in your processed cheese company, project management has been successfully introduced over the past seven years. A Project Management Office (PMO) is in place, people have been trained in project management, project reviews are held, and project managers follow a standard methodology. Many people have been certified as PMPs®. A member of your PMO recently attained her PgMP®. She has recommended that a new initiative to modernize the process cheese factory be managed as a program because it is so complex and will have a number of projects associated with it that have interdependencies. She feels it is better managed therefore as a program rather than as a large project. She also feels that if the factory modernization initiative is managed as a program, there will be more benefits as a result. A key characteristic of the program life cycle is that it—

  a. Follows a repeatable process
  b. Is nonsequential
  c. Ends with the delivery process
  d. Focuses first on benefits realization

14. Working on this program to modernize the process cheese factory, you now have seven projects in it and one operations initiative. You realize the program was set up to deliver more benefits through a program structure rather than as standalone projects. Because a program is responsible for delivering benefits to the organization, the program manager, members of the program team, project managers and team members, and other program stakeholders all have key roles and responsibilities in benefits management. These roles are set forth in the—

    a. Benefits register
    b. Benefits realization plan
    c. Benefits management plan
    d. Responsibility assignment matrix

15. As the manager of a new program to develop the next-generation heating, ventilation, and air-conditioning (HVAC) system, you have three projects in your program, and it is only the first year. You expect the program to last at least three years, and you are hopeful you will have a PMO for support. You also are sure more projects will be added as the program ensues. Therefore, you establish a process to monitor your program benefits. Following the standard benefits management life cycle, you develop this process during the—

    a. Benefits identification phase
    b. Benefits analysis and planning phase
    c. Benefits realization phase
    d. Benefits monitoring phase

16. As you move to establish program management in your processed cheese company, you are facing a lot of questions especially from project managers and the other members of the PMO since this is a culture change from the organization. You are setting up a program life cycle that is different from the project life cycle that has been followed now for seven years and will continue to be followed for individual projects. You also must train those people who will manage the programs and set up a program management methodology within the PMO. You have talked with your executives, and they plan to announce that the Project Management Office will be retitled as the Program Management Office. Within the context of the program life cycle, the program manager is primarily responsible for managing—

    a. The program governance board so that it does not interfere with the team
    b. Key stakeholders
    c. Benefits realization
    d. Individual project deliverables to ensure that they align with organizational objectives

17. Assume you have just completed a program to design and develop a new Park for your City of 10,000 people. It is different from the existing two Parks as it does not concentrate on sports and instead is devoted solely to the environment with a theme of exotic plants and lakes throughout with places to sit and observe the beauty within the Park. The purpose was to provide benefits to the residents of all ages. You want to make sure that these benefits then are sustained now that your work is done, and the Park is open to the residents of the City. The City now has the responsibility for sustaining these benefits. This is the purpose of the—

    a. Program transition plan
    b. Program road map update
    c. Transition Monitoring and Controlling process
    d. Transition Realization process

18. You are the program manager for a six-year program that is in its second year. To ensure that the benefits realization plan is on target, you perform a benefits review of the four projects that are under way. Project B is not achieving the desired benefits, and its deliverables are not being completed as planned. When you report this concern to the governance board, the executive sponsor recommends that Project B be terminated. At the program level, you—

    a. Prepare a transition request
    b. Prepare a report of lessons learned
    c. Conduct a final program review
    d. Reassign the project manager for Project B

19. Your company is a leader in the pharmaceutical industry. It has received approval from the Food and Drug Administration (FDA) for a new drug that will cure all glaucoma conditions. Although the demand for this product is high, the company has many other drugs to manufacture. You are managing a program to upgrade the manufacturing process. Because you recognize the potential benefits associated with this new product, as the program manager, you should regularly monitor the—

    a. Quality management plan
    b. Benefits realization plan
    c. Benefits register
    d. Benefits report

20. You are managing a program that lengthened existing icebreaker vessels so that they could be used in the waters surrounding Antarctica. During extensive testing off the coast of Labrador, the vessels performed well, and the reliability and maintainability (R&M) data were well within an acceptable variance range. Many of the vessels are now in use off the coast of Antarctica, and the R&M data have a much wider range of variance; vessel performance remains acceptable. It is now time to close the program. You need to—

   a. Leave in place a legacy of operational benefits sustainment
   b. Continue to provide governance oversight
   c. Support corrective actions as required
   d. Track all benefits even after the program closes

Answer Sheet

1.	a	b	c	d
2.	a	b	c	d
3.	a	b	c	d
4.	a	b	c	d
5.	a	b	c	d
6.	a	b	c	d
7.	a	b	c	d
8.	a	b	c	d
9.	a	b	c	d
10.	a	b	c	d

11.	a	b	c	d
12.	a	b	c	d
13.	a	b	c	d
14.	a	b	c	d
15.	a	b	c	d
16.	a	b	c	d
17.	a	b	c	d
18.	a	b	c	d
19.	a	b	c	d
20.	a	b	c	d

Answer Key

1. b. Sustainment of benefits

    While all are good measures of success, programs are established in order to obtain greater benefits than if the projects that comprise them were managed in a standalone fashion. The benefits are stated in the benefits realization plan, and success is measured in terms of the continued realization of benefits once the program is complete.

    PMI. *Program Management Professional* (PgMP)® *Examination Content Outline*, April 2011, 13

2. d. Program sponsor

    The program sponsor is the group or person who champions the program initiative and is responsible for providing project resources and for the ultimate delivery of program benefits.

    PMI®, *The Standard for Program Management*, 2008, 235

3. c. Improvement in the performance of business operations from the AS-IS state

    Measuring benefits should also be able to identify the improvements achieved as the new capability, process, or operation is integrated into the overall business operations, thereby providing an advantage to the organization.

    PMI®, *The Standard for Program Management*, 2008, 309

    Central Computer and Telecommunications Agency (CCTA). *Managing Successful Programmes*. London: CCTA, 1999, 89

4. d. The program is terminated

    During the Benefits Realization phase, the major work of the program is under way. This phase ends when the benefits are achieved, or the program is terminated in the Benefits Transition phase.

    PMI®, *The Standard for Program Management*, 2008, 20

5. c. Benefits realization phase

    The program management team is responsible for managing the program's projects in a consistent and coordinated fashion to achieve incremental benefits. In phase four (the benefits realization phase), the team is responsible for managing the transition from the current or AS-IS state to the target or TO-BE state.

    PMI®, *The Standard for Program Management*, 2008, 20 and 28–29

6. d. Delivery of Program Benefits phase

   This phase concludes when the program's planned benefits have been achieved, delivered, and accepted or when the program is terminated. During this phase, benefits realization reports are prepared and the Manage Program Benefits process is executed.

   PMI®, *The Standard for Program Management*, 2008, 28–29 and 66

7. b. Ensuring that the benefits delivered are in line with the original business case

   Programs are initiated to deliver benefits that may not be realized if the component projects are managed in a standalone fashion. When a program ends, the benefits delivered should be compared to those that were initially identified in the business case to ensure that the program actually delivered the full benefits for which it was created.

   PMI®, *The Standard for Program Management*, 2008, 31

8. a. Document in the final program report the reasons for the deviation

   When a program ends, the program manager assesses overall performance and shares lessons learned with all team members. Information is included in the final program report.

   PMI®, *The Standard for Program Management*, 2008, 100

9. c. Ensure as part of the transition plan that the program team members are provided advice and counsel for appropriate redeployment to other projects or programs

   A key activity of the Program Closure phase is to disband the team and ensure that arrangements are in place for appropriate redeployment of all human resources.

   PMI®, *The Standard for Program Management*, 2008, 30

10. c. A way to link the outputs to the planned program outcomes

    There are a number of key components in the benefits realization plan, which is prepared in the Define Program Goals and Objectives process and maintained throughout the program. Two key components are to ensure that the program is managed in a way that satisfies the use of the program's outputs and to link the outputs to an outcome of the program. Each benefit should be specific, measurable, actual, realistic, and time-based (SMART).

    PMI®, *The Standard for Program Management*, 2008, 109

11. b. Benefits realization plan

The benefits realization plan is drafted early and maintained throughout all phases of the program. During the Manage Program Benefits process, a benefits realization report is prepared. Among other things, this report tracks the benefits realized against the benefits delivered to the organization.

PMI®, *The Standard for Program Management*, 2008, 266

12. b. Ensuring that the benefits delivered are in line with the business case

Upon program completion, the benefits delivered should always be compared against those identified in the business case to ensure that all expected benefits were delivered.

PMI®, *The Standard for Program Management*, 2008, 31

13. b. Is nonsequential

The program life cycle is nonsequential. Throughout the life cycle, components are mobilized as appropriate so that a stream of deliverables focuses on facilitating new operations and benefits.

PMI®, *The Standard for Program Management*, 2008, 18

14. b. Benefits realization plan

A key component of the benefits realization plan, which is prepared in the early phase of the program, is a description of roles and responsibilities for benefits management.

PMI®, *The Standard for Program Management*, 2008, 109, 310

15. c. Benefits realization phase

A process for benefits monitoring is established in the benefits realization phase. At this time, the program manager and the team establish the structure in which work will occur as well as the technical infrastructure to facilitate the work. This includes establishing a framework to monitor and control the projects and to measure program benefits.

PMI®, *The Standard for Program Management*, 2008, 20, 84

16. c. Benefits realization

In contrast to the project life cycle, which focuses on producing deliverables, the program life cycle manages outcomes and benefits. The program manager, therefore, manages and accrues the program's corresponding benefits.

PMI®, *The Standard for Program Management*, 2008, 11 and 28–29

17. a. Program transition plan

The program transition plan enumerates all necessary actions that are required to transfer the program from a development state to an operational state pending approval that all requirements are complete. It is an output of the Develop Program Management Plan process.

PMI®, *The Standard for Program Management*, 2008, 83

18. a. Prepare a transition request

A transition request is an input to the Approve Component Transition process, and it is required if a project is terminated before its scheduled completion. A termination decision may be the result of a program benefits review or a change in the external environment. The transition request is also required for normal project completion.

PMI®, *The Standard for Program Management*, 2008, 270

19. b. Benefits realization plan

The benefits realization plan must be monitored regularly to determine the actual events and changes in plans at both the component and overall program level.

PMI®, *The Standard for Program Management*, 2008, 266

20. a. Leave in place a legacy of operational benefits sustainment

The Closing Process Group formalizes acceptance of the products, services, or results that define the program's successful completion. It is intended to leave in place a legacy of operational benefits sustainment, thus deriving optimal value from the program's objectives.

PMI®, *The Standard for Program Management*, 2008, 66–67

Stakeholder Management

Study Hints

The Stakeholder Management questions on the PgMP® certification exam, which constitute 16% of the exam, or 27 questions, focus on the importance of stakeholder identification, management, and engagement throughout the program's life cycle and even when the program is first being proposed. They also emphasize the link between stakeholders and effective communications, since communications are the key competency for program managers, and so much of the program manager's time is spent in communications given the large and diverse numbers of stakeholders on programs. Therefore, other questions focus on communications planning and distributing information to stakeholders in the format needed, at the desired frequency, and with the desired level of detail.

Throughout the program, stakeholders will have different levels of influence and interest in the program at different phases of the life cycle. A stakeholder analysis, therefore, is essential and is ongoing. The program manager and his or her core them must work diligently with some stakeholders, who may not be program supporters, to gain their confidence and turn them into advocates for the program. A stakeholder matrix is a useful tool to prepare and maintain.

Stakeholder engagement is essential for program success and is a way to generate and maintain program visibility. As a result, defining communications needs for different types of stakeholders and providing it as required also promotes their support for the program.

This domain covers the four processes in the Program Stakeholder Management knowledge area as well as the Plan Communications and Distribute Information processes from the Program Communications Management knowledge area.

Following is a list of the major topics covered in Stakeholder Management. Use this list to focus your study efforts on the areas that are the most likely to appear on the exam.

Major Topics

Importance of Stakeholder Management

- Definition of a stakeholder
- Types of stakeholders—internal and external
- Necessity in terms of organizational change

Plan Program Stakeholder Management

- Steps to follow to conduct a stakeholder analysis
- Preparation and contents of a stakeholder management plan
- Guidelines for program components in project-level stakeholder management

Identify Program Stakeholders

- Stakeholder register
- Impacts on the stakeholders
- Approaches to manage stakeholder relationships
- Mapping techniques to consider for categories of stakeholders
- Using contracts and Request for Proposals to identify stakeholders
- Key questions to consider in interviews with stakeholders
- Key program stakeholders
- Stakeholder inventory
- Stakeholder matrix

Engage Program Stakeholders

- Stakeholder impact and issue tracking and prioritization tool
- Program impact analysis
- Stakeholder metrics

Manage Program Stakeholder Expectations

- Effective negotiation techniques
- Conflict management approaches
- Communications skills
- Influencing skills

Plan Communications

- Determine stakeholder information and communication needs
- Define communications requirements
- Cultural and language differences

- Working with virtual teams
- Using the organization's communications strategy
- Using the program management information system
- Communication methods
- Program communications management plan
- Communications log
- Communications strategy

Distribute Information

- Providing stakeholders with timely and accurate information
- Three key channels—clients, sponsors, and component managers
- Types of communications methods
- Using information gathering and retrieval systems
- Using information distribution methods
- Providing performance reports
- Updating lessons learned

Practice Questions

1. As the program manager to develop a new source of energy that can be used in the northern and southern hemispheres when solar power is not readily available, you have a large number of stakeholders, both internal and external. You also are working with a virtual team, and many team members represent different cultures. You recognize since you are the program manager the importance of keeping all of your stakeholders informed in a timely manner by distributing various types of information. One piece of information that stakeholders need but that is often overlooked by program managers is a—

   a. Receipt of proposals
   b. Notification of responses to change requests
   c. List of preventive actions
   d. Record of training

2. You are working on a complex five-year program that has a minimum of four projects under way at any given time. A major scope change to Project L has resulted in a need to rebaseline its schedule. Consequently, because of dependencies with Project L, Project D also had to revise its schedule. These two revisions required that the program schedule be revised as well. The program schedule change has been approved and processed, and the program and component schedules are updated. Your next step is to—

   a. Inform your stakeholders
   b. Inform the project governance board
   c. Prepare a balanced scorecard report
   d. Issue a variance performance report

3. The president of your company has selected you to be the head of all eLearning and has asked that you launch a program to develop new media for delivering your company's content. The success of the program is contingent upon adopting an eLearning approach that the marketplace needs and for which it will pay a reasonable price. The program has a number of stakeholders, some of whom are supportive and some of whom are skeptical, and you anticipate many debates concerning the program's objectives. As the program manager, you recognize that you need to rely on—

   a. Leadership skills
   b. Conflict resolution skills
   c. Environmental awareness skills
   d. Diplomatic skills

4. As program manager for all eLearning in your company, BBB, you are launching your program to develop new media for delivering your company's course content. The success of your program is measured by adopting an eLearning approach that the marketplace needs and for which it will pay a reasonable price so BBB will have a competitive advantage. You have a diverse group of stakeholders, and your program has active involvement by BBB's Chief Executive Officer. As the program manager, you must ensure the performance data on your eLearning program are consolidated and routed to the intended recipients to provide a clear picture of overall program performance and especially to show how resources, which already are constrained in BBB, are being used effectively. This is done through—

   a. Targeted communications messaging
   b. The Distribute Information process
   c. Program performance and status reports prepared in the Report Program Performance process
   d. Stakeholder management as identified in the stakeholder management strategy

5. As the program manager to develop a new source of energy that can be used in the northern and southern hemispheres when solar power is not readily available, you have a large number of stakeholders, both internal and external. You also are working with a virtual team, and many team members represent different cultures. You have eight projects so far in your program and are in the executing phase. This means in regard to project and program communications with your stakeholders you should be—

   a. Determining who needs to be receiving the communications and when
   b. Distributing communications messages to stakeholders
   c. Implementing the feedback loops developed earlier in the program
   d. Building your communications infrastructure

6. Assume you are the program manager for the City of Martone, Florida, a small island off the Florida Keys. This City is noted for its exclusive resorts and is a coveted destination for people around the globe. The Martone family donated the island to the State in 1908, with the stipulation that the Martone name remain. Since then, the island has been continually developing but at a controlled rate. Three years ago, someone illegally brought large aloe lizards into the island. At first, people thought they were cute, as they were larger than the typical lizard, and they pose no threat to humans, but they now have multiplied and seem to be everywhere. They enjoy eating many of the beautiful flowering plants at the resorts. However, vacationers are complaining about these lizards, and in the past two years the number of visitors has decreased dramatically. Your job is to manage a program to contain these lizards recognizing Florida has a regulation that prevents killing any type of lizard. So far, you have identified over 50 internal and external stakeholders, and have three projects in your program. You first collected baseline data on the number of lizards and other information about them to communicate to your stakeholders and now are providing regular updates on the status and specific requirements. A key focus in performance reporting is information on—

   a. Cost and schedule status
   b. Use of resources to deliver program benefits
   c. Issues to be discussed at program governance board meetings for decisions to move to the next phase
   d. Activities to determine whether specific work results have been completed

7. Meeting stakeholder expectations is vital to program success; therefore, participation of stakeholders must be monitored to ensure that their expectations are met. You are managing a large program with diverse stakeholder groups. On this program, you have found that you often need to—

   a. Meet one-on-one with each of the 200 stakeholders on the program
   b. Facilitate negotiation sessions between stakeholders
   c. Have your enterprise program management office (EPMO) take over responsibility for stakeholder expectations management
   d. Use your stakeholder analysis chart as a key tool and technique to assist in managing expectations

8. You have been managing a complex and major program in your company, BBB. Your program involved 11 separate contracts and also two projects that were done solely with in-house resources. Your team was a virtual one, and because of budget constraints, you were unable to have a face-to-face meeting. However, you have finally finished this program and are making sure all the contracts have been completed successfully, and that the benefits have been transitioned according to your transition plan to the operations group. You are conducting a stakeholder post program implementation review now that the operations group has been managing the ongoing work for six months. At this point, your stakeholders should be most interested in—

   a. The program's earned value analysis
   b. Whether the program met all its quality goals
   c. The results achieved relative to the organization's strategic goals
   d. The lessons learned and best practices review to help other ongoing or future programs

9. You are progressing on your eLearning program. The BBB CEO so far seems to be pleased with your progress to date, and you have four projects in the program. He has commented to the Executive team that he believes this new program will definitely increase market share for BBB, and he has asked the Sales team to begin to inform customers about it. You have successfully closed the six contracts you had awarded, and the benefits from the four projects have been realized in your opinion. You are now conducting a G4 phase-gate review with your Governance Board. You and two of the Board members, who are not in the CEO's inner circle, are having a disagreement as to whether the phase has been completed successfully, and your program can now advance to the closing process. One way this can be determined is to—

   a. Take a vote of the members of the program board
   b. Compare performance to date against the exit criteria for the phase
   c. Try to reach consensus among all stakeholders
   d. Conduct an earned value analysis

10. In the most recent program performance meeting as part of the program closeout phase, you reported that the earned value data were favorable, that all performance metrics were in line with stated criteria, and that stakeholder requirements were met. Yet several stakeholders reported that the program fell somewhat short of their expectations. You assert that the program is successful because it has met all objective criteria. Your assessment is—

    a. Incorrect. Expectations are as important as requirements.
    b. Incorrect. Although expectations should be considered, they are not as important as requirements.
    c. Correct. There is no difference between expectations and requirements.
    d. Correct. The stakeholders should have expressed their expectations as requirements during the requirements-gathering phase.

11. Recently, your City has been experiencing numerous power outages because of excessive heavy rainfall and numerous hurricanes. Many residents have purchased gas generators, but they tend to not last long enough so people are also purchasing generators that use propane. However, some people do not want a large 500 to 750 gallon propane tank in their yard or lack the required space based on City ordinances. Your propane company has decided that it should set up a program that instead of having to have large propane tanks, a distribution system would be put in place to use natural gas instead. You are the manager for this program. Since natural gas is plentiful, you realize this program will provide a number of benefits for the City, its residents, and your company, CDE. You also have a large number of interested stakeholders, and they are monitoring your progress to see if this new natural gas approach will be ready before the next hurricane season. The success of your program is measured in terms of—

    a. The degree to which the program satisfies needs and benefits
    b. Earned value management
    c. Each project's adherence to its schedule
    d. Products delivered according to specification

12. You are the program manager on a highly controversial e-mail retention program for your company, AEI. More than 75 percent of the people in AEI are opposed to the program because they realize all of their e-mail messages will be archived. AEI management has informed everyone they plan to hire someone to review each e-mail to make sure it pertains to company business and is not a personal one. They also want to make sure all e-mails are written in a professional way and are ethical. You now have many conflicts as you and your team execute the five projects in your program. This program represents a major culture change for AEI as in the past it was common to discuss anything with anyone. Generally accepted methods of organizational change management are required for this program, and the person in charge of this change is—

    a. The program director
    b. The program sponsor
    c. The program governance board
    d. You, the program manager

13. As a program manager, you recognize the importance of stakeholder management. To support your efforts, especially with key stakeholders whose displeasure might hinder the program's success, you prepare a stakeholder management plan. You identify contact points on your program team for each stakeholder. You know that stakeholders must see the benefits of the program. Therefore, you need to have skills in—

    a. Strategic planning
    b. Leadership
    c. Enterprise resource management
    d. Customer relationship management

14. Each program has stakeholders. This certainly is the case in your program to contain and somehow eradicate the aloe lizards in Martone, Florida. At the time you were appointed as program manager, you and your core team immediately identified 50 key stakeholders. Now you are in the executing phase, and the number of stakeholders has increased according to your stakeholder analysis to 88. You seem to feel as if all you do all day is communicate with stakeholders and have meetings with groups of them. The purpose of program stakeholder management is to identify how the program will affect stakeholders in areas such as—

    a. The organization's culture
    b. Management of operations
    c. Corporate governance
    d. Legal policies, standards, and regulations

15. When you worked as a project manager, you learned that most project managers spend about 90 percent of their time in communications. Now as a program manager in Martone, Florida, you know you are spending almost 100% of your time in communications. It seems to never end. You have set presentations now for different groups of stakeholders but then you must continually update them to show progress, and new stakeholders seem to become interested in your progress as the program ensues. Communication planning and execution in program management therefore focus on—

    a. Reacting to stakeholder concerns
    b. Taking corrective actions in response to program issues
    c. Proactively targeting development and delivery of key messages
    d. Identifying suitable technologies for distributing program information

16. You are the program manager responsible for implementing salesmagic.com, a highly complex but powerful tool for customer relationship management. You and your team have spent three days identifying the metrics against which you will measure program performance. Your next step is to review the metrics with—

    a. Key stakeholders to gain agreement
    b. The program governance board to gain agreement
    c. The program director to gain agreement
    d. The head of sales to gain agreement

17. You are a program manager for a city transit authority. Your program has a number of projects under way to upgrade the infrastructure to current technologies and to implement a process improvement program. The transit authority's chief financial officer (CFO) has left to assume a position in a different city, and a new person has been appointed CFO. You should—

    a. Update your stakeholder inventory
    b. Appoint one of your core team members to interact with the new CFO
    c. Meet with the new CFO when it is convenient, because the CFO is not a primary stakeholder in your program
    d. Take no action at this time

18. You are a program manager for a new line of children's toys called The Destroyer. Your stakeholders—especially the members of your program governance board—have requested an analysis of any opportunities that can be leveraged as you collect and analyze performance on your program. Also, you want to identify any adverse impacts that must be corrected. After you prepare this information and consolidate it, you—

    a. Meet with your key stakeholders to inform them of your program's progress according to their specific areas of interest
    b. Make the information available through the Distribute Information process
    c. Follow the process outlined in your communications management plan
    d. Contact your governance board about any adverse trends that require immediate action to meet the required delivery date

19. Stakeholders play a critical role in the success of a program or project. As program manager for development of a next-generation motorcycle to be available in 2020, you know it is a best practice to prepare a stakeholder analysis and management plan. This should be done—

    a. During overall program planning
    b. While the business case for the program is made
    c. As the program is being initiated
    d. After the projects and other ongoing components of the program are determined

20. You are managing a program under contract with a major motion picture studio. The Statement of Work noted that you needed to interface with ten different groups of people within the studio. After your company, KSI, won this contract, you and your team recognized the importance of performing a detailed stakeholder analysis based on the Statement of Work. To conduct such an analysis, you plan to hold interviews, use focus groups, and perhaps conduct a survey. This approach enables you to—

    a. Develop a stakeholder communications strategy
    b. Prioritize stakeholders in terms of their ability to influence the program
    c. Develop a stakeholder register
    d. Identify stakeholders' attitudes toward the program

Answer Sheet

1.	a	b	c	d
2.	a	b	c	d
3.	a	b	c	d
4.	a	b	c	d
5.	a	b	c	d
6.	a	b	c	d
7.	a	b	c	d
8.	a	b	c	d
9.	a	b	c	d
10.	a	b	c	d

11.	a	b	c	d
12.	a	b	c	d
13.	a	b	c	d
14.	a	b	c	d
15.	a	b	c	d
16.	a	b	c	d
17.	a	b	c	d
18.	a	b	c	d
19.	a	b	c	d
20.	a	b	c	d

Answer Key

1. c. Notification of responses to change requests

   The Distribute Information process includes a change request log as an input to the process. Distributed information includes notifications of change requests to the program and project teams and the person requesting the change and the corresponding responses to those requests.

   PMI®, *The Standard for Program Management*, 2008, 57 and 148

2. a. Inform your stakeholders

   An output of the Monitor and Control Program Schedule process is program performance reports to provide valuable status information to stakeholders, who will then use them to make decisions about future program execution.

   PMI®, *The Standard for Program Management*, 2008, 134

3. b. Conflict resolution skills

   In the Manage Program Stakeholder Expectations process, conflict management is a tool and technique. The program manager must define how conflicts will be managed among stakeholders and should include an escalation path to ensure that stalemates do not occur.

   PMI®, *The Standard for Program Management*, 2008, 241

4. b. The Distribute Information process

   The Distribute Information process is used to convey information to program stakeholders to provide them with needed status and deliverable information. Information is also provided to team members concerning general and background information on program performance.

   PMI®, *The Standard for Program Management*, 2008, 147–148

5. b. Distributing communications messages to stakeholders

   Communication messages are an output of the Report Program Performance process and are distributed to stakeholders. Examples may include e-mails messages, voice mail messages, performance reports, presentations, updates to a central repository, and other forms of communication.

   PMI®, *The Standard for Program Management*, 2008, 156

6. b. Use of resources to deliver program benefits

   The Report Program Performance process involves consolidating performance data to provide information to program stakeholders about the use of resources to deliver program benefits. It provides information on overall program performance.

   PMI®, *The Standard for Program Management*, 2008, 152

7. b. Facilitate negotiation sessions between stakeholders

   Negotiation skills and techniques are a tool and technique in the Manage Program Stakeholder Expectations process. These skills can help the team to resolve stakeholder issues and conflicts that arise during the program. On large programs, the program manager may need to facilitate negotiation sessions among stakeholder groups.

   PMI®, *The Standard for Program Management*, 2008, 241

8. c. The results achieved relative to the organization's strategic goals

   Programs are initiated as part of an organization's portfolio, which supports strategic goals and initiatives. Ultimately, a program's measure of success is how well the strategic goals of the organization were met by investing in the program.

   PMI®, *PgMP® Examination Content Outline*, 2011, 5

9. b. Compare performance to date against the exit criteria for the phase

   It is always preferable to have an objective measure of success as opposed to relying on peoples' opinions if at all possible. Fact-based decision making is required to ensure that all program work is complete and that the intended benefits are being realized.

   PMI®, *The Standard for Program Management*, 2008, 29

10. a. Incorrect. Expectations are as important as requirements.

    Successful program managers are as concerned with meeting stakeholders' expectation as they are with meeting their requirements.

    PMI®, *PgMP® Examination Content Outline*, 2011, 14

11. a. The degree to which the program satisfies needs and benefits

    Program success can be measured using a variety of metrics; ultimately, it is measured against the needs and benefits of the stakeholders.

    PMI®, *The Standard for Program Management*, 2008, 11

12. d. You, the program manager

Program managers are the escalation point for issues, changes, risks, interfaces, and dependencies. As program manager, you must manage relationships, resolve conflicts, and deal with the political aspects of stakeholder management.

PMI®, The Standard for Program Management, 2008, 11 and 13

13. b. Leadership

Stakeholders play a critical role in determining program and project success. Because they can help or hinder a program, the program manager needs to have leadership skills to work with them.

PMI®, *The Standard for Program Management*, 2008, 12–13

14. a. The organization's culture

Program stakeholder management is concerned with how the program will affect stakeholders in areas such as the organization's culture, local population, current major issues, and resistance or barriers to change.

PMI®, *The Standard for Program Management*, 2008, 227

15. c. Proactively targeting development and delivery of key messages

The emphasis of communications planning and execution is on the proactive and targeted development of key messages. Program stakeholders should be engaged at the right time and in the right way.

PMI®, *The Standard for Program Management*, 2008, 227

16. a. Key stakeholders to gain agreement

All key stakeholders need to review and agree on the metrics against which the program will be measured. To expedite decision making, it is best to meet with as many as possible at one time.

PMI®, *The Standard for Program Management*, 2008, 236

17. a. Update your stakeholder inventory

As program manager, you manage the stakeholder inventory throughout the program and take appropriate action to handle any changes that may occur. Although the CFO may not be a primary stakeholder, he or she is important to the program and cannot be overlooked.

PMI®, *The Standard for Program Management*, 2008, 235 and 238

18. b. Make the information available through the Distribute Information process

   During the Report Program Performance process, performance information is collected, measured, and consolidated, and measurements and trends are assessed to generate improvements. Information about how resources are being used to deliver program benefits is consolidated, and the consolidated information is then made available to program stakeholders through the Distribute Information process.

   PMI®, *The Standard for Program Management*, 2008, 152

19. c. As the program is being initiated

   Stakeholders are persons who have an interest in or influence over the program. They may be internal or external to the organization, and their expectations must be managed from the beginning to the end of the program. Stakeholder considerations are stated in the program charter, which is developed during Program Initiation and should include an initial strategy to manage them.

   PMI®, *The Standard for Program Management*, 2008, 24

20. d. Identify stakeholders' attitudes toward the program

   Stakeholder analysis is a tool and technique in the Plan Program Stakeholder Management process that is used to gain an understanding of the organizational culture and the stakeholder's needs and expectations. Often this process is done through interviews, focus groups, and questionnaires and surveys.

   PMI®, *The Standard for Program Management*, 2008, 230

Governance

Study Hints

Governance is the fifth domain in program management. It represents 14% of the 170 questions, or 24 questions on the PgMP® exam. Governance transcends program management from the beginning of the program when it is first approved to be part of the portfolio to the closure of the program.

In program management, there can be several types of governance structures—one used for program approval, one used to oversee the program at the stage gates and for periodic reviews of program progress, and one used by the program manager to oversee the projects in the program. These Governance Boards, often called Program Boards or Steering Committees, each require a defined structure to promote efficiency and consistency among programs and their respective projects. A governance plan is a best practice to describe policies, procedures, and standards that the Governance Board will follow and how the stage-gate reviews will be conducted, including the requirements for each one.

An escalation process also is a best practice as the program manager may wish to escalate risks and issues to the Governance Board for resolution, and project managers may wish to do the same to the program manager.

Key performance indicators (KPIs) are useful to measure program success and to help monitor benefits throughout the life cycle. They may include items such as risks, financials, compliance, quality, safety, and stakeholder satisfaction. The program management information system is used to help facilitate tracking these KPIs. A best practice to follow is to regularly evaluate new and existing risks that impact strategic objectives and update the risk management plan as required, presenting it to the Governance Board for approval. Also, the business environment should be monitored in order to ensure the program remains in alignment with the organization's strategic objectives.

Further, emphasis is placed on contributing to an information or knowledge repository with program-related lessons learned, processes, and documentation to support organizational best practices. These lessons learned then are identified and applied to support and influence the existing program and future programs or improvements in the organization.

Major Topics

Governance Importance

- Governance and the program life cycle
- Governance at different levels
- Phase-gate reviews and the life cycle
- Aligning program goals with the strategic goals and objectives of the organization
- Ensuring value promised by the program is realized, and benefits are delivered
- Ensuring effective stakeholder communication
- Setting up measures to ensure compliance with policies
- Ensuring appropriate tools and processes are used in the program

Setting Up the Governance Structure

- Determining governance goals
- Determining governance roles and responsibilities
- Governance plan
- Component initiating criteria
- Issue escalation process
- Audit plan
- Stage-gate reviews
- Periodic health checks
- Meeting schedule

Governance Oversight

- Approving components to be in the program
- Approving closure of components and the program itself
- Monitoring program outcomes
- Ensuring best practices are being followed
- Monitoring metrics for strategic alliance
- Monitoring and controlling risk opportunities and threats
- Ensuring expected benefits are in line with those in the business plan
- Making go-/no-go decisions
- Using a decision register
- Conducting program reviews
- Updating processes, plans, roles and responsibilities
- Collecting lessons learned and updating the knowledge repository

Practice Questions

1. Within the Acme Bearing Company, management uses the terms project management and program management interchangeably, and there is no consistency across programs. Furthermore, there is no executive support to facilitate issue resolution, no direction or leadership provided to program teams, and little control over work initiatives. As an external consultant, you have been asked to provide recommendations for improvement. You prepare a report with a prioritized list of actions for Acme management. Number one on your list is to establish—

   a. A portfolio management information system
   b. Enterprise project management across all divisions
   c. A program governance model
   d. A program delivery model with supporting competencies

2. As the program manager for a new curricula of training products, you will need to work with numerous divisions within your company, many of which are located in other countries. Additionally, other projects and programs in the organization are linked to your program at various levels. Because you realize the importance of gate reviews and health checks, you need to develop a(n)—

   a. Interface management plan
   b. Integration plan
   c. Governance plan
   d. Program road map

3. As your organization's troubled program recovery specialist, you have been called in to take over a program that has had difficulties from the start. An initial assessment revealed that the project-level requirements had not been completed nor had those at the program level. Of course, they need to be finalized before work can be done. You also found that even though your program management methodology requires a Governance Board for a program of this magnitude that none had been set up. You realize this is a necessity, and stage-gate reviews must be conducted. The governance processes, procedures, and templates for programs are defined and managed by the—

   a. Program management office (PMO)
   b. Program office
   c. Program manager
   d. Program governance board

4. Assume you now have a Governance Board set up for this troubled program that has had difficulties from the start. You worked with your core team and developed program-level requirements. When you inherited the program, you learned it already had three projects, so you have had your project managers define the project-level requirements succinctly. You have been working with the project managers now on overall program planning and also on planning for their projects. You are scheduled now to meet with your Governance Board in two weeks to see if you can pass Gate Review 3 and officially begin the executing process. You realize these gate reviews are a necessity to—

a. Obtaining customer support for your work to date
b. Ensuring the customer acceptance criteria for the end products of the program will be met as planned.
c. Ensuring the risk level of the program remains acceptable to the organization
d. Assuring the ability to sustain program benefits in the long term

5. The program governance board on your program is considered to be the best in the organization because of its approach to monitoring performance. Not only do its members monitor progress reports on a routine basis, but they also specifically employ the best practice of—

a. Meeting with you quarterly to discuss status
b. Conducting client satisfaction surveys to determine whether quality is being achieved
c. Hiring an outside consultant to monitor progress reports to get an objective view
d. Reviewing program status at each phase of the program's life cycle

6. You have been managing a program to run the clinical trials for a new class of drugs that will forever eliminate prickly heat in the subtropics. Partway through the trials, you discovered that a competitor had already achieved regulatory approval to begin manufacturing and selling an identical class of drugs that will be sold at half the cost of the drug that you are developing. You met with your program governance board to discuss the situation. The board decided not to continue with the program and asked that you—

a. Prepare a program closure recommendation
b. Conduct an audit
c. Prepare a performance report
d. Conduct an impact analysis

7. You are working on a complex five-year program that has a minimum of four projects under way at any given time. A major scope change to Project L has resulted in a need to rebaseline its schedule. Consequently because of dependencies with Project L, Project D also had to revise its schedule These two revisions required that your overall program schedule be revised as well. The program schedule change has been approved, and the program and its components' schedules have been updated. As a result of these schedule changes, your original estimate is now totally out of date. Your program Governance Board now asks you to prepare the program's—

   a. Forecast
   b. Estimate at completion
   c. Cost performance report
   d. Earned value scorecard

8. Finally, your program to rebuild the water desalinization plant for Haddad, Saudi Arabia is complete. This program has been under way for more than five years. You had a number of leasing agreements on the program, and you are confident all of them have been closed successfully. You also had several subcontractors, and you have had reviews with each of them. You are meeting with your Governance Board, to obtain approval for phase-gate review G4, the final phase of the program. The purpose of this phase is to—

   a. Measure benefits realization
   b. Execute a controlled closedown
   c. Ensure that component deliverables meet requirements
   d. Integrate capabilities delivered by all components

9. You are preparing for a meeting of your governance board. You have learned that it is a best practice to meet in advance with two board members to ensure that they concur with what you plan to present. Board Member A says that your approach on some recent issues was not in line with the benefits realization plan, and she is upset with your performance. Board Member B says that he is pleased with your work; he thinks that you are realizing the benefits outlined in the benefits realization plan. On the basis of these two advance meetings, you—

   a. Continue with the governance board meeting as scheduled, because you have Board Member B's support
   b. Cancel the meeting to fully address Board Member A's concerns
   c. Work with your program team to address Board Member A's concerns before the governance board meeting
   d. Report the problem to the benefits manager

10. You are the program manager for your city's initiative to put all electrical, cable, and telephone lines underground to prevent outages during tornados and hurricanes. You have a number of subcontractors working for you, and you also have a small core team of five people. So far, you have four projects in your program, but given its complexity, you expect to have more as the program ensues. You are getting ready for a review by your Governance Board for your program. One purpose of this review is to—

    a. Initiate another project into the program
    b. Manage the program resources
    c. Identify how many project managers have earned their PMP®s
    d. Direct program communications with the public at large

11. You are the program manager on a highly controversial e-mail retention program. More than 75 percent of the organization is opposed to the program because it means that all their e-mail messages will be archived and reviewed for inappropriate, unethical, or illegal statements. You know that there will be many conflicts as you and your team execute the component projects. You inform your team that, in the case of any conflict, the first point of escalation is—

    a. The program director
    b. The program sponsor
    c. The program governance board
    d. You, the program manager

12. Although your company has been active in project management for many years, it is relatively new to program management. You became certified as a PgMP® and suggested to your supervisor that two of your current projects would be better managed as a program and discussed why program management was more appropriate. Your supervisor in turn met with some members of the executive team, and collectively, they realized a number of the existing projects in the company would be better handled through a program structure. One of the executives knew about the usefulness of governance and stage-gate reviews from his previous work in new product development, and he recommended all programs have a governance structure. Since the company is following the Project Management Institute's guidelines, this governance structure for the projects in the program is established during the—

    a. Pre-Program Preparations phase
    b. Program Setup phase
    c. Establishing a Program Management and Technical Infrastructure phase
    d. Delivery of Program Benefits phase

13. Although your company has been active in project management for many years, it is relatively new to program management. You became certified as a PgMP® and suggested to your supervisor that two of your current projects would be better managed as a program and discussed why program management was more appropriate. Your supervisor in turn met with some members of the executive team, and collectively, they realized a number of the existing projects in the company would be better handled through a program structure. One of the executives knew about the usefulness of governance and stage-gate reviews from his previous work in new product development, and he recommended all programs have a governance structure. The executives decided to use the term Governance Board but discussed use of a Program Board or a Steering Committee. The program governance falls within the corporate governance in the company. The recommended governance structure is stated in the—

    a. Program charter
    b. Program management plan
    c. Benefits realization plan
    d. Business case

14. Your program to develop the next-generation helium automobile has been completed. In retrospect, you recognize that your company's standard program governance structure was not effective, as more gate reviews were needed during the Delivery of Program Benefits phase. You recommend that the enterprise program management office (EPMO) reassess the program life cycle and the role of the governance board. This is an example of a(n)—

    a. Best practice
    b. Lesson learned
    c. Activity to be performed by the executive team
    d. Activity outside of the program manager's responsibility

15. Your program is part of a company portfolio that includes two other programs as well as three projects that are not part of any specific program. The portfolio also includes additional ongoing work. You will have a number of phase-gate reviews of your program's initiatives. These reviews will be—

    a. Carried out within the context of the corresponding portfolio
    b. Held at the key go/no-go decision points of your program
    c. Used to assess periodic project performance
    d. Held when you request them in your role as program manager

16. You are the program manager for a new version of a MP3 player. The players are manufactured by third-party companies operating plants in five countries. You have a project manager on site in each of these five countries and a total of seven projects in your program to date. Your company is working diligently to be the first to market with these new players as they are using the latest technology, and it differs significantly from that of the competition. Your company uses Steering Committees to oversee all programs for overall governance. In this program governance framework, benefits enablement is the responsibility of the—

a. Executive sponsor
b. Program board
c. Program management office (PMO)
d. Program manager

17. You are the program manager for the development of a new slot machine for the Sand Dunes casino in Macau. Your company is using program management more frequently as it realizes the benefits associated with it but operates with a balanced matrix structure. You have resources supporting your program from a variety of functional departments. Some people report to you as well as to their functional manager. This is especially the case with subject matter experts who report to the functional managers. Thus far, you have three projects in this program, and your plan is to complete development of the slot machine in six months and then complete manufacturing in an additional six months. You meet regularly with members of your governance board for phase-gate reviews. These meetings are necessary because they provide the board and other interested stakeholders an opportunity to—

a. Review program performance
b. Assess performance against the need to realize and sustain program benefits for the long term
c. Focus on the phase that was just completed to determine whether the next phase should begin
d. Assess performance of the program against expected outcomes

18. You are a program manager under contract to a government agency that is responsible for issuing visas and passports. You have been working on this program for eight years and are responsible for all the information and telecommunications functions for the agency. Your company realizes this program is essential to its success, and this is the first time it has worked for this agency. Therefore, it established a governance structure to oversee the process. One of your first roles when this governance structure was set up was to identify the governance goals and define the governance roles and responsibilities. To help you in this process, you relied on the—

    a. Program work breakdown structure (PWBS)
    b. Scope management plan
    c. Benefits realization plan
    d. Stakeholder analysis chart

19. You are preparing for a major review by your program's steering committee. The executive director of the committee is especially interested in progress on Project A, because it sets the stage for two other projects. Your program control officer informs you that Project A has a pessimistic estimate of being completed within 136 days, a most likely estimate of 121 days, and an optimistic estimate of 116 days. The expected time to complete Project A is—

    a. 120 days
    b. 123 days
    c. 127 days
    d. 130 days

20. You are the program manager for a manufacturing program. This program has been under way for three years. You are using a virtual team to manage the program, and you are unable to have face-to-face meetings of your team because of the financial situation. You have five projects in your program thus far. You just learned you needed to take immediate action in response to a quality metric. This metric indicated that the manufacturing process, Project A, exceeded parameters and therefore would affect Projects B, C, and D and the entire program. You decided you needed to meet with your program's Steering Committee because of the severity of this issue. You met with them and described the situation. Your next step should be to—

    a. Issue a change request
    b. Use the governance decision register
    c. Update the Quality Management Plan
    d. Allocate to the program a resource who is a certified Six Sigma Black Belt

Answer Sheet

1.	a	b	c	d
2.	a	b	c	d
3.	a	b	c	d
4.	a	b	c	d
5.	a	b	c	d
6.	a	b	c	d
7.	a	b	c	d
8.	a	b	c	d
9.	a	b	c	d
10.	a	b	c	d

11.	a	b	c	d
12.	a	b	c	d
13.	a	b	c	d
14.	a	b	c	d
15.	a	b	c	d
16.	a	b	c	d
17.	a	b	c	d
18.	a	b	c	d
19.	a	b	c	d
20.	a	b	c	d

Answer Key

1. c. A program governance model

    In the context of a program or a portfolio, there are five main functions of governance: facilitate decision making, provide program teams with leadership and direction, exercise program/project control, ensure consistency, and provide support for issue resolution.

    PMI®, *The Standard for Program Management*, 2008, 25

    Williams and Parr, *Enterprise Program Management Delivering Value*, 2006, 61

2. c. Governance plan

    The governance plan describes the goals, structure, roles and responsibilities, and logistics for the governance process. It includes gate review requirements and periodic health checks.

    PMI®, *The Standard for Program Management*, 2008, 249–251

3. a. Program management office (PMO)

    As part of its oversight, the project management office is responsible for defining and managing the program's governance processes, procedures, and templates.

    PMI®, *The Standard for Program Management*, 2008, 235

4. c. Ensuring the risk level of the program remains acceptable to the organization

    A phase-gate review is an objective assessment against the exit criteria of each phase to determine whether the program should proceed to the next phase. These reviews also assess the program with regard to strategic and quality-related criteria, thereby ensuring that the program and its projects are aligned with organizational strategy, that expected benefits have not changed from the original business plan, that the level of risk remains acceptable, and that best practices are followed.

    PMI®, *The Standard for Program Management*, 2008, 21–22

5. d. Reviewing program status at each phase of the program's life cycle

    One responsibility of the program governance board is to monitor program performance and progress. A key element of this activity is to conduct such reviews at each phase of the program's life cycle to determine whether the program can move to the next phase.

    PMI®, *The Standard for Program Management*, 2008, 22

6. a. Prepare a program closure recommendation

A program closure recommendation is an output of the Provide Governance Oversight process. This recommendation is typically proposed to the program sponsor for the final closure decision.

PMI®, *The Standard for Program Management*, 2008, 262

7. b. Estimate at completion

An estimate at completion is an output of the Monitor and Control Program Financials process. Revised financial information for the program should be prepared on a regular basis and communicated according to the stakeholder management plan, especially when major changes render estimates invalid.

PMI®, *The Standard for Program Management*, 2008, 226

8. b. Execute a controlled closedown

The last phase in the program life cycle is Program Closure, which focuses on a controlled closedown of the program.

PMI®, *The Standard for Program Management*, 2008, 29

9. c. Work with your program team to address Board Member A's concerns before the governance board meeting

You should proceed with the scheduled governance board meeting but be prepared to address Board Member A's concerns. Benefits are achieved in a cumulative manner. At the meeting, you can discuss the deliverables that have met requirements and describe the benefits that have been realized to date. Noting Board Member A's concerns, you can identify any risks that might affect the program and describe how you plan to mitigate them.

PMI®, *The Standard for Program Management*, 2008, 58 and 236

10. a. Initiate another project into the program

Reviews by the program's governance board are an opportunity for senior management to assess program performance before the program moves to the next phase or before another project is initiated in the program. This process can occur during any program phase except Close Program. The criteria for approval are defined in the governance plan.

PMI®, *The Standard for Program Management*, 2008, 257

11. d. You, the program manager

    Program managers are the escalation point for issues, changes, risks, interfaces, and dependencies. As the program manager, you must manage relationships, resolve conflicts and deal with political aspects of the program.

    PMI®, *The Standard for Program Management*, 2008, 11 and 13

12. d. Delivery of Program Benefits phase

    Phase four in the program life cycle is the Delivery of Program Benefits phase. This is when the work of the program through its projects and other activities begins. At this time, the program management team is responsible for managing the projects in a coordinated and consistent way, and a governance structure is established to monitor and control the projects.

    PMI®, *The Standard for Program Management*, 2008, 28

13. a. Program charter

    The primary output of program initiation is the program charter. Among other things, it includes the recommended governance structure to manage, control, and support the program as well as the governance structure for the program's components.

    PMI®, *The Standard for Program Management*, 2008, 25

14. b. Lesson learned

    In the closing phase, the program manager and team may provide feedback and recommendations on areas that are outside the scope of the program but could benefit the organization in the future.

    PMI®, *The Standard for Program Management*, 2008, 30

15. a. Carried out within the context of the corresponding portfolio

    If the program is initiated as part of a portfolio, then phase-gate reviews are held within the context of the portfolio and not as an independent process outside the purview of the portfolio.

    PMI®, *The Standard for Program Management*, 2008, 21

16. d. Program manager

    The program board is responsible for overall program governance. The program management office (PMO) supports the program manager, who has overall responsibility for benefits enablement.

    PMI®, *The Standard for Program Management*, 2008, 11–12

17. c. Focus on the phase that was just completed to determine whether the next phase should begin

Phase-gate reviews serve numerous purposes and should be held throughout the program. They focus on the phase that was just completed and result in go/no-go decisions. However, these sessions are not a substitute for periodic program performance reviews.

PMI®, *The Standard for Program Management*, 2008, 22

18. c. Benefits realization plan

Each program is expected to deliver certain benefits that may be tangible or intangible. Benefits realization planning is part of the Initiate Program process. The benefits realization plan, which is an output of the Define Program Goals and Objectives process, defines each benefit and explains how it is to be realized, maps the benefits to the program's outcomes, provides a way to measure benefits, describes roles and responsibilities, includes a communications plan, and notes transition to ongoing operations and benefits sustainment. It is a key input to the Plan and Establish Program Governance and Plan Program Quality processes.

PMI®, *The Standard for Program Management*, 2008, 30–31, 109, and 244

19. b. 123 days

At the program level, the emphasis is on interdependencies between components. PERT (program evaluation and review technique) is one tool that can be used to track the start and finish of components against planned timelines. Using PERT, the expected time is determined using the following formula:

$$P + 4 (ML) + O/6$$

Where P = pessimistic time; ML = most likely time; and O = optimistic time
In this example, the answer is 123 days.

PMI®, *The Standard for Program Management*, 2008, 127 and 131

PMI®, *PMBOK® Guide*, 2008, 150

20. b. Use the governance decision register

Decisions of the governance board or steering committee must be formally documented because these decisions are critical feedback used to improve the result of the components and the program. A governance decision register is an output of the Provide Governance Oversight process.

PMI®, *The Standard for Program Management*, 2008, 262

Practice Test 1

This practice test is designed to simulate PMI®'s 170-question PgMP® certification exam. You have four hours to answer all questions.

INSTRUCTIONS: Note the most suitable answer for each multiple-choice question in the appropriate space on the answer sheet.

1. Assume you are working to change the culture of your organization to one that views its programs and projects as strategic assets and critical to overall success. You have been working on a team to define the long-term objectives of the organization and to set forth vision and mission statements for employees that are meaningful and informative. In your efforts you recognize and your team has agreed that one of the truest measures of an organization's intent, direction, and progress is found in its—

    a. Program management office (PMO)
    b. Portfolio
    c. Strategic plan
    d. Program charter

2. Your team is located on three continents. Many team members are struggling to use the new project and portfolio management (PPM) system, and training is required. You have a PPM expert on your staff, and the PPM vendor also offers training courses. Team members work six days a week. In this circumstance, the most appropriate training approach is to—

    a. Dispatch your PPM expert to each site for individualized training
    b. Conduct synchronous webinar training so that everyone receives information at the same time
    c. Have your vendor prepare eLearning modules that team members can access at their convenience
    d. Provide audio recordings of training sessions that team members can download to their MP3 players

3. You are managing a program to develop a new source of energy in the extreme northern latitudes when solar power is not available. You have a core team and a Program Management Office to support you and the nine projects that are under way. However, your power company, DCE, is resource constrained. You are finding it difficult to obtain the key subject matter experts you need for this important program. You have been working diligently with your stakeholders to gain their support as you know stakeholder management is critical to program management. Your approach is to have effective and ongoing communications with your stakeholders. You have prepared a communications management plan for your program, and it has been approved by your sponsor and Governance Board. To complement this plan, you should prepare a(n)—

   a. Stakeholder analysis plan
   b. Information distribution plan
   c. Communications strategy
   d. Knowledge management plan

4. Assume your organization submitted its proposal to government agency ABS. After the proposal was submitted, members of your Portfolio Review Board made the decision that it should be managed as a program rather than as a project. You were listed in the proposal as the project manager if your company won the job so now you are going to be the program manager. Fortunately, you have managed programs before and have your PgMP® so program management is not new for you. The business development manager feels quite confident that your company will win this opportunity and has suggested that a program charter now be prepared. With the charter completed, once the contract is awarded, you then can move immediately into the planning phase. You are working on this charter and decided you should include—

   a. A detailed scope statement
   b. A Program Work Breakdown Structure
   c. The program's master schedule
   d. A preliminary outline of the program's organizational structure

5. You are preparing for a meeting of the governance board for your program. You have learned that it is best to contact the board members before each meeting to ensure that they concur with what you plan to present. When you speak with Board Member A, she says that your approach on some recent issues was not in line with your benefits realization plan, and she is upset with your performance as program manager. She also says that the level of risk in your program is unacceptable. Your best course of action is to—

   a. Review your benefits register and resolve any issues
   b. Update your benefits realization plan and present the revised version at the governance board meeting
   c. Proceed as planned with your meeting, as other board members have not expressed any concerns
   d. Ask your program sponsor to meet with Board Member A

6. Assume you are on a selection committee to determine which programs and projects your organization should undertake in the next year. Resources in terms of both people and funding are major constraints. You also work for a pharmaceutical company, and all your work is heavily audited to ensure generally accepted best practices are followed by your country's Food and Drug Administration; your products then must be submitted to the Food and Drug Administration for approval, which means you have legal and regulatory constraints to consider as well as you make selection decisions. Therefore, one of the key criterions that your committee uses is the benefits to be realized and sustained by the products of the programs and projects. These business benefits are identified and qualified in the life cycle during the—

   a. Benefits analysis phase
   b. Benefits planning phase
   c. Program Setup phase
   d. Benefits identification phase

7. You are excited because upon achieving your PgMP®, you have been assigned to manage a program in your motorcycle company, BCD, to design the 2025 program of vehicles to be produced. Each motorcycle is to be able to be used without helmets. Your customers have told your executives that they know helmets are required but dislike wearing them so instead they tend to purchase automobiles rather than motorcycles. Helmets are required in most states in your country so you will have many regulatory issues. Also, the motorcycles must have other safety features to make sure even in heavy traffic or inclement weather that the rider is protected, and the motorcycle must be able to travel for at least 500 miles without the need to refuel. Even with these constraints, you are pleased to be selected to be the program manager for this model year of vehicles. So far, you have five projects in your program but know others will be added. You just prepared your benefits realization plan for this program. It will be helpful because—

a. Your performance plan is tied to the benefits realization plan through the balanced scorecard approach

b. The benefits realization plan will involve all the key stakeholders in the program to get their buy in to each specific project

c. You and your team can monitor the agreed-upon benefits until the program is completed

d. You can use this plan at every meeting of your Governance Board

8. On your motorcycle program, you and your team are actively tracking the benefits identified in your plan. Your Governance Board asked you to revise your plan after they saw that there were so many intangible benefits and asked you to also include more tangible ones that were easier to track and then report to your stakeholders. You made a strong case for retaining your intangible benefits as you also felt the plan was useful as it—

a. Served as a baseline for the program with the existing metrics in it

b. Was prepared through a brainstorming session with some of the key stakeholders who then would question why some of the intangible benefits were omitted

c. Helped to better define the specific project deliverables

d. Was set up in a fashion that all the benefits would be realized at the end of the program

9. You are the program manager for your city's initiative to put all electrical, cable, and telephone lines underground to prevent outages during tornadoes and hurricanes. As program manager, you will select subcontractors to support your program. You prepare criteria for the make-or-buy decisions, as well as the criteria to select the subcontractors. The purpose of conducting a make-or-buy analysis is to—

   a. See how much cheaper it is to buy rather than to make
   b. See how much cheaper it is to make rather than to buy
   c. Outsource as much as possible in accordance with company policy
   d. Determine the optimal supply chain strategy based on a wide variety of factors

10. Because your program has the highest priority in the organization's portfolio, your governance board meets each month, and each member receives a weekly status report. The executive sponsor requests these reports to enable him to stay current on program activities and assist you with any issues that need resolution. Your customer also requests monthly meetings and a weekly teleconference. To ensure that your list of these meetings and communications is up-to-date, you should develop a(n)—

    a. Communications log
    b. Information distribution plan
    c. Communications capability matrix
    d. Information reporting schedule

11. Assume your executive management team has requested that a standard process be put in place for a business case for new programs and projects to pursue in the organization. You are the leader of a cross-functional team that is designing this process. Your executives have stressed they wish to analyze each proposal from multiple business perspectives and want a balanced view of the business opportunity to be realized as well as the business risk to do so. The first step in this generic process should be to—

    a. Determine the key milestones in the program
    b. Define the high-level requirements
    c. Define the program's mission statement
    d. Analyze program complexity and strategic alignment

12. You are managing a program with a long duration for the water management district in your county. At this time, it is scheduled to last nine years, but you believe the timeline could even be longer. You have seven projects in your program at this time, and you are only in year two. You and your program management team need to analyze any environmental or legislative changes during execution that may affect your program. This is a key activity to perform during the—

   a. Benefits Identification phase
   b. Delivery of Program Benefits phase
   c. Program Setup phase
   d. Benefits Realization phase

13. You are a program manager for a software services company. This new software will bring your company into Cloud computing. It also will replace your company's legacy finance and accounting systems. You are pleased to be the program manager, and you are to complete your program in two years. Your sponsor has asked to develop an initial cost and schedule plan for your new program. This is done in the as part of the—

   a. Program charter development
   b. Program roadmap development
   c. Business case
   d. Program management plan development

14. You are a program manager for a software services company. This new software will bring your company into Cloud computing. It also will replace your company's legacy finance and accounting systems. You are pleased to be the program manager, and you are to complete your program in two years. Since the program will last two years, you plan to use a combination of internal and external resources to complete it in this time frame. The purpose of using external resources is to assist in realizing benefits as quickly as possible. You define your resources by using the—

   a. PWBS
   b. Program charter
   c. Business case
   d. Program requirements document

15. As executive sponsor of a major program to restore coral reefs off the coast of the Maldives, you have observed conflict between the program manager and her project managers, stakeholders, and peers. Although the conflict is manageable, you are concerned about her long-term future with the organization. She is a very bright and talented individual, and you want to keep her in the organization. Therefore, you—

   a. Tell her to take a well-deserved vacation to reduce her stress level
   b. Send her to a training class on conflict management
   c. Have her go through a 360-degree feedback analysis
   d. Assign her a personal coach to uncover the causes of conflict

16. On your motorcycle program, you and your team are actively tracking the benefits identified in your plan. Your Governance Board asked you to revise your plan after they saw that there were so many intangible benefits and asked you to also include more tangible ones that were easier to track and then report to your stakeholders. However, you did revise your benefits as your executives asked and found later during the program management life cycle that you needed to add others. Some that you added included improved customer service and reduced working capital. You found, though, that employee satisfaction, which was in the first plan, was not really useful so you decided to delete this benefit and not track it; the surveys you were conducting regularly seemed to lack value and were taking time from BCD's employees as well as your own core team to analyze the data collected. Now, you have a new plan in place. Your next step is to—

   a. Begin a process to revise your benefit report and benefit register
   b. Follow the Distribute Information process to communicate the new plan to your stakeholders
   c. Discuss the new plan at your upcoming, regularly planned program status meeting with your Governance Board in two weeks
   d. Distribute your plan to your Governance Board members

17. Assume your company has fully embraced program management. It has recognized its value and has changed its Project Management Office into an Enterprise Program Management Office. You are the Director of this Enterprise Program Management Office and report directly to the CEO. You have a program life cycle, which is followed, and you and your team developed a standard but tailorable program management methodology. You also have set up a process where each program has a governance board with stage-gate reviews. Recently, you had an external *Organizational Project Management Maturity (OPM3)* assessment, and your company scored well in the best practices in the measure stage but you need to work on continuous improvement of your governance process, which means that—

    a. Only board members should be members of the organization
    b. The program sponsor makes all final decisions
    c. It is an inward-looking practice
    d. It requires monthly meetings for increased effectiveness

18. Assume you are the sponsor for a program for helping your government become a member of the Asian Union, which will be set up like the European Union. A number of stakeholders believe becoming a member of the Asian Union will be positive and will lead to more opportunities for your country; however, the Finance Minister has raised a number of objections to it. You just met with him and now are working on a way to turn him into a positive stakeholder. One approach to use is to determine—

    a. Methods of qualifying the business benefits of joining the Asian Union
    b. The specific funding model as funding is necessary to join
    c. The alignment of joining the Asian Union in terms of the country's strategic plan
    d. A high-level roadmap to set a baseline for the future work to be done

19. Working as the program manager for the Asia Union program has proved to be a challenging assignment to say the least. Not only do you have a number of stakeholders located in many different countries, you now have seven projects in your program and fortunately a PMO for support. You find it is necessary to—

    a. Differentiate between the resources assigned to the program and those at the project level
    b. Implement a team-based reward and recognition system
    c. Prepare a team charter and present it to the team
    d. Establish one person to be the sole contact with each of the different stakeholders

20. The Asia Union program continues to be a challenge, not only for you but also for your seven project managers in this program. You are continually spending the majority of your time communicating with stakeholders at all levels and in varying locations and coordinating activities. You also are preparing a number of status reports for different stakeholder groups and also for your governance board with its numerous program reviews and more rigorous stage gate reviews. Working as a program manager, you recognize the key distinctions between a project life cycle and a program life cycle. One of these distinctions is—

    a. Some projects may need to be integrated with others to provide program benefits
    b. The life cycle assists in the control and management of the project deliverables
    c. Programs have a distinct life cycle that is not extended
    d. The way the life cycle is set up means that project benefits cannot be realized immediately

21. As one of the industry's leading program management consultants, you have been asked by the Global Financial Corporation to help establish a program governance structure and then to put in place a management-by-program culture in the organization. There is a great deal of debate regarding who possesses executive ownership of the program policies. One side asserts it should be the program management office (PMO), whereas a second group of influential executives claims that it should be the executive sponsor. After numerous debates, this decision has been made, and the executive sponsor was selected. You now are establishing your core team and your first step it to—

    a. Negotiate with functional managers for key resources
    b. Identify competency requirements for each role and responsibility
    c. Establish a training program for core team members to address skill gaps
    d. Conduct a 360-degree assessment on each team member to better understand his or her strengths and weaknesses

22. Assume as you continue with this program to put in place a management-by-program culture into the Global Financial Corporation, you realize there are not that many in this worldwide corporation that possess actual experience in program management. But, your first program will be in the area of portable financial transactions by any type of device—a phone, PDA, tablet, eReader, or computer. You recognize that with this program an expert in your corporation will be needed by two of the projects in the program at approximately the same time. Both project managers have included this person in their project management plans, resource assignment matrices, and project schedules. This is an example of—

    a. An assumption
    b. A constraint
    c. Critical chain analysis
    d. An issue to be resolved by the governance board

23. One of the projects in your program has reported actuals to date of $1 million against a planned value of $500,000. You suspect that the project will run out of money soon. If it runs out of money, it will place financial constraints on your other projects and also on the entire program. Therefore, as the program manager for this program, you should—

    a. Prepare a program operational cost estimate
    b. Issue a request to terminate this project
    c. Hold regular status reviews
    d. Calculate the schedule performance index (SPI) to see how far behind schedule you are

24. You work as a program manager for a medical device company. Extensive clinical trials are typically managed as individual projects during and after product development. This is done to assess any flaws in the products before they are submitted for regulatory approval. As a program manager, you recognize that—

    a. You must define the life-cycle phases for each of these projects
    b. The major project life-cycle phases and their deliverables will remain similar
    c. The purpose of your program life cycle is to produce deliverables
    d. Each project should have a different life cycle to ensure that there are no problems with the devices that are being manufactured

25. You are managing a business process management program for a large insurance company. After six months of effort, you have noticed that the key stakeholders seem to be losing interest in the effort and that friction has surfaced between your key staff members and key client contacts. You devise a plan to uncover the reasons for these apparent issues. You advise your deputy program manager to have lunch with her client counterpart at least once a week; likewise, you will start taking the client's vice president out to dinner every month. This activity can be viewed as—

    a. Positive, because you will be building stronger relationships with your client
    b. Positive, but bordering on being unethical
    c. Negative, because it is a calculated attempt to gain information that could be obtained through more direct means
    d. Ineffective, because clients can see through such actions

26. You are the executive sponsor for a proposed program to be presented in two weeks for approval from the Portfolio Review Board in your automotive company, ABC. Your program is to develop a next generation vehicle that will not require gasoline, ethanol, or electricity. In your presentation to your Portfolio Review Board, in your business case, you want to differentiate this product. To do so, you should first—

    a. Demonstrate an understanding of the needs of the customer
    b Define the program success criteria
    c. Describe the business opportunity
    d. Analyze program risk

27. Assume you are managing a program for the National Oceanic and Atmospheric Agency (NOAA) in your country. Scientists in NOAA have been doing extensive research on global warming and have noted that the current warming of the world's oceans can cause serious diseases in the next three years. Although your government is trying to reduce funds throughout all the agencies, these data are especially alarming, and NOAA received the funds required for this program. Food poisoning and cholera are expected to result worldwide. You have these key subject matter experts assigned to your program and you have been working with them to prepare a detailed benefit realization plan. This plan is one of the key documents that now are being used by your executives in NOAA to—

    a. Determine specific projects to pursue in the program
    b. Present the business case for the program to the Office of Management and Budget
    c. Plan and establish the program governance structure
    d. Identify the program sponsor and issue a charter describing the sponsor's roles and responsibilities

28. In your program to manufacture a new series of hybrid vehicles for the 2016 year, you initially thought you would have seven projects. As you worked to develop your program charter, however, you now know you will need instead 15 component projects. You have prepared a business case for each of these projects. However, you also realize you need to conduct some feasibility studies. In the past on programs in your company, feasibility studies have focused on economic and technical feasibility. But for your program, you are also going to focus on—

    a. Developing a plan to initiate the program
    b. Engineering analysis
    c. Developing a high-level business case
    d. Benefits analysis

29. In your program to manufacture a new series of hybrid vehicles for the 2016 year, you initially thought you would have seven projects. As you worked to develop your program charter, however, you now know you will need instead 15 component projects. You have prepared a business case for each of these projects. However, you have not been successful in recruiting the specific team members you want for your program. People have been assigned to your team by other managers who contend that these people have the necessary skills for the job. Your first step is to—

    a. Complete a skill set inventory
    b. Conduct a kickoff meeting
    c. Have an informal meeting to get to know the team members
    d. Align personnel aspirations to available roles

30. So far, you have three projects identified in your program to manufacture the new series of hybrid vehicles. However, you are only in year one of this program. You recognize that at the program level, your role involves exploiting and embracing change. Also, at the program level, analysis of change requests involves identifying, documenting, and estimating the work that the change would entail. In addition, as program manager, you must—

    a. Determine whether updates to the program document repository are needed
    b. Meet with the program governance board for approval, rejection, or deferral of the request
    c. Convene a meeting of the project's configuration control board
    d. Prepare a status report

31. Finally the hybrid vehicle program is almost complete. As an experienced program manager, you know it is a best practice in program management is to identify and document lessons learned throughout the program as it moves through the various phases of its life cycle. The next step in this process is to—

    a. Formally document these lessons learned in the knowledge management system
    b. Have experts examine each one to determine whether it should be included in the organization's process asset library
    c. Analyze and archive them as part of the Closing Process Group
    d. Appoint one of the core program team members as a knowledge broker to pass on these lessons learned

32. You are responsible for developing a new line of printers using advanced laser jets for the consumer market. The customers for your products are large retail outlets and certain online outlets. As program manager, it is critical that you have a good understanding of the needs of the end user. Therefore, you—

    a. Meet with customers to obtain a profile of the buying habits of their shoppers
    b. Meet with customers to understand the wants and needs of their clients with respect to printer capability
    c. Conduct market research to see what your competitors are offering
    d. Meet with as many end users as is feasible to understand what features they would like in a printer

33. Assume you are working as a program manager under contract to the company developing the advanced laser jet printers for the consumer market. Even though you believe you have a good working relationship with the program manager at the printer company, your client has not paid its last invoice of £500,000, and it is now more than 90 days overdue. Your company's accounting policy states that any invoice that is more than 90 days late becomes bad debt. You now need to—

    a. Rebaseline your budget
    b. Update your cost management plan
    c. Take corrective action
    d. Issue a change request

34. Risk management is continual in program management. It is important in the early stages, even when approval to authorize a program has not yet been obtained. Assume you are the sponsor of a possible new program in which all asphalt on your nation's highway system would be totally replaced with a new product that would never require any maintenance. However, obviously there are going to be risks with such a new product to be developed, and you need to identify some of them to obtain approval to proceed. You also need to do some analysis after this high-level identification. Therefore, a key question to be able to answer in case your leadership asks you when you request approval to proceed is—

    a. What are the assumptions that are part of your analysis?
    b. How much do we need to set aside for contingency in our budget should the risks occur?
    c. How will these risks affect the ultimate sustainability of the product?
    d. What is the probability of success for this program?

35. Working to prepare the business case for your proposed program to develop a new product to replace asphalt on your nation's highways so maintenance will not be required, you realize the members of the Portfolio Review Board will be interested in a cost/benefit analysis as another indicator as to whether or not to proceed with this program. In preparing this cost/benefit analysis, you should—

    a. Identify tangible benefits as they can be easily quantified
    b. Identify direct benefits to your nation that will result from this program
    c. Identify tangible and intangible benefits, expressing the intangible benefits in quantifiable terms
    d. Identifying the tangible and intangible benefits showing the intangible benefits through market analysis techniques

36. As manager of a program for the Federal Trade Commission that involves changes to existing regulations throughout the agency concerning mergers and acquisitions, you have a number of key stakeholders—both internal and external—because these regulations have not been reviewed for more than 20 years. The Commission has established a Program Board, and you meet with this Board monthly to review progress. Because the Commission practices government in the "sunshine," each meeting is open to the public to attend. This means that—

    a. Public announcements concerning the program do not need to be prepared
    b. Board meeting minutes can substitute for any notifications to the public concerning the program
    c. Public announcements should be prepared
    d. A member of the core team should interface regularly with every public interest group

37. You are pleased to be appointed as the Program Manager for the development of a new ballpoint pen program. This pen will never need replacement and is to be physically appealing and available in a variety of colors. It also is to be fun to use but practical for those in a business setting. Therefore, you are developing a series of these pens and so far the program is considered to be on track. Your only key issue is that each of the stakeholders on this next-generation ballpoint pen program has different communications needs. To ensure each stakeholder receives the appropriate information he or she need in a useful format and in a timely manner, you ask a core team member to prepare a(n)—

    a. Lessons-learned process
    b. Stakeholder register
    c. Information-retrieval system
    d. Information-gathering system

38. As the program manager for a new line of children's toys, called The Destroyer, because your requirements tend to be constantly changing and because some key subject matter experts have been reassigned, you realize that you already are in a position in which a portion of your budget may be depleted, and you are not yet to the halfway point of your program. You are becoming concerned. You need to therefore consider the following as you manage your program's finances—

    a. Profit and loss
    b. Cash flow
    c. Accounts receivable
    d. Financial plan

39. You are working as program manager to develop the next-generation Segway®. One of your project managers (Project Manager A) has identified an issue that has implications for three projects (A, B, and C). You met with this project manager and concurred with her estimate of the importance of the issue. You then convened a meeting of your program governance board to determine the best way to resolve it. The governance board decided that proposed Project B is not required and that existing Project C should be terminated. The board commended you for bringing this issue to its attention. Your next step should be—

    a. Revisit and update your program plans as required
    b. Inform the client of this issue and its impact
    c. Meet with all the project managers and the core program team to discuss next steps
    d. Officially recognize and reward Project Manager A for bringing this issue to your attention

40. Assume you are managing a program for the National Oceanic and Atmospheric Agency (NOAA) in your country. Scientists in NOAA have been doing extensive research on global warming and have noted that the current warming of the world's oceans can cause serious diseases in the next three years. Because of the significance of this global warming program and the short time frame before food poisoning and cholera are expected as a result, you and your team now have seven projects in your program. You have a large number of stakeholders both internal and external, and the external stakeholders are especially interested given the danger to the citizens of your country and the world as well as the funding needed for program success. Therefore, NOAA set up a Governance Board for your program. At each gate review that is held, one of the key questions that are asked is—

    a. How corrective actions were applied to the failures encountered to date
    b. Whether the expected benefits are in line with the original business case
    c. Actual resource use versus that projected
    d. The number of issues escalated to you, as the program manager, and their effect on other aspects of the program or other programs in the agency

41. You are the program manager for a sixth-generation cell phone product. A number of component projects are associated with this program. You were on the core program team for the fifth-generation phone, so you can apply the lessons learned from that program. The schedule is the dominant constraint, and there is a chance that you will miss the user-acceptance test milestone even though it is six months away. Your next step is to—

    a. Implement your plan
    b. Inform the executive team that you will miss this critical milestone unless preventive action is taken
    c. Revisit the program architecture baseline
    d. Ask your program steering committee for additional resources to ensure that you can meet the milestone

42. In your role as program manager for your country's food safety department to ensure the safety of imported food in your country, you are facing a number of challenges. It seems as if more imported food is arriving rather than producing the food domestically. Many of the food products are totally new to your country. You lack the needed number of inspectors who have expertise in some of the exotic food that now is being imported, and you are implementing a Hazard Analysis Critical Control Program approach as part of this important program. You are working hard to keep your stakeholders, internal and external, informed of your progress and upcoming milestones in a timely manner, and you distribute a variety of different reports based on the category of stakeholders and their information requirements. However, one type that often is overlooked is—

    a. Receipt of proposals
    b. Notification of change requests
    c. List of preventive actions
    d. Record of training

43. Your company has been the leader in Segway® production since they were first made available to consumers. However, their popularity has increased tremendously since the product was first made offered, and since the production process now has been streamlined, so they are less expensive to manufacture. Therefore, sales have increased dramatically. However, recently your company has been getting a large volume of customer complaints as the battery life is only 20 miles. You have been appointed as the program manager to develop a new line of Segway® products in which the battery life will be 100 miles, yet the production process still will be one that focuses on lean manufacturing so the products can be offered to customers at a reasonable price. To set a baseline for program definition, planning, and execution, at this point, you have prepared a—

    a. Roadmap
    b. Charter
    c. Benefits assessment
    d. Program work breakdown structure

44. Assume your company has fully embraced program management. It has recognized its value and has changed its Project Management Office into an Enterprise Program Management Office. You are the Director of this Enterprise Program Management Office and report directly to the CEO. You have a program life cycle, which is followed, and you and your team developed a standard but tailorable program management methodology. You also have set up a process where each program has a governance board with stage-gate reviews. However, you want to make sure that the appropriate level of governance is applied to decision making in regard to changes in the program plan. This means you need to pay particular attention to which of the following—

    a. Managing program issues
    b. Planning and establishing the program governance structure
    c. Monitoring and controlling program changes
    d. Managing program benefits

45. As the program manager for the development of the next-generation catalytic converter, you have several major challenges. First, it is the first program in your company, second, it is highly complex, and third resources are limited. However, your program management plan has been approved, and now you are determining the required support structure and capabilities you will need for effective program management as part of the program's—

    a. Infrastructure
    b. Information technology systems
    c. Program control framework
    d. Enterprise resource planning tools

46. You have had several issues on your next-generation catalytic converter program. At first, you felt they were due to the fact that it is the first program in the company, it is highly complex, and has resource constraints. But for each issue, you have analyzed it and assigned it to an owner. Often the issue resolution has resulted in a need to make a decision, communicate that decision to those affected, and perform additional work beyond that identified in the program work breakdown structure (PWBS). For each issue, your next step is to—

    a. Update the program document repository
    b. Issue a change request
    c. Contact your customer to see whether he or she is satisfied with the resolution
    d. Close your issue register

47. You manage a program to develop a new e-commerce program for automotive parts distributors. Your organization has established this program to keep up with competitors and to increase market share, but it has recently acquired a competitor that already has a highly regarded e-commerce program in place. Your next step is to—

    a. Convene a meeting of your governance board to terminate your program
    b. Meet with each of your project managers to discuss an orderly transition to redeploy resources
    c. Revisit and update your program plans
    d. See if you can learn from the competitor

48. Your professional association in business development is increasing in terms of its membership. You also have added new chapters throughout the world in the past two years. The Executive Director of the Association asked you to lead a program to develop a body of knowledge in business development and a certification program with three levels—one for those who are relatively new to the field, one for people who have been working in the field for a least five years, plus an advanced certification for those who are considered experts in the business development field and are thought leaders. You have a core team of people to help you, but many are volunteer members of the association, and you realize how busy everyone is who is participating in their regular work at their organizations. However, the membership is committed to this body of knowledge and certification program, and recently the Executive Director authorized you to hire some consultants to help on a full-time basis for the next year. You have many stakeholders involved as volunteers and members of the association, and their knowledge and expertise are vital to the outcome of this program. However, especially since so many volunteers are involved, you have had to reach negotiated compromises with some of these stakeholders to respond to their concerns. They should be captured in the—

    a. Stakeholder management strategy
    b. Stakeholder inventory
    c. Stakeholder register
    d. Stakeholder management plan

49. You are leading a program to digitize all of the records in your nation's archives. Some of these records are extremely important but are difficult to digitize because they are ones when your country was established, approximately 500 years ago. However, it is essential that they be preserved, and the effort of your undertaking is far larger than originally anticipated. You have started with the early records and so far have three projects in your program. But, now your government is in financial difficulty, and you wonder if your proposed two new projects will be able to be funded. If not, you will definitely not meet your schedule of four years. In order to maintain funding authorization, you must—

    a. Prepare an impact analysis to show the results if the program does not receive needed funding.
    b. Conduct a benchmarking study to see how other countries have handled this type of project
    c. Estimate the high-level financial and non-financial benefits
    d. Use resource leveling to show how much longer it will take to complete the program without the two new projects

50. You have been managing a program to restructure your department within your government agency. The head of the agency informed your sponsor that she wants to change the scope of the program so that you will be working to restructure the entire agency instead. This change means that you should—

    a. Update your program architecture baseline
    b. Prepare a program architecture baseline
    c. Identify specific work tasks for each program work breakdown structure (PWBS) element
    d. Prepare a program roadmap

51. Assume you are in charge of reorganizing your government agency because its funding has been cut by 50% based on the shortfall of the overall available funds in your government. Even with the expansion of your program, to cut the funds, a number of projects and programs were terminated, and in doing so, many staff members lost their jobs. Your agency has defined rules to follow if people do lose their jobs in such situations, and now you find that many of the people who had attained their PgMPs® or PMPs® are no longer in the agency because they lacked seniority. Some of the programs, therefore, that remain now lack qualified people to manage them. In making the decisions as to which programs to terminate, one of the considerations was—

    a. The number of staff members involved
    b. The overall schedule status
    c. The funds already allocated
    d. The benefits report

52. Working as the program manager for a new program to assist people who wish to have a generator but do not want to have a giant propane tank in their yard and to replace propane with natural gas that will be easily distributed, you have a number of projects in your program. There also are many regulations and standards you must deal with as part of your program. Your company established a Governance Board, and it meets at least monthly to review progress to date, not just at stage-gate reviews. You and your team worked to identify the other stakeholders who may have an interest in or an influence over your program and to analyze them to see if they are positive or negative. Your next step is to—

    a. Develop a stakeholder management strategy
    b. Prepare a resource assignment matrix
    c. Prepare a resource management plan
    d. Develop a project stakeholder management plan

53. You are the program manager for the development of a new slot machine for the Sand Dunes casino in Macau. Your organization operates with a balanced matrix organizational structure, and you have resources supporting your program from a variety of functional departments. Some of these people report to you as well as to their respective departmental managers. You have a cost accounting system in which everyone charges time to appropriate account codes. Because your program is close to completion, you need to—

    a. Integrate this cost accounting system with the project management information system
    b. Issue a change request to close the program management plan
    c. Close the program budget to avoid non-allocable charges
    d. Use the management reserve to pay any additional charges

54. Assume you have been appointed as a program manager for an internal restructuring of your government agency. It has not been reorganized 10 years, and many new programs and projects are under way. Also, some of the existing Divisions do not seem to relate to the new five year strategic plan the agency issued six months ago, and on the surface, without detailed analysis, it is questionable that they remain necessary. You are to complete this restructuring in six months; an even shorter period of time is desirable because everyone knows about the program, and many fear they will lose their jobs after the reorganization. As you initiate the program, it is important to—

    a. Prepare a benefits analysis plan
    b. Perform an initial identification of program risks
    c. Develop a preliminary budget estimate
    d. Develop a program roadmap

55. Assume your organization is considering an internal improvement program. It is deciding whether or not it should focus on the Software Engineering Institute's Capability Maturity Model for Integration (CMMI) to obtain Level 3 and have the opportunity to bid on more U.S. Federal Government projects. The other option is to establish a program to pursue best practices in portfolio, program, and project management using the Project Management Institute's *Organizational Project Management Maturity (OPM3).* You are reviewing both possibilities to evaluate benefits and alignment with overall organizational strategic objectives. However, because of the strategic nature of programs, even those that are internal ones, it is easy to confuse the characteristics of benefits, objectives, and success criteria. A benefit can best be characterized as—

    a. The importance of the program
    b. What the individual program's projects are designed to achieve
    c. The voice of the customer (VOC)
    d. An improvement in an organization's operation

56. Assume your organization selected *OPM3,* and you hired an external consultant to perform the assessment. The consultant prepared an assessment report and an improvement report. As there are 488 Best Practices in *OPM3,* your company is so new to program management and portfolio management, it only achieved 75 of these Best Practices. You are now leading an internal program to address the consultant's prioritized improvement program. You have seven projects now in your program. As each project manager begins to identify the work to be done on their projects, you want to make sure that all work will be integrated into a program plan. The best way to ensure this linkage is through a common—

    a. Project management standard
    b. Work breakdown structure (WBS) methodology
    c. Scheduling methodology
    d. Organizational breakdown structure (OBS) methodology

57. As the program manager to integrate the back office components of your organization's system into a single system that contains data on accounting, finance, sales, business development, personnel, and portfolio, program, and project management, you have a core team of six people and six project managers, who have their PMPs®. You are using your Enterprise Program Management Office's methodology both at the program and project levels, and you also have a Governance Board that oversees your program at key stage gates and at other times. You and the six members of your core team reviewed the business case and charter and performed a comprehensive analysis and summary of how each stakeholder will be affected by the program. This is the purpose of the—

a. Stakeholder register
b. Stakeholder inventory
c. Stakeholder checklists
d. Stakeholder management plan

58. As the program manager to integrate the back office components of your organization's system into a single system that contains data on accounting, finance, sales, business development, personnel, and portfolio, program, and project management, you have a core team of six people and six project managers, who have their PMPs®. You are using your Enterprise Program Management Office's methodology both at the program and project levels, and you also have a Governance Board that oversees your program at key stage gates and at other times. You and the six members of your core team reviewed the business case and charter and performed a comprehensive analysis and summary of how each stakeholder will be affected by the program. You and your core team have identified within the organization 17 key stakeholders, and there are approximately 33 that have a peripheral interest in the program. You know you will have other stakeholders to add to this list as program progresses. The person who is responsible for providing project resources on this program is—

a. Program director
b. Program manager
c. Program sponsor
d. Head of the program management office (PMO)

59. Because of extreme droughts in Ferguson, Jordan, water restrictions have been imposed. Your company is awarded a contract to eliminate the need for these restrictions. The program includes a project to formulate and implement policies and procedures that ensure continuity of operations and performance of associated equipment. Another project will oversee improvements and modifications to existing treatment methods and facilities. A third project will design modifications to increase productivity and effectiveness. You expect other projects to be added later. Your company has a governance board in place for your program, which conducts stage-gate and other periodic reviews. You meet regularly with this board, and these meetings are necessary because they—

a. Are program performance reviews

b. Assess performance against the need to realize and sustain program benefits for the long term

c. Function as go/no-go decision points for the program

d. Assess performance of the program against expected outcomes

60. Finally, after three years of planning, your detailed design for the next-generation missile system of your country is complete. You were appointed the program manager for this program, and you now have also prepared your program management plan and schedule, as well as your subsidiary plans. Last week, your program's Governance Board approved your program management plan. Now, you are initiating the various component projects of your program, which means you are in the—

a. Program Setup phase

b. Initiation phase

c. Planning phase

d. Delivery of Program Benefits phase

61. Assume you are managing a program for the National Oceanic and Atmospheric Agency (NOAA) in your country. Scientists in NOAA have been doing extensive research on global warming and have noted that the current warming of the world's oceans can cause serious diseases in the next three years. Since the NOAA program has such high visibility in the agency and also with external organizations within your country and also around the world, it is essential that best practices be followed since there is such a high level of scrutiny about this program. You find you are constantly in meetings with key stakeholders both inside and outside of NOAA. Recently, you obtained two people in the Agency who have been certified as Six Sigma Black Belts to assist your team. They can help assure—

    a. Standard quality control inspections are being followed
    b. Audits are being conducted on a regularly scheduled basis
    c. Appropriate quality standards and measures have been defined
    d. Quality checklists are being used consistently and added to as problems are identified

62. You are pleased to be the first program manager in your company to manage a virtual team. While the company has managed programs for several years, in the past, it tended to hire subject matter experts or ask people from its offices in four other continents to meet in one place in order to work as a collocated team. It also relied extensively on contactor support. Finally, your executives have recognized that it will be cost beneficial to use a virtual team for your new program to develop a new product that combines the capabilities of a smart phone, an eBook reader, and a tablet in a single device that is less expensive with a higher quality of resolution than possible with the existing products on the marketplace. You are now evaluating the program objectives and want to make sure there is stakeholder alignment along with the ability to deliver an outstanding product. In this situation, you need to consider—

    a. Using focus groups to obtain a picture of the various attitudes of your stakeholders
    b. The cultural backgrounds of the team members
    c. The overall importance of your program in terms of the organization's portfolio of programs and projects
    d. Using market analysis

63. Your company has a career path in program management and has established standard competencies for the various positions. You were a project manager on the company's virtual team in which your program developed a new product combining the capabilities of the smart phone, eBook reader, and a tablet in a single device. You managed the integration project in your program, and you were commended by the executive team and the program manager for outstanding work. Now, you are transitioning into your first program management position. The guiding rule in your new job is to—

    a. Provide as much support as needed to project managers in their daily activities
    b. Delegate authority and responsibility to the project managers
    c. Actively manage each project until you have confidence in the project manager's ability to do so without your continual involvement
    d. Mentor project managers in their roles by working with them throughout their projects

64. As the program manager for the new landfill program for your county, you are facing a number of challenges. Your program team consists of chief engineers, regulatory specialists, project managers, and environmental engineers. You client, the county executive and Director of Public Works, now realizes just how complex your program is and today another new project was approved by your Governance Board to be added to the programs. This obviously affects your schedule and also you need more resource to best support the new project. You are especially concerned because you have a key date in which to meet a regulatory mandate and are hoping to meet it and then continue with the existing work. You have identified a large number of stakeholders, mostly in the county and the residents who have this "not in my backyard" syndrome about the landfill program, along with environmental activists. However, you recognize you need to engage each stakeholder group, even if they are negative, to ensure overall success. Recently, at some key meetings, you and your team realized some of the active stakeholders were missing. You realized some also missed the previous meeting. To identify and assess causes of nonparticipation, as a program manager, one tool to use is—

    a. Root cause analysis
    b. Cause-and-effect diagrams
    c. Variance analysis
    d. Conflict resolution strategies

65. Assume you have decided to sponsor a new program to develop a new way to determine whether or not an organization should bid on any opportunity, and the steps it should follow to predict whether the submitted proposal will be selected. This will be a quantitative model that basically can transform the way business development is handled. It will show areas of strength and areas in need of improvement and an approach to improve an organization's chances of winning the opportunity. It will be able to be used for international procurements as well as domestic and for commercial and government procurements. As the sponsor, you received approval to move to the initiating phase from your Portfolio Review Board. One objective of the Initiate Program process is to—

    a. Define the program's scope and benefit strategy
    b. Identify the program's benefits
    c. Quantify business benefits
    d. Establish a program governance process

66. Your company has established a program to manage the development of new pet food products, and you have been appointed manager of this program. It is the first program of its kind in your company; its structure was set up because numerous projects in the planning stage have dependencies and require some of the same resources. You realize that there are some commonalities among the benefits in the projects. Your program will be the first in your company to have a governance board throughout its life cycle. It has led to the company establishing program governance as a standard process, and it then enforces policies that address—

    a. Practices for capturing risks
    b. Aggregate performance of components of the portfolio
    c. Value indicators for portfolio components
    d. Models to ensure that the portfolio makes the best use of resources

67. You are the program manager for the International Air Traffic Association (IATA). The executives, representing all the airlines in the world, want to set up a global program for loyalty to airlines rather than the myriad of separate reward programs that now exist. They have built a business case for this program that shows in doing so benefits will accrue as there will be fewer disruptions to passengers and to the airlines if a flight is canceled, and the passenger could have taken a non-stop flight from his or her home airport rather than needing to travel to another airport just for the loyalty program. Of course, some of the leading airlines are resisting this approach so you have many negative stakeholders. The IATA executives recognized this issue from the outset and set up a Governance Board consisting of some of the negative stakeholders. The Board will have a number of key responsibilities one of which is—

   a. Who will determine the projects in the program?
   b. Who will ensure that benefits are realized and the value is delivered?
   c. Who will appoint the members of the core team?
   d. What will be the sponsor's role and responsibilities on the program?

68. Your organization has a defined process that it follows to determine which programs and projects should be in the portfolio, and this process is followed before leadership approval is received officially to authorize a program or project. In the past 10 years, your company, XYZ, has focused on projects. It has set up a project management methodology, which project managers are to follow, and it also has a Project Management Office. However, you recently attended a conference, and you realize since you are a member of the XYZ's Portfolio Review Board that many of the projects you are considering at your next meeting might be better managed if they were a program. After this conference, you met with other members of the Portfolio Review Board and explained how many of the existing projects in XYZ might be better organized as a program so they could then obtain more benefits than if the projects were managed in a standalone fashion. Now, with the upcoming Portfolio Review Board meeting, of the following possible key initiatives, which one would benefit by being managed as a program?

   a. Expanding a ski area
   b. Setting up a career path for people in the project management profession
   c. Upgrading the nation's airspace system
   d. Introducing a new project planning tool in a large organization

69. You are managing a program under contract with a major motion picture studio. Your contract is for three years with annual renewal possible if the program is not completed on schedule. Payment terms in your contract are 60 days. You need to hire several subcontractors to assist with the project. To protect your financial position and cash flow on the program, you should set the payment terms for your subcontractors at—

    a. 30 days
    b. 45 days
    c. 60 days
    d. 90 days

70. Finally, your program to revise and update the regulations at the Federal Trade Commission has passed stage gate four by your Program Board. You have been involving the records operation department in the program as they will be responsible for maintaining these regulations and making them easily accessible. They have been active stakeholders during the executing phase of your program management life cycle. Now, your Program Board members asked you to prepare a performance analysis report as you move to close the program. You will use a number of different tools and techniques to help you since this is one of the Commission's first completed programs and the objective is for your report to serve as a model that other programs can follow. As you prepare this report you—

    a. Collect data concerning stakeholder expectations and requirements
    b. Execute the transition plan
    c. Redeploy the personnel resources as stated in the staffing management plan
    d. Conduct a post review meeting

71. Your program is part of Portfolio X, which handles programs on the manufacturing side of new drug development and ongoing distribution of existing products. You are responsible for a program, Legacy A, to upgrade existing systems and supply chain management. Another program, New M, is responsible for all new systems. A third program, LMO, is responsible for customer relationship management and business development. Most of the systems were initially developed more than 25 years ago, and Legacy A has a number of component projects. New M handles programs involved with the scientific business units of the company. Although each program has its own governance board, the company also has a portfolio governance board. One reason for this approach is to ensure that—

    a. A common project management methodology is used across the company
    b. Issues that arise can receive visibility
    c. Benefits can be tracked in a single register
    d. Interrelationships among reported project results can be analyzed

72. As your government agency moves toward performance-based management, the senior executives issue a five-year plan with a number of initiatives. Each program and project will have key performance indicators (KPIs). Programs and projects will not be pursued without a detailed business case that is approved by a governance board composed of senior managers from each of the functional units. You are appointed as program manager to develop processes for these initiatives. The decision to set up this program is the result of—

a. Legislation
b. A regulatory requirement
c. Strategic planning
d. Scenario analysis

73. Your program to develop a 4G phone is being terminated early because your competition already has a 4G phone model on the market. Your company has initiated a program to develop a 6GXi phone, and you hope to be assigned to manage this program. At this point, you—

a. Document the current state
b. Archive your records
c. Appoint a closeout manager
d. Immediately disband your team

74. Your company is a worldwide leader in Six Sigma and the ISO 9001. Because of the importance of quality management, you appoint a member of your core program team to be responsible for quality planning on your program. At governance board meetings, he will often describe whether quality standards for the program are being met. Information is also included in program performance reports, which are also useful in terms of—

a. Performing program quality control
b. Providing governance oversight
c. Planning program quality
d. Approving component transition

75. You are the program manager for an updated enterprise resource planning system that also will include business development and knowledge management modules. Time to market is critical, and as the program manager you know other competitors' products tend to take an extremely long time to implement so with your new products you also are emphasizing ease of implementation and training end users. You will be using external contractors for part of the work. As you administer procurements, your company's program management methodology requires you to complete which of the following—

    a. Contract management plan
    b. Contract administration plan
    c. Procurement management plan
    d. Contract procurement plan

76. You are Company A's program manager for the development of an online banking system for your community bank, for which your company will realize $20 million in US dollars. The bank wants the program completed as quickly as possible and also contracted with Company B. You are now both trying to implement this system as quickly as possible. At first, it seemed as if you had a year and a half to do it but now with Company B also striving to complete the system, your Chief Executive Officer has told you it must be done in six months. So far, nine separate projects are part of the program, and you have a Governance Board overseeing it. Because it represents such a large dollar value to Company A, you have many stakeholders who are interested in it, as well as stakeholders at the bank. To track the various stakeholders, you and your team set up a stakeholder register. Ownership of the program is the responsibility of the—

    a. Executive sponsor
    b. Program board
    c. Program director
    d. Program manager

77. You are the program manager for a water-alleviation program in Ward, Florida, that requires extensive equipment. Some of this equipment represents new technology. As the program manager, you are preparing regular program performance reports, and each one discusses this equipment. A useful program performance analysis tool and technique to identify potential issues with this untested technology is—

    a. Risk analysis
    b. Forecast data
    c. Program metrics information
    d. Audit requirements

78. Your water alleviation program in Ward, Florida, is progressing. You have a core team of six people, and you have seven project managers. You were fortunate this year in that while Ward got a lot of heavy rain during the rainy season, it did not get any hurricanes. However, the Lake levels are still low, and residents cannot water more than two hour once a week until your program is complete. The City also is limited to watering only once a week as well but for four hours. You have a number of key stakeholders in the City government as well as the residents plus your own company. Therefore, you realize the importance of influencing throughout the program but especially as a tool and technique in the—

    a. Manage Program Resources process
    b. Engage Stakeholders process
    c. Identify Program Stakeholders process
    d. Manage Program Stakeholder Expectations process

79. As a program manager for the 888 series of aircraft being produced by your company, you are preparing for an important meeting of your Steering Committee to assess progress in coordinating deliverables. Because of an acquisition by your company, the committee includes two new executives. This will be their first committee meeting. You have not met them or talked to them on the phone. You are concerned that they have not read the performance reports that you provided by e-mail. For these two new members, you need to—

    a. Aggregate performance information about project and non-project work
    b. Focus on work results to date
    c. Use the earned value management system to forecast future performance
    d. Emphasize the variance reports

80. You are a member of your company's Program Selection Committee, which is trying to decide which one of four programs to launch. Your company prides itself on superior quality in the automobile parts field. Each program has prepared its business case. Proposed Program A will overlap and combine its phases, milestones, and activities. Proposed Program B will delay its schedule if necessary in a trade-off situation to ensure that quality is achieved. Proposed Program C will have a flexible structure to ensure innovative features at a minimal cost. Proposed Program D will focus on the technical features, cost, and schedule in its metrics. You select—

    a. Program A
    b. Program B
    c. Program C
    d. Program D

81. When your program is complete, it will generate more than 80 percent of the revenue earned by the company. Thus, it will have a major impact on the balance sheet. To assist you in your work, you prepared a program financial plan and established a budget baseline. Now you are tracking, monitoring, and controlling funds and expenses. Not to be overlooked in this process is—

    a. The profit the company earns
    b. The balance between profit and loss
    c. An operational cost analysis
    d. A summary of the revenue, direct cost, indirect cost, operating profit, and net profit of a company at a given point in time

82. You are the program manager for the International Air Traffic Association (IATA). The executives, representing all the airlines in the world, want to set up a global program for loyalty to airlines rather than the myriad of separate reward programs that now exist. You have worked on this program for one year, and you and your core team are slowly making progress. You have agreed with the Governance Board and the key stakeholders the value of the loyalty program and how points will be awarded. You also are about to complete a project to determine how many points to be transferred from people in existing programs to the new program. You have just prepared a request to close this project to present to your Governance Board. If they agree with your recommendation, then, your sponsor will make the final decision. As you prepare the component transition request, you also should review the—

    a. Benefits management plan
    b. Business case
    c. Benefits realization report
    d. Benefits realization plan

83. Your company is noted for its maturity and excellence in program management. It has received awards for its successes in program and project delivery. Last year, it received the Project Management Office of the Year Award, even though it really calls its PMO a Program Management Office, which it established about 12 years ago. One reason your company is a leader in the field is its reliance on the development and maintenance of organizational process assets, which may include—

    a. Environmental enterprise factors
    b. Process-related plans
    c. A portal
    d. Standards of professional conduct and responsibility

84. You meet with your Steering Committee on the 888 aircraft series program. Your program is on schedule, but the committee wants to accelerate production to beat a competitor's 480 aircraft to market. The committee provides you with 100 aerospace engineers to perform concurrent engineering in the design phase. As you work to report performance on your program and with the increase in the number of engineers, you need to—

a. Prepare a variance report
b. Prepare a project performance and status report
c. Update your program budget baseline
d. Update your program work breakdown structure (PWBS)

85. You have been a program manager for three years. You realize that a common understanding of program scope among the stakeholders leads to greater program success. Throughout the past three years, you have communicated extensively with your stakeholders and believe you are meeting most of their expectations. but some still have some doubts as to overall success. Therefore, in your last program review with your governance board, you noted this concern and now want to document a common understanding of the overall scope and have the key stakeholders sign off on it. This understanding is best documented as part of the—

a. Stakeholder management plan
b. Program scope statement
c. Program scope management plan
d. Program objectives in the program charter

86. For your program, you prepared a detailed stakeholder analysis. Stakeholder A thought that the program objectives were to deliver a detailed plan for your city's growth and development over the next 10 years; Stakeholder B thought that the purpose was to design a water-retention process to ensure that each citizen would have adequate water in the future; Stakeholder C thought that the program was to provide services to the city for its overall management by outsourcing its information technology (IT) services, personnel, and procurement functions; and Stakeholder D thought that the program was to provide a detailed workflow for all the city's functions. In the face of this lack of common understanding of the requirements, you need to prepare a—

a. Feasibility study
b. Stakeholder management plan
c. Benefits realization plan
d. Program scope statement

87. In a meeting with your program's governance board, you discussed ongoing and completed risk responses. You have been working to minimize risks, and a member of your core program team is responsible for overall risk management as her primary activity. You recently held a risk review meeting for your program, followed by a meeting with your governance board, which directed you to prepare a comprehensive update on all risks. You have prepared the risk update. Your next step is to—

    a. Update the program risk register
    b. Meet with the program's customer
    c. Enter the changes in the risk response plan
    d. Review the program issue register

88. You are a member of your insurance company's Program Selection Committee, which is considering a number of potential programs. Program A is estimated to cost $100,000 to implement and will have annual net cash inflows (ANCI) of $25,000. Program B is estimated to cost $250,000 to implement and have ANCI of $75,000. Program C is estimated to cost $600,000 to implement and have ANCI of $125,000. Program D is estimated to cost $125,000 to implement and have ANCI of $50,000. Your selection criteria are based on the shortest payback period. You recommend that your company select—

    a. Program A
    b. Program B
    c. Program C
    d. Program D

89. As an energy company "upstream" program manager, you use your program work breakdown structure (PWBS) to build your schedule. You have seven projects in your program, and it is to be completed in three years. You want to involve your team in a manner that reflects efficiency in the process. The best approach is to—

    a. Hold an off-site meeting in which project managers and your core program team work together to complete the schedule free from office interruptions
    b. Have the project managers build the detail for their projects and then roll it up into the control points and PWBS work packages
    c. Work with your core program team to develop the program schedule and then ask the project managers to use this schedule as they prepare more detailed project schedules
    d. Identify the significant milestones and build your schedule around these milestones to meet stakeholder expectations

90. Your molecular biology program is scheduled to last three years. Project A has been under way since the program began and is scheduled to be complete at the end of year 2. Project B is scheduled to begin in year 2. Project C has just begun and requires some domain-specific resources in molecular biology from both Projects A and B. Project Manager A is concerned that Project Managers B and C will require some of her key scientists; if these resources are reassigned, then the end date for Project A will slip. She has been practicing a philosophy of "no secrets" with the client and has informed Project Managers B and C that she is not willing to let any of her molecular biologists leave Project A until it is officially closed. You receive a call from the client requesting a meeting to discuss resource issues and the status of Project A. At this point, you—

    a. Meet with Project Manager A and tell her to first talk with you before she informs the client of any concerns in the future
    b. Tell Project Managers B and C that you support Project Manager A's decision not to release any of her key scientists
    c. Meet with all three project managers and inform them that you will manage any resource redeployment issues
    d. Meet with all three project managers and empower them to reach consensus on how the resources should be redeployed before you meet with the client

91. You are managing Program BBB for your manufacturing firm. Program EEE is experiencing severe resource shortfalls. The executive sponsor is the same for both programs. Your governance board holds an emergency meeting to decide what you can do to assist Program EEE. The board asks you to transfer seven of your manufacturing engineers to Program EEE and gives you the authority to contract with an outside firm for the engineering support that you need. The Procurement Department manages a basic ordering agreement with a temporary agency for such services. You must—

    a. Issue a request for proposals (RFP) so that you can contract for these services
    b. Update your program payment schedule
    c. Set up an issue tracking system
    d. Prepare nondisclosure agreements

92. You are managing a program whose budget at completion (BAC) is €420,000. The program is 10 percent complete and has an earned value of €42,000. The actual costs (AC) are €50,000. This means that—

    a. Although the program is over budget, the overrun is insignificant at this time
    b. The program is over budget by −€8,000, which is a major problem
    c. You need to calculate a new estimate to complete (ETC)
    d. The CV is €378,000, and immediate action is necessary

93. You are managing Program BBB for your manufacturing firm. Program EEE is experiencing severe resource shortfalls. The executive sponsor is the same for both programs. Your governance board holds an emergency meeting to decide what you can do to assist Program EEE. The board asks you to transfer seven of your manufacturing engineers to Program EEE and gives you the authority to contract with an outside firm for the engineering support that you need. With the change in your program BBB to use contractors for much of the manufacturing engineering work, you should—

    a. Notify your stakeholders
    b. Update your procurement management plan
    c. Prepare a contracts administration plan
    d. Approve a change to the outsourcing company's contract

94. Your company is new to program management, but it has practiced a management-by-projects culture for many years. Many people now have their PMPs® as well as advanced degrees in project management. Recently, you took a seminar at a PMI® conference on program management and suggested to your manager that the company should consider adopting program management because of its benefits to the organization. Before proceeding to take this idea to the Executive Committee, he asked you to perform an initial assessment as to why a focus on program management would add benefits. You need to therefore—

    a. Define the vision statement
    b. Show the link to corporate values
    c. Identify integration opportunities
    d. Define the objectives

95. You manage a program in the Ministry of Education. Your seven-year program is designed to ensure mandatory testing requirements for high school students throughout the country. Your program receives funding soon after the start of each fiscal year. Funds that are not spent during a fiscal year cannot be allocated to other programs or agency activities; rather, they revert to the general fund. As a program manager, you ensure that—

    a. Your program focuses on reserve analysis
    b. You spend all the money allocated in each fiscal year
    c. The program team knows how to use different budget techniques
    d. You add at least a 10 percent margin to the budget in anticipation of the reductions by the Ministry's budget office

96. Assume you are a member of a program team that is working to provide a better way to notify citizens in your City about the possibility of tornadoes. Now, the warning allows them only minutes to seek safety, and everyone believes a system such as that available for hurricanes and cyclones is necessary. As a resident of this city, you are pleased to be on the core team. Your program manager has asked you to be responsible for ensuring the program's stakeholders, of which there are many, receive information in a timely manner. Among other things, you must—

   a. Provide notifications of change requests
   b. Serve as the secretary to the program's governance board
   c. Be proactive in terms of both preventive and corrective actions
   d. Prepare a stakeholder management plan

97. Your organization is embarking on a program to establish a culture of knowledge management. You established a lessons-learned register on your last project. The enterprise program management office (EPMO) was impressed and suggested to the CEO that a program focusing on knowledge management is needed. The CEO concurred, and you were appointed program manager. Two people from the EPMO have been assigned to the core program team. They may be replaced by permanent staff during which one of the following processes?

   a. Initiate Team
   b. Acquire Program Team
   c. Manage Program Resources
   d. Human Resource Planning

98. Assume you are managing a project in your country which now allows people to buy in each state a pass to enable them to avoid the need to stop at toll booths on highways and bridges. However, each state in your country has a different type of pass so if you are in a different state, you cannot use it. As the program manager, your program's goal is to have an identical pass that every state can use on its highways and bridges. Additionally, your program will enable the pass to be used as well in airports at parking lots and garages. As you work on your program, you find there are a number of issues involved as states are reluctant to change to a new system and various stakeholders have different concerns and issues. You are working to identify, track, and close each issue as it arises. It is important to do so in tandem with—

   a. Resource control
   b. Scope control
   c. Risk management
   d. Performance reporting

99. You are an executive with a major recording studio. Four new groups have auditioned for a record contract, but you can select only one. The program to launch any group consists of Web site development, music videos, a nationwide tour, T-shirts, and a fan club. Your head of Marketing has done a net present value (NPV) for each group. Which do you choose?

Group A NPV at	Group B NPV at	Group C NPV at	Group D NPV at
5% = 5,243	5% = 2,320	5% = 6,400	5% = 3,000
10% = 2,841	10% = 1,254	10% = 3,275	10% = 2,755
15% = 1,563	15% = 688	15% = 1,679	15% = 700

You recommend that your company select—

a. Group A
b. Group B
c. Group C
d. Group D

100. You are the program manager for development of a next-generation personal digital assistant (PDA) that can be used on computers, airplanes, trains, and phones. You are in the early stages of your program, but it is ranked number 5 on your company's portfolio list. You have been asked to determine the organization's overall financial environment for the program and are doing so as part of—

a. Developing your charter
b. Establishing the program's financial framework
c. Developing the program's financial plan
d. Developing the infrastructure for the program

101. You now have five projects in your next-generation PDA program. So far, you are pleased with your core team and its progress, and you have a governance board in place to oversee your progress. They also are responsible for gate reviews. You have just completed the program work breakdown structure (PWBS) for this program. Your next step is to—

a. Generate the program schedule
b. Develop the program scope definition
c. Negotiate for project team members
d. Identify key milestones

102. You are the program manager for the International Air Traffic Association (IATA). The executives, representing all the airlines in the world, want to set up a global program for loyalty to airlines rather than the myriad of separate reward programs that now exist. On the IATA program, a number of benefits were identified in the business case and then in the benefits realization plan, which was approved by the Governance Board. You have a core team member who is maintaining a benefits register to track the status of each benefit, and you have assigned a person on your team to be the owner of each benefit. In a way, you have set this register up so it resembles the risk register you are using on your program. You found this has been a useful approach because—

    a. You need to regularly review your transition plan
    b. Some corrective actions may be required as a result of risk mitigation activities
    c. The same person who owns the benefit tends to also be a risk owner to minimize the responsibilities of your team members
    d. It is then easier to communicate benefit status to your Governance Board

103. Assume your county government decided to move into program management as it found that a number of projects under way had inter-relationships and interdependencies in terms of the benefits they were to deliver to the citizens in the county. While the county has a project management methodology it did not have one for program management so it decided to build on the best practices in the Project Management Institute's *Standard for Program Management*. You were asked to be the first program manager in the county, and you realized that while your program was to make sure everyone who entered the county was a resident, and therefore, did not need to be carefully scrutinized in case there were any later reports of violent activity, that you needed a methodology to follow so you added development of this methodology to your program. As you reviewed the guidelines in *The Standard for Program Management*, you noted that one process that was performed throughout the life cycle in this Standard is—

    a. Monitor and Control Program Schedule
    b. Benefits Realization
    c. Monitor and Control Program Performance
    d. Manage Program Issues

104. Assume you are a member of a program team that is working to provide a better way to notify citizens in your City about the possibility of tornadoes. Now, the warning allows them only minutes to seek safety, and everyone believes a system such as that available for hurricanes and cyclones is necessary. As a resident of this city, you are pleased to be on the core team. Your program manager has asked you to be responsible for ensuring the program's stakeholders, of which there are many, receive information in a timely manner. You are now preparing your stakeholder register. As you do so you want to follow best practices and have a deeper understanding of the impacts of your program on your stakeholders so you decide to use—

    a. Interviews
    b. Focus groups
    c. Questionnaires and surveys
    d. Brainstorming

105. You are managing a program that comprises new systems applications development and maintenance activities. These applications are critical to your company, as they involve access to proprietary data. The systems must be available to your clients on a 24/7/365 basis. Much of the work is to be outsourced. From a strategic perspective, your primary concern regarding this program is that—

    a. The contractor has systems capable of accommodating the applications and that all hardware and software has been updated
    b. Your legal team has reviewed all the contract's terms and conditions to ensure that your company is protected in case of default
    c. Your organization has the necessary levels of skill and expertise to manage and administer a contract of this magnitude
    d. The contractor has the appropriate tools and techniques to safeguard your intellectual property

106. Working as the program manager for this standard toll pass system, since there are about 30 such systems in existence now in your country to avoid the need for toll booths if people elect to buy these passes, you realized you needed to take the best practices of the various pass systems already in existence and incorporate them into your program. You found that one State, Virginia, had a quality plan for its pass program, while most of the other states instead were only focusing on inspection as a quality tool and technique. You decided you needed a quality management plan for your program, building on Virginia's quality plan but expanding it given the scope of your program. You then need to make sure this plan is executed at the project level. One way to do so is to—

    a. Rely on checklists
    b. Establish a quality assurance office
    c. Perform health checks
    d. Reprimand project managers who do not use them

107. You are part of a team, and you are identifying potential benefits for your program and decided to develop a high-level benefits realization plan. Everyone now is focused on employing a set of benefit measurement techniques that will provide substantive information to all stakeholders. Of the following, which is an example of a benefits measurement technique you should include in this plan?

    a. Internal rate of return (IRR)
    b. Balanced scorecard
    c. Value engineering
    d. Net present value (NPV)

108. Members of your program governance board are complaining about performance information from your program. They claim that your reports are too detailed, are too many in number, and are produced on a shifting schedule. You met with each person on the board early in the program and thought you were meeting their information requirements. You then asked your organization's Enterprise PMO for assistance. The Enterprise PMO Director recommends the development and use of—

    a. A program dashboard
    b. Standard metrics used in your industry
    c. A more comprehensive software tool
    d. The organization's standard financial reports

109. For seven years, you have managed a program that involved breakthrough scientific research. You are now in the closing stage. You have already met with each scientist involved in the program at the time his or her work was finished. You have also met with a member of your enterprise program management office (EPMO) who specializes in knowledge management to ensure that the intellectual property developed in the program is captured and documented for future reuse. You are—

a. Ensuring legal protection of this valuable asset
b. Promoting collaboration in the scientific community
c. Recognizing individual efforts as well as the efforts of the entire project team
d. Officially releasing each scientist to his or her functional organization

110. Recognizing the importance of benefits realization and management, as a program manager, it has been noted that a best practice to follow is to be able to quantify as many benefits in your benefits realization plan as possible and also to be able to communicate their status as required quickly to stakeholders. You and your core team decided that a best practice to follow in your program to develop a new drug to cure bone cancer with limited if any side effects and to beat your competitors to market even with all the federal regulations was to—

a. Use tangible benefits in your benefit realization plan
b. Have each stakeholder sign off on your benefits realization plan indicating his or her concurrence with it
c. Invite each stakeholder to regularly scheduled benefit reviews, which are included in your program's roadmap
d. Maintain a benefits register

111. As the program manager working on the development of an advanced polymer chemical for raincoats, you are in the process of assessing the feasibility of your program. In reading the latest industry journal, you discovered that a competitor is also entering the marketplace. To assess your position against that of your competitor, you conduct a—

a. SWOT analysis
b. Brainstorming session
c. Nominal group technique
d. Delphi technique exercise

112. Finally, your program to develop the advanced polymer chemical for raincoats is near to completion. You have had seven projects in your program, and the last one should finish in two months. You have been involving the people in your operations support group to be part of your program team meetings now for the last year and earlier included them on the distribution list for your status reports so they felt they were part of the team for success as you recognize transition planning is the key to benefits sustainment in program management. As a program manager, you also recognize the importance of ensuring that component transition requests are prepared. It is especially important during the—

a. Transition Planning process
b. Direct and Manage Program Execution process
c. Develop Program Management Plan process
d. Transition Execution process

113. As you work on your program to design, develop, and manufacture a class of farm equipment that can be used above the Arctic Circle, you are also maintaining spare parts inventory and also fulfilling spares requests for clients in addition to the new work in this program. You met today with the spare parts project manager, and he had a change to his project that affected his scope dramatically. When you reviewed this change with him, you realized it also would affect the scope of the manufacturing project manager's project in your program. This change request required detailed analysis for the overall impact not only to these two projects but also to your entire program. Approved change requests are—

a. An output of the Monitor and Control Program Scope process
b. Listed in the action item register
c. Returned to the person who proposed the change
d. Placed in the temporary program files.

114. On your program to design, develop, and manufacture this class of farm equipment for use above the Arctic Circle, you want to make sure that the benefits from the program will be sustainable ones. Your sponsor is interested in having regular status reports about the progress of your program especially since she is located below the Arctic Circle and rarely makes on site visits given the weather conditions to assess progress herself. To provide a clear picture of your program's performance as a while, you must—

a. Forecast information on the significant project components
b. Aggregate information across projects and non-project activity
c. Provide detailed reports on component projects at regular intervals
d. Monitor the status of the key deliverables

115. You are sponsoring a new program in your company. You have identified the benefits and objectives and submitted the documentation to the portfolio review board two weeks before its next meeting. You are competing with two other possible programs, so you decide to contact the board members to see if they have any questions about your program. Board Member A is very supportive; Board Member B has concerns about the competitive attributes of your program versus those of other programs in the pipeline; Board Member C is supportive but not enthusiastic; Board Member D is not available to talk to you; and Board Member E is skeptical about the overall program strategy. To try to increase the support of Board Members B and E, you—

   a. Align the elements of your program more closely with the company's strategy
   b. Refine your net present value (NPV) and internal rate of return (IRR) analysis
   c. Meet with the Enterprise Project Management Office director to obtain support
   d. Enlist greater support from the executive sponsor who personally knows the board members

116. You manage the development of an off-shore liquefied natural gas facility. Several contractors will be used in the component projects, and you are creating specific procurement strategies. After you determine which program work breakdown structure (PWBS) elements will be handled internally and which will be contracted, your next step is to—

   a. Follow the program scope statement
   b. Determine the program requirements
   c. Prepare a procurement management plan
   d. Use make-or-buy decision techniques

117. Assume you are leading a program in your gas company to promote more use of natural gas by customers. Your country has a large supply of untapped natural gas, and your company is privileged to have access to this supply. You have identified a number of benefits to the use of natural gas and one of them is environmental since it is much cleaner. It also is more cost effective. However, everyone resists change, and people are having trouble understanding the benefits of this program and how to best present these benefits to consumers, especially when the natural gas production facilities in your company are fully operational. This means that as the program manager because there is so much uncertainty among consumers about natural gas, and a major educational initiative is a project in the program, that you need to convince them the risks associated with natural gas are low. As you do so, it is important therefore to concentrate on—

    a. Solely financial benefits
    b. Both direct and tangible benefits
    c. Intangible benefits and tangible benefits
    d. Measurable benefits

118. Assume you are leading a program in your gas company to promote more use of natural gas by customers. Your country has a large supply of untapped natural gas, and your company is privileged to have access to this supply. You have identified a number of benefits to use of natural gas and one of them is environmental since it is much cleaner. Your benefits realization plan for your natural gas program has been approved by your Governance Board, and it also is a subsidiary plan to your overall program management plan. You have set up measurement criteria for each of the benefits you identified in your plan. You now want to establish a baseline for the benefits in the plan. As you establish your baseline, you have collected some key organizational, financial, and operational metrics against which you can measure improvements. A key task to consider as you establish the baseline is—

    a. Devise a strategy to collect baseline data such as using questionnaires and interviews
    b. Review your cost estimates
    c. Assess process interdependencies
    d. Determine the appropriate infrastructure needs

119. Finally after four years of planning, your program management plan to convert customer relationship management software, supplier management software, human resource software, and telecom systems from legacy systems to an integrated platform was approved. At last, you are working to execute your plan, and you have four projects in your program thus far. Since the executing process is under way, this means emphasis now is on implementing approved change requests, maintaining decision logs, and performing impact analysis. These tasks are done—

    a. Under the supervision of the individual project managers
    b. By the program manager, based on his or her scope of authority
    c. After approval by the program's governance board
    d. As directed by the program management methodology

120. Finally after four years of planning, your program management plan to convert customer relationship management software, supplier management software, human resource software, and telecom systems from legacy systems to an integrated platform was approved. At last, you are working to execute your plan, and you have four projects in your program thus far. As you build individual and group competencies to enhance the performance of your program, you should also—

    a. Conduct performance assessments and place reports in the Human Resources files
    b. Communicate personnel performance to each team member's line manager
    c. Communicate personnel performance to the Vice President for Human Resources
    d. Rely on the Chief Learning Officer to conduct competency assessments

121. You are preparing for a meeting of your program's governance board. Your program coordinator is using earned value (EV) to track and monitor performance and to forecast future performance. On your program, the planned value (PV) is $30,587 and the EV is $26,365. At this point, your program is 70 percent complete, so you can tell your governance board that your schedule performance index (SPI) is—

    a. 0.959, and you are not experiencing any schedule problems
    b. 0.959, and you will have problems meeting your scheduled end date
    c. 0.86, but it will be easy to recover from this performance
    d. 0.86, and it will be difficult to recover from this performance

122. You are assuming a position in a company that has not had much experience with program management. You will be leading the program team and performing a business function for your program. The business case has already been made, and the program is scheduled to move into the Program Initiation phase. As the program manager, your most important competency is—

    a. Communication
    b. Political skills
    c. Strategic visioning
    d. Leadership

123. Assume you are managing a program at your University to establish a Master of Science degree in Program Management. Already, the University's Master of Science degree in project management is well recognized, and it has been accredited by leading organizations. However, many people have been inquiring if instead they could get their degrees in Program Management as their organizations have set up a career path, which has the Program Manager at a far higher level than that of a Project Manager, and also the organizations are using programs more often now than individual projects. You want to make sure the new program is different than the project management degree, and, therefore, you need totally different courses at a higher level. Your business case for this program was approved by the University's trustees, and you are pleased to be its program manager. The trustees asked for a benefits realization plan, which you prepared, and they signed off on and approved. However, they felt for reporting purposes to a Governance Board that it would be helpful to prioritize the benefits you have identified and will report on during meetings of the Governance Board. One approach to consider is to ensure—

    a. The identified benefits support best practices
    b. The benefits are aligned with the University's strategic objectives
    c. A benefit owner is assigned
    d. Realistic measures of these benefits can be prepared

124. Working on this program to establish a Master of Science degree in Program Management, assume you have a meeting coming up with your Governance Board in two weeks. Its purpose is to serve as a gate review for you to proceed to the executing phase in your program life cycle. You need to demonstrate at this stage gate review how you will report and track the benefits from your program. However, in your work in planning, you have identified a number of key factors external to your program that affect the proposed benefits, one of which is that your leading competitor in this field and located in your state also is looking into such a program and plans to offer it in an on-line fashion; your University only operates in a face-to-face mode. You know how important it is to track benefits and learning about this other University's plans to offer the degree on line is a key benefit that you had not planned for but now feel it is essential. The new benefit actually represents a—

    a. New project
    b. Risk opportunity
    c. Major issue
    d. New program

125. As a program manager, you recognize the importance of effective risk management. You want to maximize any risks that may be opportunities that can benefit your program and the organization. As you prepare your program risk management plans, you decide to hold a risk planning meeting. After the meeting is over, you should—

    a. Determine the specific risk categories that affect your program
    b. Prepare a budget for risk management on your program
    c. Share the results with component managers
    d. Identify program risks and document their characteristics

126. As program manager for the development of a new drug, you are pleased that it has finally received regulatory approval, and you can move on to the manufacturing and distribution phase. You have been managing this program now for eight years, and you had six projects in it. To protect intellectual property, your company has—

    a. Obtained a patent
    b. Obtained a license for exclusive distribution
    c. Worked to ensure a positive reception for the product from end users and the medical field
    d. Signed a nondisclosure agreement with the government

127. As the program manager for a new pipeline system that has as its goal no potential incidents of any type, you have a major challenge as your company in the past has had a poor safety record. This program is complex, and this goal will be difficult to achieve. However, after working to plan the program for three years, your Steering Committee met and approved your program management plan. As you move to approve components to be part of your program, you need to review the

    a. Component charter
    b. Change requests
    c. Go/no-go decisions
    d. Governance plan

128. As the program manager for a new pipeline system that has as its goal no potential incidents of any type, you have a major challenge as your company in the past has had a poor safety record. This program is complex, and this goal will be difficult to achieve. However, after working to plan the program for three years, your Steering Committee met and approved your program management plan. So far, three projects have been chartered to be part of your program, and others may be added later. You have staffed your program team with a variety of in-house staff members, selected consultants, and several new full-time employees. It is now time to—

    a. Prepare your team development plan
    b. Update your program resource plan
    c. Prepare your resource management plan
    d. Update your staffing management plan

129. Assume you are working for a leading training company in portfolio, program, and project management as well as in business analysis and contract administration. Your leading competitor has just announced that it will launch in one month a new training approach using videos. The instructors will be on each video, and it will be able to be viewed by students at any time in an asynchronous way, and at other times, students will be able to interact directly with the instructor and also with other students in the class. Your CEO realizes such an approach will be highly beneficial and is superior to the on-line training your company offers, which is only asynchronous with people looking at slides, and the instructor discusses each slide. In fact, the CEO has had complaints about the boring nature of your firm's on line training, while people are very impressed with the face-to-face offerings. You have been selected as the program manager for this new video approach, and you need to have it available for all of your courses by the end of the year so you are not lagging that much behind the competition. So far, you have five projects in this video program, and you have been working closely with your project managers in communications planning. You have found which of the following to be especially useful to you in this regard—

    a. Communications strategy
    b. Communications requirements analysis
    c. Lessons learned database
    d. Program charter

130. Assume you are working for a leading training company in portfolio, program, and project management as well as in business analysis and contract administration. Your leading competitor has just announced that it will launch in one month a new training approach using videos. The instructors will be on each video, and it will be able to be viewed by students at any time in an asynchronous way, and at other times, students will be able to interact directly with the instructor and also with other students in the class. Your CEO realizes such an approach will be highly beneficial and is superior to the on-line training your company offers, which is only asynchronous with people looking at slides, and the instructor discusses each slide. In fact, the CEO has had complaints about the boring nature of your firm's on line training, while people are very impressed with the face-to-face offerings. You have been selected as the program manager for this new video approach, and you need to have it available for all of your courses by the end of the year so you are not lagging that much behind the competition. So far, you have five projects in this video program, and you have been working closely with your project managers in communications planning. Finally, you Governance Board approved your communications plan for this program. However, you realize the importance of refining your communications strategy and tactics so you should consult the—

    a. Program management plan
    b. Program work breakdown structure (PWBS)
    c. Governance plan
    d. Organizational communications strategy

131. You are a member of your organization's Program Selection Committee, which is conducting an off-site meeting to review the company's five major strategic goals, all of which are weighted equally. Goal 1 is to produce the highest possible quality products; goal 2 is to provide outstanding customer relationship management; goal 3 is to reduce reliance on external supply sources and maximize internal resources; goal 4 is to reduce manufacturing costs; and goal 5 is to maximize productivity. You are considering four programs and will recommend one to the CEO. Program A partially supports goal 1, fully supports goals 2, 3, and 4, and does not support goal 5. Program B fully supports goals 1, 3, 4, and 5, but does not support goal 2. Program C fully supports goals 1 and 2, partially supports goals 3 and 4, but does not support goal 5. Program D partially supports goals 1, 2, and 5, and fully supports goals 3 and 4. Considering this information, your recommendation should be to select—

    a. Program A
    b. Program B
    c. Program C
    d. Program D

132. You are preparing for a major Steering Committee review of your program. The executive director is especially interested in progress on Project A, as it provides the foundation for two other projects. Your program control officer informs you that Project A has a pessimistic estimate of being completed within 55 days, a most likely estimate of 42 days, and an optimistic estimate of 22 days. The expected time to complete Project A is—

    a. 35 days
    b. 37 days
    c. 41 days
    d. 45 days

133. Stakeholder management is especially important in program management. As a program manager, you consider the interests and concerns of all your stakeholders for program success. You manage communications to ensure that your stakeholders are informed about what is happening on your program and so that you can resolve any issues of importance to them. This is done as part of your responsibilities in which process?

    a. Communications Control
    b. Engage Program Stakeholders
    c. Manage Program Stakeholder Expectations
    d. Communications Planning

134. Assume you are managing a program so your organization, a Fortune 50 company, has a standard program management system (PMIS) that all programs in all of its 90 business units will use. Such a common PMIS is a major internal program, and as a result, you have a limited budget to work with to make sure it is a success and is adopted by the heads of the business units and its program managers. You are following guidelines in the Project Management Institute's *Standard for Program Management* as you prepare this PMIS. You find the Monitor and Control Program Financials process is one that is both proactive and reactive. An example of being proactive is—

    a. Dealing with unanticipated events
    b. Responding to necessary but unplanned activities that negatively affect the budget
    c. Responding to necessary but unplanned activities that positively affect the budget
    d. Using cost forecasting techniques on a regular basis

135. You are Company A's program manager for the development of an online banking system for your community bank, for which your company will receive $20 million. Because the bank would like to implement this system quickly, it has also contracted with Company B. You must implement your system completely in six months to ensure that you beat Company B's schedule. Your management at the highest level is totally committed to this program and it is the number one program in Company A's portfolio. As a result, your phase-gate reviews will be handled by—

    a. Your program's governance board in its meetings
    b. By your CEO
    c. By your executive sponsor
    d. Your company's corresponding portfolio

136. As a program manager in your country's food safety department, you are managing a program to ensure the safety of imported food in your country. This program resulted from many people becoming sick because of imported shrimp, poultry, and beef. This program is using public money and will last for several years; therefore, as the program manager, you need to—

    a. Have a thorough understanding of the financial environment
    b. Develop a plan for each of the components in your program
    c. Have your project managers use earned value management to track all expenses
    d. Set up a project management information system to track resource plans and use

137. Each of the projects in your program prepares a project risk management plan to describe how risk management is structured. Each project manager also prepares risk response plans for each of the key identified risks. As program manager, you review the risk response plans to—

    a. Establish triggers for the project risks
    b. Determine actions that could affect other components
    c. Identify intra-project risks
    d. Establish a contingency reserve

138. Your organization is ISO 9001 certified. As program manager, you have arranged for a member of your company's Quality Assurance Program (a Black Belt in Six Sigma) to support your program. This team member reports directly to you and by dotted line to the manager of the Quality Assurance Department. In his first audit, he finds that one of the projects includes several key service management activities that have not met quality requirements. Your next step is to—

    a. Facilitate an off-site meeting of your core program team to determine how best to handle this deficiency
    b. Convene a meeting of your program governance board to request that an additional resource be added to serve as a project manager for these activities
    c. Issue a change request for corrective action
    d. Assign these functions to the project manager to make sure that they are done properly

139. You are Company A's program manager for the development of an online banking system for your community bank, for which your company will receive $20 million. Because the bank would like to implement this system quickly, it has also contracted with Company B. You must implement your system completely in six months to ensure that you beat Company B's schedule. Your management at the highest level is totally committed to this program, and it is the number one program in Company A's portfolio. One of your first tasks was to work with your sponsor and specify the purpose of the phase-gate reviews and when they will be held on this program. One goal of these reviews is to—

    a. Monitor the business environment for changes
    b. Ensure generally accepted best practices are being followed
    c. Ensure the program charter remains viable
    d. Identify the key decision makers and stakeholders associated with this program

140. You manage a program for the Occupational Safety and Health Administration (OSHA) to make all the agency's regulations performance based and applicable to any industry group. You identify 50 external stakeholders who are active participants in this process and 30 who are interested but not active, along with 75 interested internal stakeholders. This stakeholder identification is your responsibility in which one of the following processes?

    a. Engage Program Stakeholders
    b. Manage Program Stakeholder Expectations
    c. Report Program Performance
    d. Direct and Manage Program Execution

141. As manager of a program for the Federal Trade Commission that involves changes to existing regulations throughout the Commission, you have a major challenge as the majority of the regulations have not been reviewed for more than 20 years. Others of course have been added. Your role is to make sure in your program that all of the regulations are current and also are easily accessible by all stakeholders. You have a total of seven projects in your program, and since your program is a government mandated one, you have a governance board for your program that meets at least monthly and at key stage gate reviews. The person who is responsible for ensuring program success is the—

    a. Program director
    b. Commission Chairman
    c. Executive sponsor
    d. Director of the Enterprise Program Management Office

142. Assume you are working in a company, CDE, which specializes in new product development. The CDE executives are concerned because its last two products in the on-line music industry were late to market, and by the time they were on the market, competitors had products out with more attractive features to customers. As a result, CDE is in jeopardy of losing its market share in on-line music for mobile phones and tablets and also in games for these phones and tablets. You are now in process of working with your R&D team to determine a new product to propose to CDE's executives. Given the last two experiences, you believe you should include all of the following items in your business case but you especially need to focus on a—

    a. Existing work under way
    b. High-level net present value analysis
    c. High-level roadmap
    d. Competitive analysis

143. You are managing a program to develop a new source of energy in the extreme northern latitudes when solar power is not available. Working with your core program team and your governance board, you have identified a number of component projects. Your company has several key projects under way, and resources will be difficult to acquire for this new program. In determining whether you will use internal or external resources, you should consider—

    a. The availability of key staff members
    b. Your ability to negotiate with functional managers for the needed staff
    c. Previous work by the staff as a successful team
    d. The availability of off-shore employees to drive down costs

144. Assume you are managing a program at your University to establish a Master of Science degree in Program Management. Already, the University's Master of Science degree in project management is well recognized, and it has been accredited by leading organizations. However, many people have been inquiring if instead they could get their degrees in Program Management as their organizations have set up a career path, which has the Program Manager at a far higher level than that of a Project Manager, and also the organizations are using programs more often now than individual projects. In your role of establishing this Masters of Science degree in Program Management, your benefit realization plan includes both tangible and intangible benefits. You recognize the demand for the degree and it in turn will lead to new income to the University. It also will enhance customer satisfaction with the University and will demonstrate to the overall project management community that it is following the trends in the profession. You expect a large number of people to enroll in the program based on the interest now in obtaining the PgMP® credential. Your program will help provide the credit hours required to obtain the PgMP®. You have seven projects in your program and are fortunate to have a Program Office with a small core staff to support you. You have asked the Program Office to determine an easy but meaningful way to report on the realization of benefits from your program and then to provide this information to your stakeholders—both internal and external. By tracking the benefits during the program rather than after the degree is in place and students have enrolled offers a number of benefits in itself, one of which is—

   a. Provides an opportunity to publicize the program
   b. Encourages ownership of the solution
   c. Ensures funding limits are not exceeded
   d. Ensures the available information is of the highest quality

145. As you work on your program to improve the economic growth of your country, you are following a program management methodology that your agency's Center of Excellence in Program Management prepared. It follows many of the processes that the Project Management Institute has set forth with some tailoring to meet the unique needs of your agency. You realize that although a number of processes have close connections with other program processes, that is particularly the case between—

   a. Plan Program Quality and Plan Program Procurement
   b. Plan for Audits and Engage Program Stakeholders
   c. Develop Program Financial Plan and Plan Program Stakeholder Management
   d. Plan Program Quality and Conduct Program Procurements

146. As the program manager for a multinational project headquartered in Sweden, you have adopted English as the common language for use on the project. However, most of your team members are located in Asia, and many of them do not speak English as their primary language. You have decided, therefore, to adopt the common English vocabulary of 4,000 words to facilitate the communication process. This decision should be stated in the—

    a. Communications requirements
    b. Program management plan
    c. Communications management plan
    d. Program scope statement

147. Working on your program to improve the economic growth of your country, you know from the business case there are many risks and issues. However, the business case only presented a high-level view of them. You then held a risk planning meeting with your stakeholders to help prepare a risk management plan, and you have set up a process to track issues. Now, you and your core program team are working to identify risks that could affect your program building on those in the business case. You and your team are clarifying the definition of each risk and grouping them by cause. This means you are using which of the following techniques?

    a. Flowcharts
    b. Influence diagrams
    c. Root cause identification
    d. SWOT analysis

148. However, as you work on this program to improve the economic growth of your country, now you have another problem. A key member of your program staff has been complaining lately of the company's vacation policies. He would like to take more time off but has not yet accrued enough time to do so. You are concerned that he is going to leave the company, so you monitor his e-mail, in accordance with company policy, to see whether he is sending his resume to other companies. The act of sending out his resume would be called a—

    a. Risk trigger
    b. Risk event
    c. Misuse of the company's e-mail policy
    d. Violation of the company's code of ethics

149. As manager of a program for the Federal Trade Commission that involves changes to existing regulations throughout the Commission, you have a major challenge as the majority of the regulations have not been reviewed for more than 20 years. Others of course have been added. Your role is to make sure in your program that all of the regulations are current and also are easily accessible by all stakeholders. You have a total of seven projects in your program, and since your program is a government mandated one, you have a governance board for your program that meets at least monthly and at key stage gate reviews. You and your core team have prepared a governance plan that you will present at the board's next meeting in two weeks. As you prepared this plan, it was beneficial to review the—

 a. Governance structure and composition
 b. Gate review requirements
 c. Commission's quality standards
 d. Strategic directive

150. As part of your stakeholder management activities, your core program team meets with each of the stakeholders you have identified as critical to program success. During these meetings, the team members assigned to work with specific stakeholders try to gauge their attitudes toward risk, identify their perceptions, and better understand how they might respond. This approach is especially useful to you in the—

 a. Plan Program Risk Management process
 b. Plan Program Quality process
 c. Analyze Program Risks process
 d. Plan Program Stakeholder Management process

151. You are sponsoring a new program that will focus on a new product in which educators can immediately determine whether or not a student is plagiarizing, whether the student has cited the reference correctly, or whether it is an entirely new idea. The program will have a number of components to it because one project will involve setting up an approach to quickly search all existing references in a quick and easy fashion, another project will enable a student then to receive immediate feedback along with the professor, one project will protect student privacy, and a fourth project will be one to show the student how a reference should be cited effectively. In this program you want to evaluate its program objectives, and you realize you need to address a number of concerns to satisfy all the involved and committed stakeholders. One of these considerations in this situation is—

 a. Cultural considerations
 b. Ethical concerns
 c. Sustainability issues
 d. Technological changes

152. As manager of a program for the Federal Trade Commission that involves changes to existing regulations throughout the Commission, you have a major challenge as the majority of the regulations have not been reviewed for more than 20 years. Others of course have been added. Your role is to make sure in your program that all of the regulations are current and also are easily accessible by all stakeholders. You have a total of seven projects in your program, and since your program is a government mandated one, you have a governance board for your program that meets at least monthly and at key stage gate reviews. Your program is to be completed in a year and a half, and you are now at the half-way point. As you have been managing this program, it has been extremely helpful to you to—

   a. Have a program management information system
   b. Use your benefit delivery plan
   c. Have a change management specialist as a member of your core team
   d. Use benchmarking with other government agencies who have already conducted similar programs to update regulations

153. Assume you are managing a program at your University to establish a Master of Science degree in Program Management. Already, the University's Master of Science degree in project management is well recognized, and it has been accredited by leading organizations. However, many people have been inquiring if instead they could get their degrees in Program Management as their organizations have set up a career path, which has the Program Manager at a far higher level than that of a Project Manager, and also the organizations are using programs more often now than individual projects. Managing this program for the new Masters of Science degree in Program Management means among other things that the University will need to hire a director and a small staff to review student applications, publicize the program at a variety of events, hire faculty to teach the courses, and determine when new courses should be added. You have completed five of the seven projects in your program so far. In the last meeting with the Governance Board, when it was time to transition one of the projects, this meant it was then time to hire the program director and a couple of people for supporting roles. This project had outlined all the support tasks that needed to be done and included items such as the job descriptions for the program director and his or her staff members, the criteria to use to select the program director and staff, and methods to evaluate their performance. Now the director has been hired. You therefore should as a best practice—

   a. Involve the new director in all meetings with all stakeholders
   b. Ensure the new director understands the benefits of this program and how they will be sustained
   c. Ask the director to serve as the project manager for the two remaining projects on the program
   d. Ask the Governance Board to add the new director to be a member to oversee the remaining projects on the program

154. Finally, your program to rebuild the water desalinization plant for Ferguson, Saudi Arabia is complete. This program has been under way for more than five years. You had a number of leasing agreements on the program, and you are confident all of them have been closed successfully. You also had several subcontractors, and you have had reviews with each of them. You are meeting with your Governance Board, to obtain approval for phase-gate review G4, the final phase of the program. You have made a recommendation to the Board to close the program. The person who will make the official decision is—

    a. Executive director
    b. Program sponsor
    c. Governance Board members as they approve G4
    d. Head of the PMO

155. Your organization has just announced that funds will be cut by 10 percent. Even though you are still in the planning phase of your program life cycle, and your program is considered a high priority in your company's portfolio, unfortunately, your program is not exempt from these budget cuts. But, you do have an advantage because your executive team is interested in your program because it is required for your company's continued viability in the production of sport utility vehicles. Your executive team has mandated certain delivery dates, which you felt were feasible until these budget cuts were announced. Still, you must meet them so you have prepared a new program roadmap and a new master schedule. You now must communicate these changes to your stakeholders. As the program manager, you administer three different but equally important communications channels, one of which is—

    a. Component managers
    b. Core program team
    c. Functional managers
    d. Program managers

156. You have been working on a new product development program for your company, which specializes in farm equipment. Your product is to combine an easy-to-use tractor with a more complex crawler so the customer does not have to purchase two separate items and can use the combination product to meet a number of unique needs. You just found out from your portfolio manager that the company plans to acquire a competitor that specializes in riding lawn mowers. You have now suggested to your Governance Board that you add a project to your program to also combine a mower into the new product of your program. You believe such an improvement will—

    a. Increase the benefits to be realized by the product
    b. Result in a longer timeline but will be one that customers should find of use
    c. Can position your company well in the marketplace
    d. Will lead to improved customer relationship management

157. The contractor working on your program is losing money on the contract and asks that you terminate the agreement. She says that if you do not, she will simply stop working because she cannot afford to continue. If she does stop work, she will—

    a. Be held in contempt of court
    b. Default and be subject to legal action
    c. Terminate the contract for convenience
    d. Terminate the contract for cause

158. Your program communications management plan shows the various items to be distributed to your stakeholders; their purpose, frequency, and format; and the person responsible for each. As you work on your program, you follow this plan for formal communication of program information. You now have your process in place to distribute information to your stakeholders at the time and frequency they require. Your next task is to—

    a. Update the communications requirements analysis
    b. Prepare a lessons-learned process
    c. Prepare standard information requests
    d. Update the communications log

159. You are a program manager under contract to a government agency that is responsible for issuing visas and passports. You have been working on this program for eight years and are responsible for all the information and telecommunications functions for the agency. Your company realizes this program is essential to its success, and this is the first time it has worked for this agency. Therefore, it established a governance structure to oversee the process. A best practice to follow after each governance meeting is to—

    a. Update the governance plan based on decisions made
    b. Document decisions in a decision register
    c. Meet with your core team and project managers and inform them of the results of the governance board meeting
    d. Meet with your program sponsor to discuss your next steps

160. Assume you have been maintaining a benefit register once your program's benefit realization plan was prepared. Because of the importance of benefits management on programs, you are fortunate that a member of your core team has expertise in this area and have appointed her to serve as the business benefits manager of your program, working closely with the Program Management Office in your company. She will work closely with you and the other core team members as she will be maintaining the register, preparing the benefit reports, and also conducting benefit reviews. One of the key purposes of the benefit reviews is to—

    a. Create benefit ownership
    b. Address the risk of operational areas that fail to commit to the benefits
    c. Establish an approach to prioritize benefits that are in the realization plan
    d. Review the benefits realization plan and implement improvements based on lessons learned to date

161. Your company, a member of the Fortune 500, is well known around the world as it is the leading producer of the top selling cereal. The cereal is nutritious, is one that both adults and children both enjoy, and has been on the market for over 40 years. Your company, though, is interested now in moving into the ice cream market. This will be a major change, and you have been asked to be the program manager for a new line of 12 different ice cream types. The development of this product is in your company's strategic plan, but it is so radically different from the cereal products for which you company is well known. Before going further and finalizing your charter, you feel it is important to talk with organizational leaders to address the program's—

    a. Attractiveness
    b. Readiness
    c. Vision
    d. Funding methods

162. Assume that your ice cream product line has been officially approved, and you are the program manager for this new program in your company. Because it is considered to be such a breakthrough program, it is ranked number three in your company. It has the support and visibility of the executive team. You are now in the Initiate Program process and are seeking formal acceptance of the program charter from the steering committee. After the committee's sign-off is obtained, you can be assured that—

    a. The stakeholders will support the program until completion
    b. The steering committee will generally rule in your favor on controversial issues
    c. The program is viewed as a way to achieve the organization's strategic benefits
    d. Funding will be available whenever required to achieve objectives

163. You are working to plan your ice cream program for your Fortune 500 company, which is so well known around the world for its cereal products. Because it is venturing into ice cream, all resources are being provided internally, and everyone on the team is signing a confidentiality agreement so competitors are not aware of this new program. However, already resources are scarce in the organization working on cereal products. You have prepared your schedule and in doing so assumed the needed resources would be available. However, in a meeting with your steering committee, you now realize you will need to do a lot of negotiating for resources. You decided since this program is ranked number three on the priority list that you should use—

    a. Market analysis
    b. Critical chain
    c. Resource leveling
    d. Resource optimization

164. You are enjoying your work as the program manager for the new ice cream program for your Fortune 500 company, which is so well known around the world for its cereal products. Because it is venturing into ice cream, all resources are being provided internally, and everyone on the team is signing a confidentiality agreement so competitors are not aware of this new program. However, already resources are scarce in the organization working on cereal products. You have prepared your schedule and in doing so assumed the needed resources would be available. However, in a meeting with your steering committee, you now realize you will need to do a lot of negotiating for resources. Fortunately, you have been successful and have three experienced project managers so far assigned who are supporting the three projects thus far in the program. It is important now that these project managers have been assigned that you evaluate their performance according to the—

    a. Project plan
    b. Program plan
    c. Benefits realization plan
    d. Resource plan.

165. You are working to plan your ice cream program for your Fortune 500 company, which is so well known around the world for its cereal products. Because it is venturing into ice cream, all resources are being provided internally, and everyone on the team is signing a confidentiality agreement so competitors are not aware of this new program. However, already resources are scarce in the organization working on cereal products. You have prepared your schedule and in doing so assumed the needed resources would be available. However, in a meeting with your steering committee, you now realize you will need to do a lot of negotiating for resources. Now you are in year two of your program, and you have four projects, and each one is comprised of people who are pleased to be working on their respective projects and the overall program. Many view being on this program as a way to advance in their careers as the program has high corporate visibility. Because of your work in program management, you recognize changes occur on programs, especially given that programs represent a change of some type. Therefore, you and your core team prepared a change management plan. You find it is especially helpful in terms of which of the following types of changes—

    a. Benefits
    b. Stakeholder expectations
    c. Market conditions
    d. Rewards

166. You are working to plan your ice cream program for your Fortune 500 company, which is so well known around the world for its cereal products. Because it is venturing into ice cream, all resources are being provided internally, and everyone on the team is signing a confidentiality agreement so competitors are not aware of this new program. However, already resources are scarce in the organization working on cereal products. You have prepared your schedule and in doing so assumed the needed resources would be available. However, in a meeting with your steering committee, you now realize you will need to do a lot of negotiating for resources. Now you are in year two of your program, and you have four projects, and each one is comprised of people who are pleased to be working on their respective projects and the overall program. Many view being on this program as a way to advance in their careers as the program has high corporate visibility. However, now, you have some new members of your steering committee, and they have been working in different business units of the company. New member E believes the program is too risky, and new member F is also a risk avoidance person. You realize the next meeting of your steering committee could be quite contentious, and you decided to evaluate the risks of your stakeholders. It is especially important as you perform this evaluation to consider the views of your—

    a. Sponsor
    b. Head of the Steering Committee
    c. Enterprise PMO Director
    d. Portfolio Manager

167. You are responsible as the program manager for the development of a new gas transmission pipeline that will span three countries. You are in the early phases, and one of the countries involved has major concerns that the pipeline will impact areas detrimental to the environment. It wants additional information about the program before it will provide the needed permits and approval. Your managers recognize that such approval is paramount for the program to proceed and have asked you to prepare a—

    a. Feasibility study
    b. Roadmap
    c. Mission statement
    d. Vision statement

168. Although your company has been active in project management for many years, it is relatively new to program management. You became certified as a PgMP® and suggested to your supervisor that two of your current projects would be better managed as a program and discussed why program management was more appropriate. Your supervisor in turn met with some members of the executive team, and collectively they realized a number of the existing projects in the company would be better handled through a program structure. One of the executives knew about the usefulness of governance and stage-gate reviews from his previous work in new product development, and he recommended all programs have a governance structure. Such a process now has been implemented. The effectiveness of the governance process is best handled through—

    a. Regularly scheduled reviews
    b. Program performance reports
    c. Formal gate review decision requests
    d. Use of your program management plan

169. You are a program manager in your agency. Your enterprise program management office (EPMO) has a program management information system (PMIS) and a methodology for projects that are undertaken in your agency programs. You have decided to use the agency's PMIS for your program. It will be especially helpful to you in—

    a. Plan Communications
    b. Monitor and Control Program Risks
    c. Develop Program Financial Plan
    d. Provide Governance Oversight

170. Assume you are managing a program at your University to establish a Master of Science degree in Program Management. Already, the University's Master of Science degree in project management is well recognized, and it has been accredited by leading organizations. However, many people have been inquiring if instead they could get their degrees in Program Management as their organizations have set up a career path, which has the Program Manager at a far higher level than that of a Project Manager, and also the organizations are using programs more often now than individual projects. Finally your program to establish the Masters of Science degree in Program Management is complete. You have completed the transition plan to the program director and his staff, and people at the University are pleased with how you managed this program and achieved the benefits in your benefit realization plan. To help future programs at the University, they asked you to identify what you believe is the value of benefits management. As a first step you suggest that—

    a. Each program have an individual on the core team that is responsible for the program's business benefits
    b. Involving as many stakeholders as possible, both internal and external to the program, in the benefits identification process to help secure their buy-in to its goals and objectives
    c. The program be set up with a viable business case that has a list of initial benefits to be achieved
    d. Establish from the start of the program methods to use to measure each identified benefit and ways to track its achievement

Answer Sheet for Practice Test 1

1.	a	b	c	d
2.	a	b	c	d
3.	a	b	c	d
4.	a	b	c	d
5.	a	b	c	d
6.	a	b	c	d
7.	a	b	c	d
8.	a	b	c	d
9.	a	b	c	d
10.	a	b	c	d
11.	a	b	c	d
12.	a	b	c	d
13.	a	b	c	d
14.	a	b	c	d
15.	a	b	c	d
16.	a	b	c	d
17.	a	b	c	d
18.	a	b	c	d
19.	a	b	c	d

20.	a	b	c	d
21.	a	b	c	d
22.	a	b	c	d
23.	a	b	c	d
24.	a	b	c	d
25.	a	b	c	d
26.	a	b	c	d
27.	a	b	c	d
28.	a	b	c	d
29.	a	b	c	d
30.	a	b	c	d
31.	a	b	c	d
32.	a	b	c	d
33.	a	b	c	d
34.	a	b	c	d
35.	a	b	c	d
36.	a	b	c	d
37.	a	b	c	d
38.	a	b	c	d

39.	a	b	c	d		61.	a	b	c	d
40.	a	b	c	d		62.	a	b	c	d
41.	a	b	c	d		63.	a	b	c	d
42.	a	b	c	d		64.	a	b	c	d
43.	a	b	c	d		65.	a	b	c	d
44.	a	b	c	d		66.	a	b	c	d
45.	a	b	c	d		67.	a	b	c	d
46.	a	b	c	d		68.	a	b	c	d
47.	a	b	c	d		69.	a	b	c	d
48.	a	b	c	d		70.	a	b	c	d
49.	a	b	c	d		71.	a	b	c	d
50.	a	b	c	d		72.	a	b	c	d
51.	a	b	c	d		73.	a	b	c	d
52.	a	b	c	d		74.	a	b	c	d
53.	a	b	c	d		75.	a	b	c	d
54.	a	b	c	d		76.	a	b	c	d
55.	a	b	c	d		77.	a	b	c	d
56.	a	b	c	d		78.	a	b	c	d
57.	a	b	c	d		79.	a	b	c	d
58.	a	b	c	d		80.	a	b	c	d
59.	a	b	c	d		81.	a	b	c	d
60.	a	b	c	d		82.	a	b	c	d

83.	a	b	c	d
84.	a	b	c	d
85.	a	b	c	d
86.	a	b	c	d
87.	a	b	c	d
88.	a	b	c	d
89.	a	b	c	d
90.	a	b	c	d
91.	a	b	c	d
92.	a	b	c	d
93.	a	b	c	d
94.	a	b	c	d
95.	a	b	c	d
96.	a	b	c	d
97.	a	b	c	d
98.	a	b	c	d
99.	a	b	c	d
100.	a	b	c	d
101.	a	b	c	d
102.	a	b	c	d
103.	a	b	c	d
104.	a	b	c	d

105.	a	b	c	d
106.	a	b	c	d
107.	a	b	c	d
108.	a	b	c	d
109.	a	b	c	d
110.	a	b	c	d
111.	a	b	c	d
112.	a	b	c	d
113.	a	b	c	d
114.	a	b	c	d
115.	a	b	c	d
116.	a	b	c	d
117.	a	b	c	d
118.	a	b	c	d
119.	a	b	c	d
120.	a	b	c	d
121.	a	b	c	d
122.	a	b	c	d
123.	a	b	c	d
124.	a	b	c	d
125.	a	b	c	d
126.	a	b	c	d

127.	a	b	c	d
128.	a	b	c	d
129.	a	b	c	d
130.	a	b	c	d
131.	a	b	c	d
132.	a	b	c	d
133.	a	b	c	d
134.	a	b	c	d
135.	a	b	c	d
136.	a	b	c	d
137.	a	b	c	d
138.	a	b	c	d
139.	a	b	c	d
140.	a	b	c	d
141.	a	b	c	d
142.	a	b	c	d
143.	a	b	c	d
144.	a	b	c	d
145.	a	b	c	d
146.	a	b	c	d
147.	a	b	c	d
148.	a	b	c	d

149.	a	b	c	d
150.	a	b	c	d
151.	a	b	c	d
152.	a	b	c	d
153.	a	b	c	d
154.	a	b	c	d
155.	a	b	c	d
156.	a	b	c	d
157.	a	b	c	d
158.	a	b	c	d
159.	a	b	c	d
160.	a	b	c	d
161.	a	b	c	d
162.	a	b	c	d
163.	a	b	c	d
164.	a	b	c	d
165.	a	b	c	d
166.	a	b	c	d
167.	a	b	c	d
168.	a	b	c	d
169.	a	b	c	d
170.	a	b	c	d

Answer Key for Practice Test 1

1. b. Portfolio

   The portfolio is where investment decisions are made, resources are allocated, and priorities are identified. Thus, it is one of the truest measures of the organization's intent. Program components must be aligned with the organization's strategy to clearly show why they are being undertaken.

   PMI®, *The Standard for Program Management*, 2008, 10

2. c. Have your vendor prepare eLearning modules that team members can access at their convenience

   Considering your team members' various locations and work schedules, the best option is to provide them with training that they can access when time permits. Although MP3 recordings can be accessed on an as-needed basis, audio recordings are much less effective than eLearning modules in helping people to learn a software system.

   PMI®, *The Standard for Program Management*, 2008, 180

   PMI. *Program Management Professional* (PgMP)® *Examination Content Outline*, 2011, 10

3. c. Communications strategy

   Because programs typically span a longer period and involve more stakeholders than a single project, it is important to ensure that the methodologies used to communicate among the stakeholders are effective. A communications strategy promotes timely and relevant stakeholder communications, which help to ensure that all have their issues and concerns thoroughly addressed.

   PMI®, *The Standard for Program Management*, 2008, 147

4. d. A preliminary outline of the program's organizational structure

   The charter should contain a discussion of the resources needed and their costs. Training requirements can also be included. A preliminary outline of the program's organizational structure can accompany this section.

   PMI®. *The Standard for Program Management*, 2008, 24, 75

5. a. Review your benefits register and resolve any issues

   Stakeholders play a critical role in program success. During program execution, the program manager must resolve issues and maintain the benefits register. As issues are resolved, the benefits register may require updates. It is maintained during the benefits realization phase of the benefits management life cycle during the Delivery of Program Benefits phase of the program life cycle.

   PMI®, *The Standard for Program Management*, 2008, 20

6. d. Benefits identification phase

   Benefits identification corresponds to the Pre-Program Preparation Phase in *The Standard for Program Management* or to the Strategic Program Management domain in *The Examination Content Outline*. This is the phase in which benefits are identified and qualified.

   PMI®, *The Standard for Program Management*, 2008, 20

7. c. You and your team can monitor the agreed-upon benefits until the program is completed

   The benefits realization plan is prepared during the Define Program Goals and Objectives Process. It identifies the business benefits and documents the plan for realizing them. Then, the team uses the plan to monitor each of the agreed-upon benefits in the plan throughout the program until it ends.

   PMI®, *The Standard for Program Management*, 2008, 109

8. a. Served as a baseline for the program with the existing metrics in it

   The benefits realization plan identifies how and when benefits will be realized. Its measurement criteria are used to ensure the benefits are fully realized as planned. When the plan is developed with the measurement criteria in it, it then sets a baseline for the program and it is then communicated to stakeholders, including sponsors.

   PMI. *Program Management Professional* (PgMP)® *Examination Content Outline*, 2011, 13

9. d. Determine the optimal supply chain strategy based on a wide variety of factors

Make-or-buy decisions are business decisions that can have far-reaching impacts on any organization. A decision, for example, to outsource an operation could lead to a lack of core competency in that area. Make-or-buy decisions determine which program elements will be delivered using internal resources as compared to those that will be obtained from outside suppliers.

PMI®, *The Standard for Program Management*, 2008, 187 and 190

10. a. Communications log

The communications log is an output of the Plan Communications process. It identifies the who, what, when, how, and why for each form of communication. After the communications framework has been developed and agreed to, the next step is to identify and put into place the components (that is, the processes and technical elements) that will enable the communications to be executed.

PMI®, *The Standard for Program Management*, 2008, 147

11. d. Analyze program complexity and strategic alignment

An initial program assessment should be performed, which includes defining program objectives, requirements, and risks to ensure program alignment with the organization's strategic plan, objectives, priorities, vision, and mission statement.

PMI®, *The Standard for Program Management*, 2008, 9

PMI. *Program Management Professional* (PgMP)® *Examination Content Outline*, 2011, 6

Milosevic, Dragan Z., Martinelli, Russ J., and Waddell, James M. *Program Management for Improved Business Results*. Hoboken, NJ: John Wiley & Sons, 2007, 150–151

12. b. Delivery of Program Benefits phase

Environmental changes are critical, because they can affect the program management plan or any anticipated benefits. As a result, they are an area of emphasis in the Delivery of Program Benefits phase; these changes must be identified and analyzed.

PMI®, *The Standard for Program Management*, 2008, 28

13. d. Program management plan development

The detailed program management plan, which is prepared in the Program Setup phase in the *Standard for Program Management* or the Planning phase in the life cycle in the *Examination Content Outline*, contains information on program deliverables and when they will be completed. This plan includes a detailed initial cost and schedule plan to set up the program and outlines plans for the remainder of the program.

PMI®, *The Standard for Program Management*, 2008, 26

14. a. PWBS

The program work breakdown structure (PWBS) formalizes the program scope in terms of deliverables and the work that must be done. It also defines the required resources to perform the work using a task responsibility matrix as a tool and technique.

PMI®, *The Standard for Program Management*, 2008, 116–117

15. c. Have her go through a 360-degree feedback analysis

A 360-degree feedback analysis is an excellent mechanism to look broadly at a person's management, leadership, and interpersonal skills. It can provide an excellent foundation for future development as well as providing key insights by the people that work with her on a daily basis.

PMI. *Program Management Professional* (PgMP)® *Examination Content Outline*, 2011, 10

16. b. Follow the Distribute Information process to communicate the new plan to your stakeholders

When plans are updated, they require approval at certain levels. They also then need to be distributed to key stakeholders including sponsors. This should be done following the Distribute Information process set up for the program.

PMI®, *The Standard for Program Management*, 2008, 260

17. c. It is an inward-looking practice

In the Provide Governance Oversight process, the governance plan is executed. This process ensures that a governance process is in place and working effectively to improve all aspects of program management.

PMI®, *The Standard for Program Management*, 2008, 260

18. b. The specific funding model as funding is necessary to join

    The financial environment for a program must be determined. There are a variety of funding methods to consider and they range from funding from a single organization (or in this case the country), those managed within a single organization but funded separately, or those entirely managed and funded by outside the organization. Once the funding model is determined, then the high-level financial benefits of the program can be determined.

    PMI®, *The Standard for Program Management*, 2008, 210

    PMI. *Program Management Professional* (PgMP)® *Examination Content Outline*, 2011, 6

19. a. Differentiate between the resources assigned to the program and those at the project level

    An accountability matrix is useful on programs. It can identify and assign program roles and responsibilities in order to build the core team. It is also helpful to differentiate between the program and project resources.

    PMI. *Program Management Professional* (PgMP)® *Examination Content Outline*, 2011, 8

20. a. Some projects may need to be integrated with others to provide program benefits

    In a program, some projects may produce benefits that can be realized immediately, and others may deliver capabilities that must be integrated with those of other projects to realize benefits. The program life cycle may be extended as some projects transition and others begin.

    PMI®, *The Standard for Program Management*, 2008, 29

21. b. Identify competency requirements for each role and responsibility

    After the competence requirements are identified, then we can negotiate for team members, assess their strengths and weaknesses, and build a training plan. Core team assignments are an output of the Develop Program Infrastructure process.

    PMI®, *The Standard for Program Management*, 2008, 86

22. a. An assumption

An assumption is a common input to most program management processes. Assumptions are considered to be true, real, or certain. In this situation, both project managers have assumed that this critical resource will be available as required. The program manager must work to resolve this situation, and the resolution should be noted in the program management plan.

PMI®, *The Standard for Program Management*, 2008, 27 and 38

23. c. Hold regular status reviews

Status reviews of component financial expenditures are a tool and technique in the Monitor and Control Program Financials process. These reviews should be held regularly to ensure compliance with contracts and with the cost and schedule baselines.

PMI®, *The Standard for Program Management*, 2008, 225

24. b. The major project life-cycle phases and their deliverables will remain similar

Although the type of program may influence the life cycle, the primary life-cycle phases and their deliverables are similar.

PMI®, *The Standard for Program Management*, 2008, 19

25. a. Positive, because you will be building stronger relationships with your client

Provided the client's code of ethics does not prohibit such entertainment activities, internal politicking is a skill and competency that successful program managers practice. In this instance, such activity can be very helpful in uncovering underlying problems.

PMI. *Program Management Professional* (PgMP)® *Examination Content Outline,* 2011, 14

26. a. Demonstrate an understanding of the needs of the customer.

The business case must demonstrate an understanding of the needs, business benefits, feasibility, and program justification. To do so, skills in feasibility analysis and marketing are required. The business environment and customer requirements information are necessary to build the business case.

PMI®, *The Standard for Program Management,* 2008, 23

PMI. *Program Management Professional* (PgMP)® *Examination Content Outline,* 2011, 6

Milosevic, Dragan Z., Martinelli, Russ J., and Waddell, James M. Program Management for Improved Business Results. Hoboken, NJ: John Wiley & Sons, 2007, 281–283

27. c. Plan and establish the program governance structure

The benefits realization plan is an input to the Plan and Establish Program Governance Structure process. It is necessary because value is delivered when the benefits then are used. The Governance Board further will use the plan as it oversees the program and determines whether the benefits are being realized and also to provide feedback to the program management team.

The Standard for Program Management, 2008, 247

28. b. Engineering analysis

Activities in the Program Initiation phase often include feasibility studies, because programs may be desirable but not worthwhile to pursue. Feasibility studies are a tool and technique in the Initiate Program process and are performed early in the life cycle to determine viability. Engineering analysis is appropriate to include given the scenario for this program.

PMI®, *The Standard for Program Management,* 2008, 311

29. a. Complete a skill set inventory

Regardless of the assertions made by the other managers who provided the team members, it is important to fully understand what skill sets each member has. After a skill set inventory is completed, team assignments can be made.

PMI. *Program Management Professional* (PgMP)® *Examination Content Outline,* 2011, 10

30. a. Determine whether updates to the program document repository are needed

    Changes affect the various program-level processes. As part of the Monitor and Control Program Scope process, updates to the document repository may be required based on the nature of the change.

    PMI®, *The Standard for Program Management*, 2008, 82, 124

31. c. Analyze and archive them as part of the Closing Process Group

    Lessons learned are an output of many program management processes. They should be identified during the life of the program and should be inputs to the Close Program process, where they are analyzed and archived.

    PMI®, *The Standard for Program Management*, 2008, 39

32. d. Meet with as many end users as is feasible to understand what features they would like in a printer

    In this situation, the program manager has two clients: the retail store that places orders for the printer and the end user who actually uses the product. To ensure that the best product is made that will satisfy the needs of the marketplace, the program manager should meet with as many end users as is feasible.

    Dragan Z., Milosevic, Russ J. Martinelli, and James M. Waddell. *Program Management for Improved Business Results*. Hoboken, NJ: John Wiley & Sons, Inc., 2007, 366

    PMI®, *The Standard for Program Management*, 2008, 235

33. c. Take corrective action

    Bad debt is money that is not collectible and is therefore worthless. As a result, it is deemed an expense to the business rather than revenue, because the business incurred the expense of providing a service or product for which it was not paid. In response to this problem, you need to take corrective action, which is an output of the Monitoring and Controlling Program Financials process.

    PMI®, *The Standard for Program Management*, 2008, 226

34. d. What is the probability of success for the program?

Even before programs are authorized, risks must be identified and analyzed. The risk analysis serves to answer questions at this stage such as the probability of success for the program, what will be done to scrutinize the probability of success, how will the known risks be avoided or mitigated, and whether the level of risk prevents program investment.

PMI®, *The Standard for Program Management*, 2008, 23

PMI. *Program Management Professional* (PgMP)® *Examination Content Outline*, 2011, 6

Milosevic, Dragan Z., Martinelli, Russ J., and Waddell, James M. *Program Management for Improved Business Results*. Hoboken, NJ: John Wiley & Sons, 2007, 283

35. c. Identify tangible and intangible benefits, expressing the intangible benefits in quantifiable terms.

The cost/benefit analysis should answer questions such as how much will the program cost to implement, how much work the program will contribute to the bottom line, and is the program worth investing in terms of achievement of specific business objectives. It includes tangible and intangible benefits. The intangible benefits should be expressed in quantifiable terms such as dollars gained or saved, hours saved, and gross margin increase.

PMI®, *The Standard for Program Management*, 2008, 23

PMI. *Program Management Professional* (PgMP)® *Examination Content Outline*, 2011, 6

Milosevic, Dragan Z., Martinelli, Russ J., and Waddell, James M. *Program Management for Improved Business Results*. Hoboken, NJ: John Wiley & Sons, 2007, 282–283

36. c. Public announcements should be prepared

Distributed information concerning the program should be provided in useful formats and using the appropriate media. Public announcements communicating information useful to the general public should be prepared as appropriate.

PMI®, *The Standard for Program Management*, 2008, 148

37. b. Stakeholder register

The Distribute Information process involves providing timely and accurate information to program stakeholders in useful formats and using appropriate media. A key input to this process is a stakeholder register, which lists the primary stakeholders of the program, their roles and responsibilities, and their expectations. Use of a stakeholder register helps to ensure that their information needs are identified and can be met.

PMI®, *The Standard for Program Management*, 2008, 149 and 313

38. d. Financial plan

The program financial plan is a subsidiary plan to the program management plan and documents all financial aspects of the program.

PMI®, *The Standard for Program Management*, 2008, 216

39. a. Revisit and update your program plans as required

Planning is an iterative process. When a significant event affects the program and renders current plans inadequate or ineffective, the next step for a program manager is to revisit and update the plans to ensure their ongoing usefulness. Many processes result in the need to update the program management plan and its subsidiary plan.

PMI®, *The Standard for Program Management*, 2008, 39

40. b. Whether the expected benefits are in line with the original business case

One of the most important points of program governance is gate reviews to ensure program components are being managed effectively. At each gate review, questions focus on the program and its components to ensure they are still aligned with the organization's strategic objectives, expected benefits to see if they are in line with the original business plan, whether the level of risk remains acceptable, and whether best practices are being followed.

PMI®, *The Standard for Program Management*, 2008, 250

41. c. Revisit the program architecture baseline

The program architecture baseline is the output of the Develop Program Architecture process. It is useful in examining current risks and determining whether new risks exist.

PMI®, *The Standard for Program Management*, 2008, 114 and 162

42. b. Notification of change requests

   During the Distribute Information process, information that is distributed includes notification of change requests to the program and project teams, and eventually, notification of the responses to the change requests through use of the change request log, which contains data on approved, rejected, or modified change requests.

   PMI®, *The Standard for Program Management*, 2008, 149, 269

43. a. Roadmap

   The roadmap is an important document that is used throughout the program. In the early stages, a high-level roadmap is important to have milestones and preliminary estimates and also to set a baseline for program definition, planning, and execution.

   PMI. *Program Management Professional* (PgMP)® *Examination Content Outline*, 2011, 6

44. c. Monitoring and controlling program changes

   During the Monitor and Control Program Changes process, decisions to accept, reject, or modify change requests are made by the people who have the designated authority to do so. As change decisions are made, the program team ensures that the changes are made to the program plan and communicated to the components for implementation or action.

   PMI®, *The Standard for Program Management*, 2008, 64 and 267–268

45. a. Infrastructure

   The Develop Program Infrastructure process investigates, assesses, and plans the support structure to enable the program to achieve its goals. It considers the unique challenges and needs of the program and how program components interact. The program's management and technical infrastructure support the program and its projects as expected benefits are delivered. This infrastructure includes program-specific governance processes and procedures.

   PMI®, *The Standard for Program Management*, 2008, 84–86

46. b. Issue a change request

   Change requests are an output of the Manage Program Issues process. The change request, once approved, may then involve another process for further action. At the end of the program, each change request should be analyzed to provide feedback and recommendations for future programs or projects in the organization.

   PMI®, *The Standard for Program Management*, 2008, 30 and 97

47. c. Revisit and update your program plans

Acquisitions and mergers are unplanned events. When they occur, they should trigger a review of existing program plans to see whether updates are required to ensure ongoing usefulness.

PMI®, *The Standard for Program Management*, 2008, 46

48. a. Stakeholder management strategy

Stakeholder management strategy updates are an output of the Engage Program Stakeholders process. Stakeholder meetings often are held to capture issues and concerns, which can be subsequently addressed by the program manager and his or her team.

PMI®, *The Standard for Program Management*, 2008, 239

49. c. Estimate the high-level financial and non-financial benefits

It is essential to estimate the high-level financial and non-financial benefits of the program in order to both obtain funding for it and also to maintain funding authorization for the program. This approach as well drives the prioritization of the projects in the program.

PMI. *Program Management Professional* (PgMP)® *Examination Content Outline*, 2011, 6

50. a. Update your program architecture baseline

The program architecture baseline is an output of the Develop Program Architecture process and describes the various program components that need to be in place to produce the desired benefits. Given this change in scope, this baseline requires updates.

PMI®, *The Standard for Program Management*, 2008, 114

51. d. The benefits report

Programs are established to deliver benefits. The benefit realization plan is a key document; while some programs do not deliver benefits until the program is complete, others deliver them incrementally. The benefits report becomes a key document as it measures each component against the benefit realization plan. It is then analyzed by the program team and reported to executives, who may cause the component to be realigned, started early, or in this situation, terminated.

PMI®, *The Standard for Program Management*, 2008, 266, 270

52. a. Develop a stakeholder management strategy

An output of the Identify Program Stakeholders process is a stakeholder management strategy. It captures mitigation approaches flowing from the identify Program Stakeholders process, which outlines the steps to take to manage the program's impact on stakeholders.

PMI®, The Standard for Program Management, 2008, 236

53. c. Close the program budget to avoid non-allocable charges

As an output of the Monitor and Control Program Financials process, the program budget is closed as the program comes to a close, the final financial reports are distributed in accordance with the stakeholder management plan, and any unused funds are returned to the funding organization.

PMI®, *The Standard for Program Management*, 2008, 226

54. d. Develop a program roadmap

During the Program Initiation phase, the program roadmap is prepared. Among other things, it describes the links between the planned and prioritized work, and it shows how program components are organized. It also provides a chronological representation of the program's intended direction.

PMI®, *The Standard for Program Management*, 2008, 78

55. d. An improvement in an organization's operation

A benefit is an improvement to the operation of an organization. Benefits may include increased profits, improved growth, or improved employee morale.

PMI®, *The Standard for Program Management*, 2008, 309

Williams and Parr, *Enterprise Program Management Delivering Value*, 2006, 178–179

56. b. Work breakdown structure (WBS) methodology

Because the WBS defines all work in a project and program, this is the best tool to use for integration. The program work breakdown structure (PWBS) typically corresponds to the first one or two levels of the WBS of each component project. As the PWBS is developed, the management planning process is a key tool and technique to use.

PMI®, *The Standard for Program Management*, 2008, 115–117

57. b. Stakeholder inventory

   As an output of the Identify Program Stakeholders process, the stakeholder inventory provides a complete and comprehensive overview of how the program's stakeholders will be affected by the program. It also provides an assessment of likely stakeholder responses, identified stakeholder issues, and planned approaches to mitigate negative stakeholder reaction.

   PMI®, *The Standard for Program Management*, 2008, 235

58. c. Program sponsor

   The program sponsor is the group or person who champions the program initiative, is responsible for providing project resources, and ensures the ultimate delivery of program benefits.

   PMI®, *The Standard for Program Management*, 2008, 235

59. c. Function as go/no-go decision points for the program

   Phase-gate reviews serve numerous purposes and should be held throughout the program. They focus on the phase that was just completed and reflect go/no-go decisions, but they do not substitute for periodic performance reviews.

   PMI®, *The Standard for Program Management*, 2008, 21, 250, and 262

60. d. Delivery of Program Benefits phase

   Phase four in the program life cycle is the Delivery of Program Benefits phase. Its purpose is to initiate the various component projects in the program and coordinate deliverables to create the incremental benefits.

   PMI®, *The Standard for Program Management*, 2008, 28

61. c. Appropriate quality standards and measures have been defined

   The benefits realization plan is an input to the Plan Program Quality process. Program quality is defined primarily by successful benefit realization; therefore, with a complete understanding of the scope and nature of the program's benefits, the program manager then can define appropriate quality standards and measures.

   PMI®, *The Standard for Program Management*, 2008, 255

62 b. The cultural backgrounds of the team members

The scenario is one in which virtual teams will be used for the first time, and the organization has locations in four continents. To ensure stakeholder alignment and program deliverability, cultural considerations are critical.

PMI. *Program Management Professional* (PgMP)® *Examination Content Outline,* 2011, 6

63. b. Delegate authority and responsibility to the project managers

Program managers are not project managers. Program managers focus on coordination among the projects and ongoing activities that make up the program and on ensuring that expected benefits from the program are realized. Program managers address issues at a higher level and are not involved in day-to-day project management activities.

PMI®, *The Standard for Program Management,* 2008, 11–12

64. a. Root cause analysis

Stakeholder metrics are an output of the Engage Program Stakeholders process. It is important to identify risks caused by nonparticipation, which can be done by analyzing participation trends and using root-cause analysis.

PMI®, *The Standard for Program Management,* 2008, 58 and 238

65. a. Define the program's scope and benefit strategy

The Initiate Program process helps to define the program's scope and benefits expectations and ensures that the authorization and initiation of the program are linked to the organization's ongoing work and strategic priorities.

PMI®, *The Standard for Program Management,* 2008, 24, and 74–75

66. a. Practices for capturing risks

Organizations that conduct program governance activities typically have policies for capturing risks and issues, benefits measurements, and lessons learned. Program governance monitors and reviews program progress and the delivery of coordinated benefits from component projects.

PMI®, *The Standard for Program Management,* 2008, 21

67. b. Who will ensure that benefits are realized and the value is delivered?

In preparing a governance plan for a program, one of the key items in the plan is the program governance roles and definitions. They include among other things, who will ensure that benefits are realized and the value is determined. This shows the importance of the benefit realization plan to the Plan and Establish Program Governance Structure process.

PMI®, *The Standard for Program Management*, 2008, 249

68. c. Upgrading the nation's airspace system

An upgrade to the nation's airspace system would consist of numerous projects as well as ongoing work. If these projects were managed in a coordinated way, then you would have better control over them and would obtain greater benefits.

PMI®, *The Standard for Program Management*, 2008, 5

69. d. 90 days

Establishing a longer period of time to pay your subcontractors than the payment terms you have with the studio ensures that you will have the cash to pay your subcontractors without the need to borrow money or take it from savings.

Milosevic, Martinelli, and Waddell, *Program Management for Improved Business Results*, 2007, 358–359

PMI®, *The Standard for Program Management*, 2008, 197

70. a. Collect data concerning stakeholder expectations and requirements

The performance analysis report is prepared in the closing phase. It gathers final values and compares them with planned values for quality, cost, schedule, and resource data to determine program performance. The project manager uses data on stakeholder expectations and requirements to determine whether these requirements were met.

PMI. *Program Management Professional* (PgMP)® *Examination Content Outline*, 2011, 14

71. b. Issues that arise can receive visibility

Program governance processes and procedures should be structured and implemented such that critical issues will receive appropriate visibility for their potential effects across other portfolios in the organization.

PMI®, *The Standard for Program Management*, 2008, 96

72. c. Strategic planning

    Programs are undertaken for a variety of reasons; one reason is to implement the organization's strategic plan. The starting point for a program may be a desired future organizational environment, as stated in the organization's strategic plan. It is necessary to know the strategic drivers and the program's link to the organization's strategic objectives, which are stated in the program charter.

    PMI®, *The Standard for Program Management*, 2008, 24

73. a. Document the current state

    During the Closing processes, it is important to demonstrate that the benefits have been delivered and the scope of work has been fulfilled. If the program is terminated early, then the current state should be documented.

    PMI®, *The Standard for Program Management*, 2008, 66 and 98

74. b. Providing governance oversight

    Program performance reports are used in providing governance oversight. They support program oversight and control so that the governance board can monitor program results and ensure good practices are being followed.

    PMI®, *The Standard for Program Management*, 2008, 259 and 261

75. a. Contract management plan

    During the Plan Program Procurements process, the contract management plan is prepared based on the specified items or services within the contract. It is used for contract administration.

    PMI®, *The Standard for Program Management*, 2008, 191

76. c. Program director

    The program director is the individual with executive ownership of the program.

    PMI®, *The Standard for Program Management*, 2008, 234

77. a. Risk analysis

    Program performance analysis, a tool and technique of the Monitor and Control Program Performance process, includes gap analysis, risk analysis, issues analysis, and trend and probability analysis. Risk analysis emphasizes real-time monitoring of program risk as critical for success.

    PMI®, *The Standard for Program Management*, 2008, 95

78. d. Manage Program Stakeholder Expectations process

Influence is the ability to affect the beliefs, actions, and attitudes of other people and is a tool and technique in the Manage Program Stakeholder Expectations process.

PMI®, *The Standard for Program Management*, 2008, 241

79. a. Aggregate performance information about project and non-project work

The Report Program Performance process consolidates performance data to provide stakeholders with information about how resources are being used to deliver program benefits. It emphasizes aggregating performance information about the entire program, as well as project and non-project work, to provide a clear picture of overall performance information.

PMI®, *The Standard for Program Management*, 2008, 152

80. b. Program B

Program B is quality-driven, as illustrated by its strategy to delay the schedule if necessary in a trade-off situation. Its competitive attribute is superior quality, which aligns with the organization's culture and environment.

Milosevic, Martinelli, and Waddell, *Program Management for Improved Business Results*, 2007, 75–76

PMI®. Program Management Professional (PgMP)® Examination Content Outline, 2011, 6

81. c. An operational cost analysis

Program operational cost analysis is a tool and technique in the Monitor and Control Program Financials process. It is necessary because costs associated with program management and the infrastructure must be monitored and controlled.

PMI®, *The Standard for Program Management*, 2008, 225

82. c. Benefits realization report

While the component transition request is a key input to the Approve Component Transition process, the other key input is the benefits realization report. The component project must provide the specific benefits for it as outlined in this report; if the benefits were not provided, then, the component may be terminated.

PMI®, *The Standard for Program Management*, 2008, 270

83. b. Process-related plans

Organizational process assets (a process asset library) are key inputs to many program management processes. They may include the organization's knowledge bases, may exist in paper or electronic format, and may include process-related plans, policies, procedures, and guidelines institutionalized by the organization.

PMI®, *The Standard for Program Management*, 2008, 14

84. c. Update your program budget baseline

In this situation, and as an output of the Monitor and Control Program Financials process, you need to update your program budget baseline to reflect the addition of these resources to your program, because this change has significant cost impacts.

PMI®, *The Standard for Program Management*, 2008, 226

85. b. Program scope statement

The program scope statement defines the scope of the program as well as the limitations, expectations, and business impact of the program. It also describes each project and its resources as well as organizational needs and requirements, initial high-level product requirements, and the program's vision, assumptions, and constraints. This statement helps the program team to perform more detailed program planning.

PMI®, *The Standard for Program Management*, 2008, 106

86. d. Program scope statement

The program scope statement is the basis for future program decisions and establishes the expectations of the endeavor. It articulates the scope of the program—generally, what is included and what is excluded. This is especially important if a stakeholder might erroneously assume that a particular product, service, or result is a program component.

PMI®, *The Standard for Program Management*, 2008, 108

87. a. Update the program risk register

Updates to the program risk register are an output of the Monitor and Control Program Risks process. The risk monitoring program tracks the progress of each program risk and includes meeting minutes, actions implemented, and information on results. The project managers provide information about their projects to the program manager and other interested stakeholders.

PMI®, *The Standard for Program Management*, 2008, 183

88. d. Program D

The payback period can be determined by dividing the initial fixed investment in the program by the estimated annual net cash inflows. In this example, the payback period for Program D is 2.5 years, so it should be selected.

PMI®, *Program Management Professional* (PgMP)® *Examination Content Outline,* 2011, 6

Milosevic, Martinelli, and Waddell, *Program Management for Improved Business Results*, 2008, 21 and 42

89. b. Have the project managers build the detail for their projects and then roll it up into the control points and PWBS work packages

The Develop Program Schedule process is both a top-down and a bottom-up approach. The program schedule is created with the PWBS as the starting point. Individual project managers then build the details for their specific projects, and these details are then incorporated into the management control points for the program packages of the PWBS. Project schedule information is an input to this process.

PMI®, *The Standard for Program Management*, 2008, 8 and 127–128

90. c. Meet with all three project managers and inform them that you will manage any resource redeployment issues

The Manage Program Resources process is ongoing throughout the program. As projects are authorized, resources may need to be redeployed. This redeployment is handled by the program manager at the program level. It may require other program process activity if the project managers are unable or unwilling to release the required resources.

PMI®, *The Standard for Program Management*, 2008, 57 and 91

91. b. Update your program payment schedule

As an output of the Administer Program Procurements process, updates to the program payment schedule may be needed as resources are obtained through basic ordering agreements and as resources are reassigned. A payment control system, which is a tool and technique in this process, ensures that any problems in the payment process can be resolved in a timely manner.

PMI®, *The Standard for Program Management*, 2008, 201 and 203

92. a. Although the program is over budget, the overrun is insignificant at this time

    The cost variance (CV) is calculated by subtracting the actual cost (AC) from the earned value (EV); that is, CV = EV − AC, or €42,000 − €50,000 = −€8,000, which is insignificant compared to the budget at completion (BAC).

    PMI®, *The Standard for Program Management*, 2008, 133

93. b. Update your procurement management plan

    As an output of the Administer Program Procurements process, updates to the program procurement management plan are important for the program team to communicate with sponsors and customers. The plan must be updated on a regular basis to reflect approved changes and corrections.

    PMI®, *The Standard for Program Management*, 2008, 203

94. d. Define the objectives

    Before moving forward, an initial program assessment should be conducted to ensure the program's alignment with the organization's strategic plan, objectives, priorities, and mission statement. This is done by defining program objectives, requirements, and risks.

    PMI. *Program Management Professional* (PgMP)® *Examination Content Outline*, 2011, 6

95. c. The program team knows how to use different budget techniques

    The Budget Program Costs process establishes program budgets. It should consider any financial constraints on the budget, which may be a consequence of fiscal year budget planning cycles or funding limits for particular periods. Because programs can span multiple planning periods, the program team may use different budget techniques over the program life cycle.

    PMI®, *The Standard for Program Management*, 2008, 222

96. a. Provide notifications of change requests

    All stakeholders should receive timely information about the program. The program's communications channels must be administered; information such as status updates and notifications of change requests and the corresponding responses must be provided; and responses must be made to governmental and regulatory agencies.

    PMI®, *The Standard for Program Management*, 2008, 147–148

97. c. Manage Program Resources

Many organizations set up a program team to participate in initiation or program start-up and then replace team members with permanent staff during the Manage Program Resources process, which tracks and adapts the use of program resources throughout the life cycle.

PMI®, *The Standard for Program Management*, 2008, 91

98. c. Risk management

It is important to carry out the Manage Program Issues process in tandem with program risk management so that unresolved issues do not affect overall program progress, especially because risk assessment is an integral part of issues management and the risk register is an input to the process.

PMI®, *The Standard for Program Management*, 2008, 96–97

99. c. Group C

Using net present value (NPV) as a selection criterion, a dollar a year from now is worth less than a dollar today. The more the future is discounted (that is, the higher the discount rate), then the lower the NPV of the program. If the NPV is higher, then the program is rated higher than others. In this example, Group C has the highest NPV and should be selected.

PMI. *Program Management Professional* (PgMP)® *Examination Content Outline*, 2011, 6

Milosevic, *Project Management ToolBox: Tools and Techniques for the Practicing Project Manager*, 2003, 42–44

100. b. Establishing the program's financial framework

The purpose of this process is to assess the overall financial environment for the program and to identify funding sources for the identified milestones. The key output is the program financial framework plan to coordinate the available funds, constraints, and how payments will be made.

PMI®, *The Standard for Program Management*, 2008, 207 and 213

101. a. Generate the program schedule

Upon completion of the program work breakdown structure (PWBS), realistic schedules can be built, cost estimates can be developed, and the program's work can be organized.

PMI®, *The Standard for Program Management*, 2008, 114

102. b. Some corrective actions may be required as a result of risk mitigation activities

    As a program manager, one must analyze and update the benefit realization and sustainment plans for uncertainty, risk identification, risk mitigation, and risk opportunity in order to determine if corrective actions are necessary and then communicate them to stakeholders.

    PMI. *Program Management Professional* (PgMP)® *Examination Content Outline*, 2011, 13

103. c. Monitor and Control Program Performance

    This process, which includes collecting, measuring, and disseminating performance information and assessing overall program trends, is performed throughout the program's life cycle.

    PMI®, *The Standard for Program Management*, 2008, 93

104. b. Focus groups

    Focus groups are a tool and technique in the Identify Program Stakeholders process and are used to solicit feedback from stakeholder groups regarding their attitudes toward the program and appropriate approaches for impact mitigation. Open-ended questions help participants to interact with one another, thus resulting in a deeper understanding of program needs.

    PMI®, *The Standard for Program Management*, 2008, 234

105. d. The contractor has the appropriate tools and techniques to safeguard your intellectual property

    Intellectual property (IP) is the lifeblood of any company. Outsourcing a project or group of projects to a contractor provides the contractor the opportunity to work with and manipulate your IP. You need to be absolutely certain that the contractor has safeguards in place to protect your IP.

    PMI. *Program Management Professional* (PgMP)® *Examination Content Outline*, 2011, 9

106. c. Perform health checks

Regular quality reviews and project management health checks are best practices to assess performance against expected and desired outcomes. Health checks are also used to gauge whether the program benefits will be realized in the long term. They are less formal than phase-gate reviews, but they are useful to focus on such areas as quality planning to ensure that the overall program is successful.

PMI®, *The Standard for Program Management*, 2008, 251 and 263

107. b. Balanced scorecard

The balanced scorecard is a benefits measurement technique that includes a set of performance measures. These measures cover a range of areas that reflect and show a balanced view of organizational performance. Internal rate of return (IRR) and net present value (NPV) are financial analysis techniques, and value engineering is a technique used to reduce costs in product development.

David Williams and Tim Parr, *Enterprise Program Management Delivering Value,* 2006, 287

108. a. A program dashboard

A dashboard highlights and briefly describes or illustrates through the use of colors—red (bad), yellow (warning), green (good)—the status of various aspects of the program. It is simple and easy to interpret, making it a useful communication tool at the executive level. Methods to represent status reports are dashboards, memos, and presentations to stakeholders.

Milosevic, Martinelli, and Waddell, *Program Management for Improved Business Results*, 2007, 330–336

PMI®, *The Standard for Program Management*, 2008, 156

109. a. Ensuring legal protection of this valuable asset

It is important not only to capture and document knowledge assets from each project and the intellectual property that has been developed, but also to do so in a manner that ensures legal protection of these assets. This is necessary to ensure that data privacy and confidentially laws are not violated.

PMI®, *The Standard for Program Management*, 2008, 66

110. d. Maintain a benefits register

    A benefits register is a best practice and can be easily translated into a benefits report. It is useful to report the benefits and their status to stakeholders following the communications management plan.

    PMI. *Program Management Professional* (PgMP)® *Examination Content Outline*, 2011, 13

111. a. SWOT analysis

    A SWOT (strengths-weaknesses-opportunities-threats) analysis provides information that is helpful when matching an organization's resources and capabilities to the competitive environment in which it operates. It is used in feasibility studies as a tool and technique in the Initiate Program process.

    PMI®, *The Standard for Program Management*, 2008, 77

112. c. Direct and Manage Program Execution

    The Direct and Manage Program Execution process focuses on managing the execution of the program management plan. As components close on transition requests, assesses them, and forwards requests the governance board for decisions.

    PMI®, *The Standard for Program Management*, 2008, 86

113. a. An output of the Monitor and Control Program Scope process

    Approved change requests are outputs of the Monitor and Control Program Scope process. These change requests are ones that fall within the program manager's authority and are approved or rejected.

    PMI®, *The Standard for Program Management*, 2008, 90 and 123

114. b. Aggregate information across projects and non-project activity

    Performance reporting aggregates all performance information for both project and non-project activity. It consolidates performance data to provide stakeholders with information regarding the use of resources to deliver program benefits.

    PMI®, *The Standard for Program Management*, 2008, 152

115. a. Align the elements of your program more closely with the company's strategy

     Programs represent change, and the strategic value of each program should be explicit and driven by the business strategy of the organization. Organizations determine a strategic direction on the basis of competitive attributes that, in turn, focus and define the content of program management elements.

     PMI. *Program Management Professional* (PgMP)® *Examination Content Outline*, 2011, 6

     Milosevic, Martinelli, and Waddell, *Program Management for Improved Business Results*, 2007, 75–76

116. d. Use make-or-buy decision techniques

     After you analyze the PWBS, scope statement, and product description, you apply make-or-buy decision techniques to determine which of the PWBS elements will be produced using internal resources and which will be obtained from outside suppliers.

     PMI®, *The Standard for Program Management*, 2008, 187

117. c. Intangible benefits and tangible benefits

     In identifying benefits and preparing a benefits realization plan, categories of benefits are useful. They should be both tangible and intangible, along with risk avoidance.

     PMI. *Program Management Professional* (PgMP)® *Examination Content Outline*, 2011, 13

     Williams, D. and Parr, T., *Enterprise programme management*, 2006, 179

118. a. Devise a strategy to collect baseline data such as using questionnaires and interviews

     Before setting the baseline, the benefits realization plan and its measurement criteria need to be developed. The baseline then serves as a control tool or mechanism to manage changes to benefits and costs through the implementation of the program. A number of key tasks are recommended including devising a strategy to collect baseline data such as by using questionnaires, interviews, reports, by location, and the organization structure.

     PMI. *Program Management Professional* (PgMP)® *Examination Content Outline*, 2011, 13

     Williams, D. and Parr, T., *Enterprise programme management*, 2006, 180

119. b. By the program manager, based on his or her scope of authority

    During this process, change requests that clearly fall within the program manager's level of authority are approved or rejected.

    PMI®, *The Standard for Program Management*, 2008, 90

120. b. Communicate personnel performance to each team member's line manager

    Line managers typically assign resources to programs and projects. It is important for the program manager to communicate personnel performance to line managers so that it can be used as input for salary reviews, future development, and so on.

    PMI. *Program Management Professional* (PgMP)® *Examination Content Outline*, 2011, 10

121. d. 0.86, and it will be difficult to recover from this performance

    The SPI is EV/PV. In this case, it is 0.86, which means you are 14 percent behind schedule. It will be difficult to recover.

    PMI®, *The Standard for Program Management*, 2008, 133

    PMI®, *PMBOK® Guide*, 2008, 183

122. a. Communication

    A successful program manager must have a special blend of knowledge, skills, and competencies. The most important is communication skills to deal with all program stakeholders.

    PMI®, *The Standard for Program Management*, 2008, 12–13

123. b. The benefits are aligned with the University's strategic objectives

    It is important to prioritize benefit delivery especially on those programs in which benefits are delivered incrementally. Proof of early benefits also assists in securing funding to continue the program. In prioritizing benefits, items to consider include alignment with strategy, short-and long-term expected results, expertise of the resources available, and the probability of success

    Williams, D. and Parr, T., *Enterprise programme management*, 2006, 181

124. b. Risk opportunity

Benefits realization requires analysis throughout the program.
This scenario is an example of a risk opportunity, which if accepted by
the Governance Board, then will lead to the need to update the benefit
realization plan and also the sustainment plan.

PMI. *Program Management Professional* (PgMP)® *Examination Content
Outline*, 2011, 11

125. c. Share the results with component managers

The Plan Program Risk Management process has two tools and
techniques: risk planning meetings and analysis and lessons learned
reviews. An integrated program risk management process is evidenced
by the fact that results are shared with the component project managers.

PMI®, *The Standard for Program Management*, 2008, 163

126. a. Obtained a patent

Intellectual property must be captured and documented for future use.
Patents are used to protect intellectual property that is developed in
a program.

PMI®, *The Standard for Program Management*, 2008, 66

127. a. Component charter

The Approve Component Initiation process involves performing
program management activities to initiate a component in the program.
Each component requires a charter before it can begin its work.

PMI®, *The Standard for Program Management*, 2008, 258

128. b. Update your program resource plan

The output of the Manage Program Resources process is the updates to
the program resource plan. Changes in the assignment of program staff
are reflected in this update.

PMI®, *The Standard for Program Management*, 2008, 93

129. d. Program charter

During the Plan Communications process, the program charter is a key
input because it helps to determine the communications requirements
based on the overall program requirements, business needs, purpose,
and other relevant information.

PMI®, *The Standard for Program Management*, 2008, 144

130. b. Program work breakdown structure (PWBS)

     As an input to the Distribute Information process, the PWBS is useful in communicating the program's size and complexity as well as other characteristics.

     PMI®, *The Standard for Program Management*, 2008, 149

131. b. Program B

     Programs should have a strategic fit with the organization's long-term goals. In selecting a program to pursue, this is one area to consider. In this example, Program B fully supports four of the five goals.

     PMI®, *The Standard for Program Management*, 2008, 23

     Milosevic, Martinelli, and Waddell, *Program Management for Improved Business Results*, 2007, 286

132. c. 41 days

     At the program level, the emphasis is on interdependencies between components. PERT (program evaluation and review technique) is one tool that can be used to track the start and finish of components against planned timelines. Using PERT, the expected time is determined by the following formula:

     $$P + 4 (ML) + O/6$$

     Where P = pessimistic time; ML = most likely time; and O = optimistic time

     PMI®, *The Standard for Program Management*, 2008, 127 and 131

     PMI®, *PMBOK® Guide*, 2008, 150

133. c. Manage Program Stakeholder Expectations

     The Manage Program Stakeholder Expectations process involves managing stakeholder communications to satisfy requirements and resolve issues.

     PMI®, *The Standard for Program Management*, 2008, 228 and 239

134. d. Using cost forecasting techniques on a regular basis

     Forecasting techniques are a tool and technique in the Monitoring and Controlling Program Financials process. Estimates to complete and estimates at completion are earned value metrics that help to predict future cost performance against the baseline and to predict the final program costs.

     PMI®, *The Standard for Program Management*, 2008, 225

135. d. Your company's corresponding portfolio

Governance structures differ based on numerous factors with the purpose to monitor and review the progress of the program and delivery of the benefits from the project and non-project work. In cases in which a program is initiated as part of a portfolio, reviews are carried out within the context of the portfolio.

PMI®, *The Standard for Program Management*, 2008, 21

PMI. *Program Management Professional* (PgMP)® *Examination Content Outline*, 2011, 15

136. a. Have a thorough understanding of the financial environment

Programs using public money are often complex, expensive, and of long duration. The program manager needs to have a thorough understanding of the financial environment as noted in the Establish Program Financial Framework process.

PMI®, *The Standard for Program Management*, 2008, 210

137. b. Determine actions that could affect other components

Program management should support the risk activities of the program components. The program component's risk response plans should be reviewed to assess proposed actions that could affect the program risk responses for better or for worse. These component plans are an input to the Plan Program Responses process. This enables response mechanisms that could benefit more than one component to be suggested and implemented.

PMI®, *The Standard for Program Management*, 2008, 177

138. c. Issue a change request for corrective action

Audits take time and are performed during program execution or after the program is complete. All decisions and change requests should be documented. When the audit is complete, results are recorded, and feedback is then provided to the governance board if changes are needed to address audit concerns, in which case change requests will be required.

PMI®, *The Standard for Program Management*, 2008, 253–254

139. b. Ensure generally accepted best practices are being followed

Gate reviews serve a number of different purposes. In addition to ensuring that identified good practices are being followed, they also serve to ensure alignment of the program and its components with the organization's strategic goals that expected benefits are in line with the business plan, and that the level of risk is acceptable to the organization.

PMI®, *The Standard for Program Management,* 2008, 21 and 250

140. b. Manage Program Stakeholder Expectations

Because the program is large, expensive, and long in duration, it is necessary to ensure that communications are managed to satisfy stakeholder requirements, that effective negotiation techniques are used if stakeholders have conflicts, and that stakeholder participation is monitored. These activities will help to ensure that expectations are met, which is vital to program success. This is part of the Manage Program Stakeholder Expectations process.

PMI®, *The Standard for Program Management,* 2008, 239

141. c. Executive sponsor

The executive sponsor is the individual or group responsible for providing program resources and ensuring program success; typically the executive sponsor is a senior manager responsible for defining the direction of the organization and investment decisions.

PMI®, *The Standard for Program Management,* 2008, 245

142. d. Competitive analysis

Competitive analysis or market analysis is useful to help identify organizational benefits for the potential program. A well-developed business case will include a certain level of analysis and comparison against real or imagined alternative efforts. Such comparisons generate substantive debate with respect to the best solution.

PMI®, *The Standard for Program Management,* 2008, 77

PMI. *Program Management Professional* (PgMP)® *Examination Content Outline,* 2011, 6

143. a. The availability of key staff members

Resource availability indicates the availability of the personnel, assets, materials, or capital resources that are required to accomplish the program's goals. It is an input to the Manage Program Resources process.

PMI®, *The Standard for Program Management,* 2008, 92

144. b. Encourages ownership of the solution

A regularly scheduled benefit report is essential in stakeholder communication in terms of achieving the planned benefits. It also is helpful to ensure ownership of the solution and benefits within the relevant business area, reduces the risk of "optimistic" reporting from the program team, and enables benefits reports to be available within regular management reports.

Williams, D. and Parr, T., *Enterprise programme management,* 2006, 181–182

145. a. Plan Program Quality and Plan Program Procurement

The Plan Program Quality and Plan Program Procurement processes are closely related, because both can benefit from standardizing product specifications and tests and by establishing economies of scale. The quality improvement plan focuses on ways to increase customer value by analyzing processes to identify waste and non-value added activities. It includes targets for improved performance as well as process metrics.

PMI®, *The Standard for Program Management,* 2008, 254–255

146. c. Communications management plan

The communications management plan should contain a glossary of common terminology for use on the project. This is where you would specify use of the 4,000-word common English vocabulary.

PMI®, *The Standard for Program Management,* 2008, 147

147. c. Root cause identification

Root causes are the fundamental conditions or events that may give rise to a risk. Program-specific risk activities include determining the primary causes of a program's risks, which can be done by sharpening the definition of each risk and grouping risks by cause. More effective risk responses can be prepared after the root causes are identified.

PMI®, *The Standard for Program Management,* 2008, 167

148. a. Risk trigger

A risk trigger is a sign that a particular risk may occur.

PMI®, *The Standard for Program Management,* 2008, 180

Ward, *Dictionary of Project Management Terms,* 2008, 389

149. d. Strategic directive

    Decisions made resulting from the program's governance process may affect strategic alignment and program benefit delivery, which means it is necessary to have an understanding of the overall strategic directive for the program.

    PMI®, *The Standard for Program Management*, 2008, 247

150. a. Plan Program Risk Management process

    Stakeholder risk tolerance is identified in the program stakeholder management plan, which is an input to the Plan Program Risk Management process. Each stakeholder has specific attitudes toward risk that can affect the program and the risk response that is selected.

    PMI®, *The Standard for Program Management*, 2008, 162

151. b. Ethical concerns

    In evaluating program objectives ethical concerns are a key consideration. In this example, student privacy is an example of an ethical concern to satisfy.

    PMI. *Program Management Professional (PgMP)® Examination Content Outline*, 2011, 6

152. a. Have a program management information system

    An effective program management information system is essential in program management and in the planning and establishing the governance structure. It provides tools and mechanisms to store information about the program and a quick way to retrieve needed information. It provides a mix of manual and automated tools, techniques, processes, and procedures to help the program team provide effective oversight of the program.

    PMI®, *The Standard for Program Management*, 2008, 248

    PMI. *Program Management Professional (PgMP)® Examination Content Outline*, 2011, 15

153. b. Ensure the new director understands the benefits of this program and how they will be sustained

    A benefits transition plan is required for all programs. In this case, it is essential to then transition the benefits to the new program director. One approach to help sustain the benefits is to involve the new director in preparing this plan and making sure the director understands the benefit realization plan and reports prepared to date.

    PMI. *Program Management Professional* (PgMP)® *Examination Content Outline*, 2011, 13

154. b. Program sponsor

    When the last component in the program has closed, the process is for the Governance Board to review the overall program delivery and benefits realization and make a recommendation as to whether the program should be closed; this recommendation then is proposed to the program sponsor for the final closure decision.

    PMI®, *The Standard for Program Management*, 2008, 262

155. a. Component managers

    A program has three major communications channels: clients, sponsors, and component managers.

    PMI®, *The Standard for Program Management*, 2008, 147

156. a. Increase the benefits to be realized by the product

    The purpose of programs is to attain more benefits than if the projects were managed in a standalone fashion. This scenario shows the program manager is exploiting the strategic opportunities for change with the merger in order to maximize benefit realization for the company.

    PMI. *Program Management Professional* (PgMP)® *Examination Content Outline*, 2011, 7

157. b. Default and be subject to legal action

    When a contractor refuses to perform according to the terms and conditions of a contract, he or she is in default and is subject to legal action. Although it is unfortunate that the contractor is not making money on the program, that is not grounds for refusing to live up to her end of the agreement. The organization's contract closure procedure, a tool and technique in the Close Program Procurements process, outlines the requirements for contract termination, including verification criteria to protect the organization from breach of contract.

    PMI®, *The Standard for Program Management*, 2008, 205

158. d. Update the communications log

> The outputs of the Distribute Information process include program performance reports as well as updates to lessons learned, the program communications plan, and the communications log.

> PMI®, *The Standard for Program Management*, 2008, 151–152

159. b. Document decisions in a decision register

> Governance board decisions using meeting minutes, action item logs, or other forms of decision reports should be documented in a governance decision register. These decisions are used as feedback to improve the results of the components and overall program.

> PMI®, *The Standard for Program Management*, 2008, 262

160. d. Review the benefits realization plan and implement improvements based on lessons learned to date

> Benefit reviews can be conducted throughout the program. They enable the program team among other things to review the effectiveness of the benefits strategy and make changes to it based on lessons learned, inform stakeholders of progress, identify further benefits to the program, assess overall performance to date, and provide an opportunity to publicize the program and its success thus far.

> PMI. *Program Management Professional* (PgMP)® *Examination Content Outline*, 2011, 11;

> Williams, D. and Parr, T., *Enterprise programme management*, 2006, 182

161. b. Readiness

> In it important to evaluate the organization's capability for new products by consulting with its leaders to develop, validate, and assess the program's objectives. Readiness analysis can help to establish new benefits from the program, ensure resources are available, and evaluate the current state to prioritize requirements.

> PMI. *Program Management Professional* (PgMP)® *Examination Content Outline*, 2011, 6

162. c. The program is viewed as a way to achieve the organization's strategic benefits

The Initiate Program process requires formal acceptance of the program scope by the steering committee, by a portfolio management body, by an external funding organization, or at the organizational executive level. This acceptance acknowledges the necessity of the program to achieve strategic benefits.

PMI®, *The Standard for Program Management*, 2008, 74–75

163. c. Resource leveling

Resource leveling is a useful approach to show the impact on the schedule if the resources are not available as planned. It is also a way to optimize the program plan by leveling the resource requirements in order to gain efficiencies and maximize productivity/synergies among constituent projects.

PMI. *Program Management Professional* (PgMP)® *Examination Content Outline*, 2011, 9

164. a. Project plan

Project managers' performance is evaluated according to their ability to execute the project according to the project plan. This approach is used to then maximize their contribution to achieving program goals.

PMI. *Program Management Professional* (PgMP)® *Examination Content Outline*, 2011, 10

165. d. Rewards

Each program should manage changes in accordance with the change management plan. The purpose is to control scope, quality, schedule, cost, contracts, risks, and rewards.

PMI. *Program Management Professional* (PgMP)® *Examination Content Outline*, 2011, 11

166. a. Sponsor

In stakeholder management, it is important to evaluate any risks to the program identified by stakeholders, and it is especially important to evaluate those of the sponsor, since the sponsor is the champion for the program and is providing its resources and funding. As necessary, this evaluation should be part of the risk management plan.

PMI. *Program Management Professional* (PgMP)® *Examination Content Outline*, 2011, 14

167. c. Mission statement

The purpose of the mission statement is to describe why the program is important and what it needs to achieve. It is done by evaluating stakeholders' concerns and expectations in order to establish program direction.

PMI. *Program Management Professional* (PgMP)® *Examination Content Outline*, 2011, 6

168. a. Regularly scheduled reviews

Governance board meetings are the most common method used to perform governance oversight activities. Regularly scheduled review meetings with well-planned agendas and documented decision records enhance the effectiveness of the governance process.

PMI®, *The Standard for Program Management*, 2008, 262

169. a. Plan Communications

In this process, the PMIS provides the vehicle for program reporting and communicating with stakeholders. It also is used to communicate status, changes, and performance.

PMI®, *The Standard for Program Management*, 2008, 145

170. c. The program be set up with a viable business case that has a list of initial benefits to be achieved

A business case is required for each program, and as part of it, benefits are identified for the program. This business case should be reviewed and updated throughout the program and be realistic so people will commit to it to help achieve overall program success.

Williams, D. and Parr, T., *Enterprise programme management,* 2006, 185

PMI®, *The Standard for Program Management*, 2008, 23

Practice Test 2

1. Finally both the Boeing 787 and the Airbus 380 are operational. Assume you are the Program Manager now for the Boeing 797. You have reviewed all the lessons learned from the work done on the 787 as you are determined this time that the 797 will be in service before the scheduled date. However, the 797 uses new technology, and you have different subcontractors than those of the 787. Your executive managers recently returned from the Paris Air Show and already have some orders, and you and your team are just identifying the various projects that will comprise this important program. You have been asked since you are the program manager to provide your sponsor and your governance board with regular updates on the status of the program's benefits, and you need to be able to measure the benefits that have accrued during each reporting period. You decided to track the benefits in a—

    a. Benefits register
    b. Benefits realization report
    c. Benefits control system
    d. Benefits monitoring system

2. You are working to establish program management in your organization. You recognize since you are working in the Portfolio Management Office that there are many benefits to be attained if projects that are somehow related can be part of a program structure so through the program, more benefits can be attained than if they were managed separately. You recognize the importance to aligning program goals and benefits with long-term organizational goals. Therefore, you realize as the company embraces program management, you will need to hire people as program managers, or appoint people from within the organization, who have skills in—

    a. Leadership
    b. Organizational awareness
    c. Political awareness
    d. Strategic visioning

3. Your organization has a defined career path in project and program management and you are now a program manager. Earlier, you spent time as a project team member, you then became a junior project manager and got your PMP®. From there, you began to lead more complicated projects and received your Master's degree in Project Management from a leading University in your country. When PMI announced the PgMP® certification, you asked if you could move into a program management position so you could gain the hours needed to qualify for this credential. This is your first program management job. There are various phases in the program life cycle in your company, which follows the PMI® Standard; the longest is—

a. Program Initiation
b. Delivery of Program Benefits
c. Program Setup
d. Pre-Program Preparations

4. You are working for pharmaceutical company, GenBioform, as program manager for the development of a breakthrough drug to inhibit the growth of cancer tumors and eliminate the need for chemotherapy or radiation treatments. Your CEO is determined that your company will be the first to get approval from the Food and Drug Administration (FDA) for this new drug. You have performed an in-depth analysis of stakeholders in your company and have identified the following key external stakeholders: consumer groups, oncologists, the FDA, and cancer patients. Your next step is to—

a. Finalize the results of your stakeholder identification and analysis by preparing a transition plan
b. Note stakeholder considerations in your program charter
c. Rank the stakeholders by importance and assign key team members to work with the top two
d. Ask your Marketing Department to perform an analysis of the competition

5. You are working for pharmaceutical company, GenBioform, as program manager for the development of a breakthrough drug to inhibit the growth of cancer tumors and eliminate the need for chemotherapy or radiation treatments. Your CEO is determined that your company will be the first to get approval from the Food and Drug Administration (FDA) for this new drug. You have performed an in-depth analysis of stakeholders in your company and have identified the following key external stakeholders: consumer groups, oncologists, the FDA, and cancer patients. You receive many requests for information from your stakeholders. You have structured your program processes so that information requests are a standard output from many processes used in your company. These requests should—

   a. Be handled according to the communications management plan

   b. Flow to the Distribute Information process

   c. Be the specific responsibility of the person designated to work with each identified stakeholder

   d. Flow to the Report Program Performance process

6. You are working for pharmaceutical company, GenBioform, as program manager for the development of a breakthrough drug to inhibit the growth of cancer tumors and eliminate the need for chemotherapy or radiation treatments. Your CEO is determined that your company will be the first to get approval from the Food and Drug Administration (FDA) for this new drug. You have performed an in-depth analysis of stakeholders in your company and have identified the following key external stakeholders: consumer groups, oncologists, the FDA, and cancer patients. You receive many requests for information from your stakeholders So far on your program, with its six projects, you have had a number of change requests, which is not surprising given the complexity of the program. At the program level, analysis of change requests involves identifying, documenting, and estimating the work the change would entail. As program manager, you also need to—

   a. Determine any program management processes that must be revisited

   b. Meet with the program governance board for approval, rejection, or deferral of the request

   c. Convene a meeting of the project's configuration control board

   d. Prepare a status report

7. The emphasis at your logistics company has always been to 'do projects right'. Therefore, your management established a Project Management Office, with the responsibility to develop a methodology that project managers would follow that was consistent across the organization. This has proven to be effective. Now the organization is doing the same for program management. Since it has been successful in 'doing projects right' and is 'doing programs right', the organization now has implemented portfolio management to ensure it is 'doing the right programs and projects'. In terms of the expected benefits of a program, the first step is to—

   a. Formalize benefits at the portfolio level
   b. Develop a benefits management plan
   c. Map each benefit proposed to a portfolio outcome
   d. Assign responsibility for benefits realization to the program manager and the governance board

8. You are managing a systems integration program for your company, Globus Enterprises, which is under contract to the government of Moldova. This program includes a hardware systems project and an information systems project; other projects are expected to be added as the program progresses. Because this program will include numerous projects, you have decided to—

   a. Have each project use a distinct life cycle as defined by the program management office (PMO)
   b. Define a common life-cycle model for the various projects
   c. Set up a governance structure for each project in the program to assess progress according to the established life cycles
   d. Prepare the project management plans

9. You have been appointed program manager for the closing phase of the systems integration program for Globus Enterprises, under contact to the government of Moldova. The original program manager, most staff members, and the technical team members have moved on to other projects and programs. As the closing program manager, you must ensure that all administrative activities are complete. One best practice is to review the—

   a. Program work breakdown structure (PWBS)
   b. Change request plan
   c. Program management plan
   d. Quality management plan

10. You are pleased to finally move into a program management position in your city, and as the program manager for the new wastewater treatment initiative, you have now completed your program management plan. You have selected project managers and also a core team and had defined criteria to help you evaluate the various candidates. You are fortunate that you have worked with two of the people before on specific projects, but the others are new to you, and the team has not worked together previously as a team. As a program manager, you must be an effective leader. A key area of focus is—

  a. Ensuring task delivery
  b. Adding value to decision making
  c. Setting directives and procedures
  d. Establishing program direction

11. You are managing a program that comprises new systems application development and maintenance activities. These applications are critical to your company, CDE, as they involve access to proprietary data. The systems must be available to your clients on a 24/7/365 basis. Much of the work on you program will be outsourced as you have an aggressive schedule to meet; fortunately CDE has a qualified vendor list to simplify the acquisition process. This program has high visibility in CDE. You and your core team realize the high level of interest and have worked hard to identify the key stakeholders and determine their position toward your program. You have prepared your stakeholder management plan, and it has been approved by your sponsor and Governance Board. Now, the next step for you and your team is to—

  a. Provide guidelines for project-level stakeholder management
  b. Prepare a stakeholder inventory
  c. Ensure the stakeholder management plan supports CDE's strategic plan
  d. Communicate to all stakeholders a need for change to the new systems applications

12. On your new 797 program, you have a larger number of stakeholders than did your counterpart program manager on the 787. You have reviewed all the lessons learned from the work done on the 787 as you are determined this time that the 797 will be in service before the scheduled date. However, the 797 uses new technology, and you have different subcontractors than those of the 787. There is even greater interest from people inside the organization, external to the organization, and there are more suppliers than before. You are working actively to identify early all the key stakeholders and prepare and follow a stakeholder engagement plan. To date, you find the stakeholder's major interests are in the program's benefits. However, the program is progressing as planned. In your plans, you have decided to conduct an overall review of the program's benefits with the stakeholders during the—

    a. Execution phase
    b. Delivery of Program Benefits phase
    c. Program Closing phase
    d. Program Setup phase

13. Change is inevitable in programs and projects. As the manager of your company's natural gas distribution program, you are pleased to have this program as it is ranked number one in the company's portfolio. So far, you have five separate projects, and the program is scheduled to last four years. You have your core team staffed as well as the needed staff members for these five projects. You also set up a configuration management system as part of your program management information system (PMIS). It includes a change management subsystem that enables you to review change requests and work with your change control board during the—

    a. Delivery of Program Benefits phase
    b. Program Execution phase
    c. Project Execution phase
    d. Monitoring the Benefits phase

14. Now that you have moved into this program management role in your manufacturing company, you realize your work really involves active involvement with stakeholders at a variety of levels. It is also compounded because on your program you have external stakeholders involved and need to spend time communicating with this group. Additionally, your Governance Board is extremely interested in your program and wants to meet more regularly than solely at phase-gate review sessions. They have requested these other meetings in order to—

    a. Ensure expected benefits are in line with the original business plan
    b. Focus on alignment of the program and your projects in it with the organization's strategic plan
    c. Determine if the level of risk still remains acceptable to your organization
    d. Focus on areas rather than specific points to ensure the overall program is successful

15. As a program manager in an aerospace organization, you are managing the next fighter plan. In the early stages, it is known as F200. It will serve a variety of needs once it is completed, and it will not require your country to have a series of fighter planes available. Because you have a large number of components, you need to prioritize them—its projects as well as ongoing activities. Because you have set up your benefits life cycle, you should do the prioritization during the—

    a. Benefits identification phase
    b. Benefits analysis and planning phase
    c. Benefits planning phase
    d. Benefits realization phase

16. As you work to propose a program to your Portfolio Review Board to develop a new colon cancer detecting approach that does not involve any pre-preparation work or after effects to patients, you want to also to identify high-level financial and non-financial benefits for this program. You also want to make sure the benefits are congruent with the funding goals for the program as the financial organization will not be a passive stakeholder. One business case driver for financial management that often is overlooked is—

    a. Mission statements
    b. Reducing risks
    c. Increasing efficiency
    d. Streamlining administration

17. As the program manager for the landfill program for your county, you have assembled your program team. It consists of civil engineers, regulatory specialists, project managers, and environmental engineers. You know you will add some key subject matter experts as required. You also will have contractors on your team. You are working hard to achieve the county's desired due date for program completion. You have a number of administrative functions to comply with that are part of the City's methodology. At the program level, these administrative functions are best handled by a(n)—

    a. Program management office (PMO)
    b. Program Core Team
    c. Program Office
    d. Office of Administrative Services

18. Now that you have moved into this program management role in your manufacturing company, you realize your work really involves active involvement with stakeholders at a variety of levels. It is also compounded because on your program you have external stakeholders involved and need to spend time communicating with this group. Additionally, your Governance Board is extremely interested in your program and wants to meet more regularly than solely a phase-gate review sessions. While you have two projects in your program, the Manufacturing Director at your company, CCC, has requested that you add another project to your program. Criteria for initiating a project is contained in the—

    a. Program management plan
    b. Program business case
    c. Program charter
    d. Governance plan

19. As the program manager working to upgrade and integrate the back office components of your organization's systems, you have five projects in your program. You realize all programs, and projects, have risks associated with them, and some of the high-level risks are in your program charter. Since risks and issues or major program concerns are components of your overall program management plan, a key result of the program life cycle during the Program Setup or the Planning phase is—

    a. Risk response plans for each project
    b. Risk identification
    c. Risk management consolidation
    d. Risk tolerances of program stakeholders

20. You are a program manager and are responsible for a major project to integrate the back office components of your organization's systems. You have five projects in your program. You realize all programs, and projects, have risks associated with them, and some of the high-level risks are in your program charter. You have a core team of six people and six project managers. For consistency and to promote best practices, you want to ensure that the project managers adhere to the company's project management methodology. This is done during the—

    a. Program Setup phase
    b. Program Execution phase
    c. Delivery of Program Benefits phase
    d. Monitoring and Controlling phase

21. You are the program manager to restructure your department within your government agency. The head of the agency informed your sponsor that she wants to change the scope of the program so you will be working to restructure the entire agency instead of just one department. The Agency Administrator felt this change would be beneficial as the Agency also has to undergo some funding cuts in the next three fiscal years. This represents a major change to your program. You decided before moving forward was that your best course of action was to—

    a. Inform your team and involve them in planning the next steps
    b. Meet with your program sponsor
    c. Convene a meeting of your Governance Board
    d. Meet with the Director of the Enterprise Program Management Office as obviously you now need additional resources for your program

22. As the program manager for the systems integration program for Globus Enterprises, which is under contract to the government of Moldova, you have a number of projects in your program. First, your program includes a hardware systems project. Second, you have an information systems project. Now, you recently added a software engineering project, and you plan to add a verification and validation project in the fourth quarter. Other projects also are on your roadmap. Your overall program success is measured in terms of—

    a. Benefits delivery
    b. Earned value
    c. Each project's adherence to its schedule
    d. Products delivered according to specification

23. For success in any program, it is necessary to identify the key stakeholders and their specific interest in or influence over the program's objectives. This identification process should begin even when the program's business case is being prepared and before it is submitted to the organization's leadership for approval. In your proposed colon cancer detection program, already you have identified the financial organization as one that will not be a passive stakeholder should your program be selected and authorized to proceed. Before presenting your business case to the executive team, you decided to—

    a. Work closely with each member of the financial group to develop quantifiable benefits such as NPV, IRR, and the payback period
    b. Evaluate your proposed program's alignment to the strategic plan by consulting with organizational leaders
    c. Identify the financial constraints that will affect development of the budget for your program
    d. Estimate the costs of the program

24. As you met with the organizational leaders for your colon cancer detection program that does not involve any pre-preparation work or after effects to patients to determine whether or not they felt the program was in alignment with organizational objectives, you used these meetings to obtain support and also to identify your key stakeholders. You decided to begin the development of a stakeholder register. The person who is responsible for ensuring program success is the—

    a. Executive sponsor
    b. Program board
    c. Program director
    d. Program manager

25. You are managing a major curriculum redesign program in your training company. Now, the company's focus is on general managerial skills and specific courses for business analysts. At the last strategic planning meeting, the CEO set forth a three-year plan with a major goal to be the leading provider of portfolio, program, and project management training in your country; it still will offer general managerial and business analyst training. You are the program manager for this new initiative. You recognize key differences between a project life cycle and a program life cycle, one of which is that the program life cycle—

    a. May be extended as some projects transition or others begin
    b. Assists in the control and management of the project deliverables
    c. Is distinct and may not be extended
    d. May be set up such that project benefits cannot be realized immediately

26. You are the program manager to restructure your department within your government agency. The head of the agency informed your sponsor that she wants to change the scope of the program so you will be working to restructure the entire agency instead of just one department. The Agency Administrator felt this change would be beneficial as the Agency also has to undergo some funding cuts in the next three fiscal years. You now have acquired additional resources for this major change and have re-structured your program. You realize, however, that with this change, you should have—

    a. Followed appropriate procedures and guidelines
    b. An appropriate governance structure in place
    c. Updated all your plans
    d. Communicated with every stakeholder

27. You are managing a landfill program for your county. Your program team consists of civil engineers, regulatory specialists, project managers, and environmental engineers. You also have a number of internal and external stakeholders. Your client, the county executive, has informed you that your program must be completed no later than September 15, 2013, to comply with a regulatory mandate. The county executive has imposed—

    a. A constraint
    b. An assumption
    c. A dependency
    d. A risk

28. When you were a project manager, you found the risk register to be an extremely useful tool. Now that you are a program manager, you ask your project managers to use a risk register, and you assign a member of your core program team to identify, analyze, and track program-level risks. Because of the large number of changes expected on your program, you decide to set up a change request log. This log is a(n)—

    a. Tool and technique used in the Monitor and Control Program Changes process
    b. Output of the Monitor and Control Program Performance process
    c. Input to the Monitor and Control Program Changes and Distribute Information processes
    d. Tool and technique used in both the Monitor and Control Program Changes process and the Monitor and Control Program Performance process

29. You have been appointed program manager for the closing phase of Program CCC. The original program manager, most staff members, and the technical team members have moved on to other projects and programs. As closing program manager, you must ensure that all administrative activities are complete. In the Close Program Procurements process, each contract in the program must be closed according to its terms and conditions. As manager for the closing phase of Program CCC, you focus on contract documentation. Sixty-two contracts were awarded during the life of this program. You contact the Contracts Department and a contracts specialist assists you. As you work through this process, you review—

   a. The procurement management plan
   b. The contract management plan
   c. Delivery notices
   d. Contract closure procedures

30. Assume you are managing the reward loyalty operational activity for your airline. Members have been complaining about the difficulty of actually using an award, especially your elite members who tend to fly on your airline at least one million miles per year. You feel you will lose elite members to other airlines unless the program changes dramatically, and you believe it needs to offer more possible rewards in conjunction with free stays at leading hotels of the world and also free car rentals. You have received authority from your Portfolio Review Board to establish a new program to emphasize improvements in how rewards are to be handled. You now are in the Initiating process. The key output of it is—

   a. Identification of the program manager
   b. The program charter
   c. The benefits analysis plan
   d. Feasibility studies

31. Assume you are managing the reward loyalty operational activity for your airline. Members have been complaining about the difficulty of actually using an award, especially your elite members who tend to fly on your airline at least one million miles per year. You feel you will lose elite members to other airlines unless the program changes dramatically, and you believe it needs to offer more possible rewards in conjunction with free stays at leading hotels of the world and also free car rentals. You have received authority from your Portfolio Review Board to establish a new program to emphasize improvements in how rewards are to be handled. You realize that informal alliances are an important consideration, especially when decisions are made that affect aspects of the program. This need means that the program manager requires which one of the following skills?

    a. Interpersonal
    b. Political
    c. Organizational
    d. Stakeholder management

32. Assume that you have completed your program to re-design your organization's approach to how it works with other companies. Rather than bidding on contracts as a single organization, you have set up a program to use consortiums for any contract over $10 million US. You designed as separate projects the various mechanisms to best work with other companies so the consortium members are viewed as ones that trust one another, and the program processes are effective and embraced. Now that the process is in place and has been followed, it is time to close this program. The closing process formalizes acceptance of the program's—

    a. Plan
    b. Benefits
    c. Knowledge assets
    d. Governance recommendations

33. You are responsible for business development in your division, which is a subsidiary of a large defense contractor. Recently, you attended a conference and learned that many of your competitors are focusing on continuous improvement in the area of sales strategies and techniques and are conducting maturity assessments. When you returned to your office, you prepared a business case and recommended that such a program be initiated. One of the criteria you used was—

    a. Representatives from each business unit in the organization would participate in the program
    b. The program duration would be short because a maturity assessment typically can be conducted in three months
    c. It would be necessary to set up some specific projects as a result of the improvement plan from the maturity assessment, but these projects would be unique to each business unit
    d. The benefits that would accrue from the program would be independent of specific deliverables of the various associated projects

34. Your company has established a program to manage the development of new pet food products, and you have been appointed manager of this program. It is the first program of its kind in your company; its structure was selected because numerous other projects in the planning stage have dependencies and require some of the same critical resources. Because you manage the various interfaces among your projects, you should examine the—

    a. Program architecture baseline
    b. Program governance structure
    c. Program roadmap
    d. Program risk management plan

35. You are the program manager for a program that is using multiple suppliers. Even though you have signed partnering agreements with each supplier, you know performance problems will surface, especially with this program because more than 75 percent of the work is being done by third-party suppliers. Also, your company has not worked with five of these suppliers in the past, and two are start-up companies. You have identified the various stakeholders on this program and classified them. The stakeholder responsible for ultimately delivering the benefits on this program is the—

    a. Head of your Governance Board
    b. Program Director
    c. Head of your Program Management Office
    d. Program Sponsor

36. Because of extreme droughts in Haddad, Jordan, water restrictions have been imposed. Your company is awarded a contract to eliminate the need for these restrictions. The program includes a project to formulate and implement policies and procedures that ensure continuity of operations and performance of associated equipment. Another project will oversee improvements and modifications to existing treatment methods and facilities. A third project will design modifications to increase productivity and effectiveness. As program manager, you will manage, contract, and provide oversight for capital improvement projects. You will need various types of resources and a variety of office supplies. To assist in managing contracts, you should—

   a. Conduct inspections and audits
   b. Identify the program funding source
   c. Prepare a program financial framework
   d. Use written deviations

37. You are the program manager for a program that is using multiple suppliers. Even though you have signed partnering agreements with each supplier, you know performance problems will surface, especially with this program because more than 75 percent of the work is being done by third-party suppliers. Also, your company has not worked with five of these suppliers in the past, and two are start-up companies. Many in your organization are interested in this program and especially how the integration efforts will be accomplished given the large number of suppliers involved. It is important in this situation to ensure—

   a. A contact change control system is in place
   b. A contract administrator is a member of your core team
   c. Important interfaces are managed
   d. Key stakeholders have active involvement in the program at all times

38. As a program manager in the Department of the Interior, you are working on ways to ensure continued availability of water resources. You have a number of projects in your program, but you are particularly interested in the effect of earthquakes on water resources. You have appointed a manager for this project, and he has assembled an outstanding team that does impressive work. You have already determined your program's budget requirements for the next fiscal year; your governance board concurs with your financial analysis and includes your requirements in the budget submitted to the Office of the Secretary. However, the Office makes 10 percent cuts across the board, thus forcing you to eliminate the earthquake analysis project. Your next step is to—

    a. Disband your team
    b. Assign the project manager to another project so that he does not lose his job
    c. Update your program plans as required
    d. Make another attempt to secure funding for this project

39. Your program in the Department of Interior to work on was to ensure continued availability of water resources to the citizens of your country has a number of projects, now seven are under way, and unless there are no other budget cuts, you expect at least three more to be added. You know this program has a number of challenges, as already the earthquake project and its effect on water resources has been cut. You also know that your program has some interfaces with other programs and projects under way within the Interior Department. In most programs, there is a core infrastructure which is the—

    a. Governance board
    b. Program management team
    c. Program management office (PMO)
    d. Program office

40. As the manager of a major program in your company, you have access to various supporting resources. Your organization uses a balanced matrix organizational structure, and supporting resources come from a variety of functional departments. Some of the people who support your program report to you as well as to their department managers. In the company's cost accounting system, everyone charges time to appropriate codes. One member of your program team regularly prepares resource deviation reports. These reports are an—

    a. Output of the Monitor and Control Program Performance process
    b. Output of the Manage Program Resources process
    c. Input to the Report Program Performance process
    d. Input to the Provide Governance Oversight process

41. You have been appointed program manager to develop digital yo-yos. You are excited by this challenge, and when you learned of this possible opportunity, you decided to attain your PgMP® and also take a course on managing programs for best practices. This is your first time as a program manager, and this program is ranked number three in your organization. You are preparing a high-level program plan and must include a statement as to why the program is important and what it will achieve. Such a plan and associated statement constitute your program's—

    a. Justification
    b. Vision
    c. Charter
    d. Values

42. As you continue with the digital yo-yo program, you are excited about the opportunity to manage this initiative for your company. You realize, though, for success on this program, you need an outstanding team, and you have been negotiating for the best and the brightest people to manage the seven identified projects that will comprise the program as well as to be in your Program Management Office. It has been a difficult process working with the company's department managers to obtain needed resources. You know for success you also need—

    a. A determination of contractor resources for your use
    b. Agreement among the team as to the program values
    c. Standard measurement criteria
    d. Risks identified by stakeholders

43. You are a program manager in a global software company that uses virtual teams. Work is passed 24/7 from team members on one continent to those on another continent. You have adopted the common 4,000-word English vocabulary for use on all your projects; however, nine different languages are spoken by your team members. Which of the following is a key input to your program to ensure that you do not make the same mistakes made on previous initiatives?

    a. Historical information
    b. Common messages
    c. Communications technologies
    d. Communications management plan

44. As the program manager for a new wastewater treatment initiative in your city, you must deliver both tangible and intangible benefits. You must also identify the interdependencies of the benefits delivered in various projects in your program. This means that you must map benefits to program outcomes. In terms of the benefits management life cycle, this is done during the—

    a. Benefits identification phase
    b. Benefits setup phase
    c. Benefits analysis and planning phase
    d. Benefits execution phase

45. You are managing a program that comprises new systems application development and maintenance activities. These applications are critical to your company, CDE, as they involve access to proprietary data. The systems must be available to your clients on a 24/7/365 basis. Much of the work on you program will be outsourced as you have an aggressive schedule to meet; fortunately CDE has a qualified vendor list to simplify the acquisition process. This program has high visibility in CDE. You and your core team realize the high level of interest and have worked hard to identify the key stakeholders and determine their position toward your program. You decided to use mapping to help develop a stakeholder matrix to put stakeholders into certain categories. One of the advantages of the mapping approach is that it—

    a. Can be done easily through brainstorming sessions
    b. Shows the stakeholder's attitude toward the program
    c. If done correctly, can promote stakeholder engagement
    d. Shows the type of stakeholder who defines the command, control loops, and communication mechanisms

46. Working as the primary contractor to CDE on this new systems application development and maintenance program, this award is a great opportunity for your company, XYZ. You are pleased to have the greatest part of the work on this program and you are fortunate to be XYZ's program manager. CDE set up partnering relationships with all the contractors so everyone is working closely as a team to meet the aggressive schedule in the Statement of Work. Your CEO wants your part of this program to be completed at least two months earlier than scheduled to maintain a positive relationship with CDE for future opportunities. He asked you to prepare a plan as to how you were going to interface with all the stakeholders on this program especially the CDE personnel. This is your first program to manage for CDE, and you have three projects in it. Before preparing your stakeholder management plan, you decided to conduct a stakeholder analysis. Your first step is to—

    a. Brainstorm the possible stakeholders to get a complete list of them

    b. Evaluate the degree of support or opposition each stakeholder has regarding the program

    c. Gain an understanding of CDE's culture, attitudes, and communications requirements

    d. Perform a detailed review of the Statement of Work and other key documents already completed

47. Your company is noted for its maturity and excellence in program management. It has received awards for program and project delivery. In a recent assessment by a person certified by PMI® as an *OPM3*® Professional, out of the possible 488 Best Practices that can be achieved, your company had achieved 405 of these Best Practices. People seem dedicated to the success of the company and in its portfolio management process as well as its management of programs and projects. One reason for your company's success is that it relies on the development and maintenance of organizational process assets, which are also known as—

    a. Environmental enterprise factors

    b. A process asset library

    c. A portal

    d. Standards of professional conduct and responsibility

48. You are the program manager for a global Fortune 100 software company. The company has determined that it must pursue Cloud Computing, and it wants to use agile methods as it enters this market to speed the time to complete the Cloud Computing program and to develop a marketing campaign for it. You also know you will need to do extensive testing before the program is complete. You have identified the strategic area for your program, and you have identified the key stakeholders as you consulted with organizational leaders. Your next step is to prepare a(n)

    a. Business case for each of your projects
    b. Initial plan to set up the program management office (PMO)
    c. High-level plan
    d. Communications management plan for your program's stakeholders

49. As the program manager for global Fortune 100 software company. The company has determined that it must pursue Cloud Computing, and it wants to use agile methods as it enters this market to speed the time to complete the Cloud Computing program and to develop a marketing campaign for it. You also know you will need to do extensive testing before the program is complete. You have identified the strategic area for your program, and you have identified the key stakeholders as you consulted with organizational leaders. You are responsible for ongoing management of program benefits. You must ensure that the program transition activities provide for continued management of benefits through the framework of—

    a. Ongoing operations
    b. Transfer of the benefits to the customer
    c. Program closure
    d. Consolidation of the benefits

50. You are the legacy system conversion program manager in your company. You need to upgrade the company's business development/sales tracking system, which was developed in C++. Your governance board recognizes the importance of improving other projects in this upgrade so there is an integrated system for all applications in your company. You now have projects in your program to also upgrade the accounting/financial management system, interface them to the program management information system, and add a knowledge management system. You have a complex program. With these additional projects, you and your core team realize you need to upgrade your stakeholder management plan. You re-did your initial stakeholder analysis before this update. The last step in this process is to—

    a. Prepare a stakeholder register
    b. Determine how receptive the stakeholder is to communications from the program
    c. Prioritize stakeholders in a matrix according to their ability to influence the program outcomes, either positively or negatively
    d. Determine the degree of support or opposition the stakeholder has for the program's objectives

51. You are the program manager for a program that is using multiple suppliers. Even though you have signed partnering agreements with each supplier, you know performance problems will surface, especially with this program because more than 75 percent of the work is being done by third-party suppliers. Also, your company has not worked with five of these suppliers in the past, and two are start-up companies. Many in your organization are interested in this program and especially how the integration efforts will be accomplished given the large number of suppliers involved. Today, one of the suppliers responsible for project D informed you that he did not have sufficient financial capacity and resources to continue on the program and was going to declare Chapter 11 and file then for bankruptcy. Obviously, this change involves other projects on your program and the entire program's ability to deliver its benefits on time. You have decided that the best course of action is to first—

    a. Call an immediate meeting with your program team
    b. Contact the Procurement Department to obtain their services in obtaining another qualified supplier
    c. Contact the suppliers with whom you have had positive working relationships in the past to see if they can take on this company's work
    d. Follow the issue escalation process

52. As the manager for a water-gasification program that will provide potable sparkling mineral water from public water fountains in Garvey, England, you have leased some of the needed equipment. Unfortunately, you have found that on two of your projects, some of these leased resources did not meet specifications. The project managers on Projects A and D advised you of their concerns because they were concerned that overall program progress might be affected. You decided to compare the potential effects of these issues to the tolerances established in the Program Management Plan. A tool and technique to use is—

    a. Issues analysis
    b. Stakeholder risk tolerance
    c. Risk audit
    d. Project management information system

53. Assume you are managing the next generation SMART car so it runs entirely on ethanol rather than gasoline now that your country has ethanol stations in all major cities and on interstate highway systems. Your executives believe this type of SMART car will increase in popularity. As the program manager, you also are to ensure that it is equipped with the latest safety prevention systems in order that people will want to drive it on interstate highways given its small size. You also want a version that will appeal to taller people. Since there are a number of benefits associated with this new line of SMART cars, you decided to use a benefit register to track the benefits accrued by each of the projects in your program so your organization can realize them and then through its dealers be able to sustain them. As the program manager, you maintain this benefits register during which of the following phases in the benefits management life cycle?

    a. Benefits identification
    b. Benefits analysis and planning
    c. Benefits transition
    d. Benefits realization

54. You have successfully finished your new line of SMART cars, and they have been well received. In all, you have four different models, all using ethanol and all with advanced safety measures. They also are environmentally efficient. They also have the latest safety prevention system so people can drive them on interstate highway systems. One model is designed especially for taller people; another is a convertible; a third is a station wagon; and a fourth is a coupe. Now that the cars are being purchased, to derive the optimal value from the work you and your team accomplished, as the program manager, you should—

    a. Conduct team satisfaction surveys
    b. Leave a legacy of operational benefits sustainment
    c. Ask an independent party to contact end users to ensure the effectiveness of customer relationship management
    d. Provide support to end users throughout the product life cycle

55. As the key member of your company's Program Selection Committee, you are responsible for deciding which programs to undertake. Your Committee meets on a quarterly basis and then selects new programs and projects as appropriate and also then rebalances the company's portfolio accordingly. As you consider the proposed business case for a new program and assess the suggestions of the other committee members, a key factor is—

    a. Constituent component identification and definition
    b. Total available resources
    c. Overall stakeholder interest
    d. The program's feasibility study

56. You are the program manager for a program that is using multiple suppliers. Even though you have signed partnering agreements with each supplier, you know performance problems will surface, especially with this program because more than 75 percent of the work is being done by third-party suppliers. Also, your company has not worked with five of these suppliers in the past, and two are start-up companies. Many in your organization are interested in this program and especially how the integration efforts will be accomplished given the large number of suppliers involved. Given the extensive work being done by suppliers, you expect you will have more internal audits than usual on your program. Their specific timing should be—

    a. In your program's roadmap
    b. Set forth in your audit plan
    c. Set forth in your program plan
    d. In your program schedule

57. You are the program manager to restructure your department within your business unit. The head of the company informed your sponsor that she wants to change the scope of the program so you will be working to restructure the entire company instead of just one department. The CEO felt this change would be beneficial as the company also has to undergo some funding cuts in the next three fiscal years. However, to overcome these funding cuts, she wants you to then head up a new program so the company can pursue international markets. You prepared a stakeholder register as part of your planning efforts for the restructured program, and the person who has the executive ownership of your program is the—

   a. CEO
   b. Director of the Enterprise Program Management Office
   c. Program director
   d. Program Governance Board

58. You are managing a program in your company, and you are following the phases articulated in the Project Management Institute's *The Standard for Program Management*. Your governance structure has five phases, and you have just received approval from the executive sponsor of the program board to move into the fourth phase of the program. At this time, you will concentrate on—

   a. Program-specific tools
   b. Delivering benefits
   c. Understanding strategic benefits
   d. Establishing a program infrastructure

59. You are the program manager for a program that is using multiple suppliers. Even though you have signed partnering agreements with each supplier, you know performance problems will surface, especially with this program because more than 75 percent of the work is being done by third-party suppliers. Also, your company has not worked with five of these suppliers in the past, and two are start-up companies. Many in your organization are interested in this program and especially how the integration efforts will be accomplished given the large number of suppliers involved. Recently, your organization made a major change in its financial management policies and now is requiring a 10% retainage as part of each supplier's contract. This means that—

   a. You require a person specializing in contracts and procurement management to be a member of your core team
   b. Suppliers are now a major stakeholder
   c. You need to actively work to rewrite each contract and then submit it to your Contracts Department
   d. A supplier engagement plan should be prepared

60. Assume that you are the program manager for a product to be delivered to an external customer and that you are now planning your program. This new product is to be completed in two years. So far, you have three projects in your program and plan to add several more as the program continues. You believe you have an excellent team with the key competencies to assist you in the program. You also are glad to have a governance board. However, to minimize the potential for conflicts between you and your project managers and between you and your governance board, you should use which one of the following tools and techniques?

    a. Tolerances
    b. Planning techniques
    c. Best practices library
    d. Review meetings

61. You are managing a program to produce the next generation of hurricane-, tornado-, and typhoon-resistant glass. Technical specialists in your company will support each of the projects in this program. Four projects are in process. Project A is fully staffed; Project B has about 75 percent of the staff members it needs; and Projects C and D are about to begin, but these two projects will require the services of several key specialists now working on Projects A and B. You tell Project Manager A that he must release two staff members to support Project C and three to support Project D. He uses resource leveling to analyze this change and tells you that the end date for Project A will need to be extended, as he will be understaffed. The program governance board and the executive sponsor agree to extend the schedule for Project A. The five specialists are released to the other projects. Your next step is to—

    a. Commend Project Manager A for his willingness to release these resources
    b. Meet with the five people involved and tell them they must move to the new projects
    c. Update the program-level documentation and records
    d. Pacify Project Manager A by seeing whether Project Manager B can release two resources from her project

62. You are managing a program to produce the next generation of hurricane-, tornado-, and typhoon-resistant glass. Technical specialists in your company will support each of the projects in this program. Four projects are in process. Project A is fully staffed; Project B has about 75 percent of the staff members it needs; and Projects C and D are about to begin. Your program team identifies several issues that force you to modify program requirements. Some changes are minor, but one issue requires a program scope change. Your next step is to—

    a. Involve the program's governance board in its resolution
    b. Prepare a change request
    c. Update the program management plan
    d. Update the scope statement

63. You are the legacy system conversion program manager in your company. You need to upgrade the company's business development/sales tracking system, which was developed in C++. Your governance board recognizes the importance of improving other projects in this upgrade so there is an integrated system for all applications in your company. You now have projects in your program to also upgrade the accounting/financial management system, interface them to the program management information system, and add a knowledge management system. You have a complex program, and it now has increased risks with the variety of systems involved. Your sponsor is aware of these increased risks. Plus, your executive team has set an aggressive time table to complete the program. Another problem is resource requirements as the accounting system was written in COBOL, and you will need to outsource this project. You should therefore update a number of the plans you have prepared with the first one to—

    a. Update your communications management plan
    b. Update your schedule management plan
    c. Update your financial management plan
    d. Update your risk management plan

64. You are the legacy system conversion program manager in your company. You need to upgrade the company's business development/sales tracking system, which was developed in C++. Your governance board recognizes the importance of improving other projects in this upgrade so there is an integrated system for all applications in your company. You now have projects in your program to also upgrade the accounting/financial management system, interface them to the program management information system, and add a knowledge management system. You have a complex program. With these additional projects, you and your core team realize you need to upgrade your stakeholder management plan. This is especially important because—

a. You lack needed resources now for some of the new projects
b. There are broad interdependencies between these projects
c. You will be spending more time communicating with more groups
d. You realize you will require strong leadership skills to deal with the complexity of this program

65. Assume you have just been named program manager to develop and manufacture a new drug designed to have fewer side effects than the existing ones on the marketplace to strengthen bones and help to minimize bone cancer. This will be a breakthrough product for your company and also for patients. You know competitors also are working on similar drugs, but members of your team of experts believe you can get your drug to market quickly including obtaining the needed regulatory approval. A number of benefits therefore will be associated with this program. Development of program-level benefits is the responsibility of the—

a. Program office
b. Program management office (PMO)
c. Program manager
d. Program team

66. Your company is a leader in the pharmaceutical industry. It has received approval from the Food and Drug Administration (FDA) for a new drug that will cure all glaucoma conditions. Although demand for the product is high, your company has many other drugs to manufacture. You are managing a process to upgrade the manufacturing process, and your CEO has given you an aggressive schedule, especially so the glaucoma drug can reach its numerous possible patients. You have five projects in this program, and you are getting ready for your second gate review on it. Although it is cumbersome assembling all the required materials for these reviews, you know they are useful as they ensure—

    a. Expected benefits are in line with the original business plan
    b. Lessons learned are collected in order to prevent any future problems and improve overall processes
    c. Alternatives can be uncovered when problems are identified
    d. Processes and procedures are being used as designed

67. You are the program manager to restructure your department within your government agency. The head of the agency informed your sponsor that she wants to change the scope of the program so you will be working to restructure the entire agency instead of just one department. The Agency Administrator felt this change would be beneficial as the Agency also has to undergo some funding cuts in the next three fiscal years. As you prepared your stakeholder inventory, especially to consider the involvement of external organizations, it was helpful to you to use—

    a. Expert judgment
    b. Brainstorming
    c. Organizational analysis
    d. Focus groups

68. As a program manager for Destruct, AB, a leading defense contractor, you must determine which components should be part of your program. You are pleased to be the program manager, and while you have managed programs in the past at another defense contractor, this is your first opportunity to manage a program for Destruct AB. Your program involves the development of the next generation parachute. It is to be completely safe, easy to deploy, and available in one year at a reasonable price. Your executives want it to be completed at the time of the next Paris Air Show. When you do this, you are working in the—

    a. Benefits planning phase
    b. Pre-Program Preparations phase
    c. Program Initiation phase
    d. Component identification phase

69. It is easy to focus primarily on the benefits programs will deliver to the organization and the deliverables the projects in each program will produce. Many organizations though do not have a clear understanding of all of the programs and projects that are under way, and many people do not want to disclose some 'pet' program they are working on as they believe they are breakthrough initiatives for the company. However, assume you are in an organization that lacks such a list of all the work in progress, and your company needs such a list as the executives have mandated that a portfolio management process be followed. The executives plan to meet monthly to review the existing portfolio and determine whether or not new programs and projects should be added and others deferred or terminated. The overall objective is to ensure the—

    a. Programs and projects in the portfolio are focused on delivering lasting results and benefits

    b. The portfolio's strategy is one in which it focuses on preventing poor return on investments in the programs and projects pursued

    c. Program and project inputs are emphasized along with direct program deliverables and metrics

    d. The emphasis continues on the triple constraint as programs and projects to pursue are considered

70. Assume you are working toward your doctoral degree in program management part-time as you work in your City government office that oversees all existing regulations and standards. You have suggested based on your studies that many of the existing projects to overhaul and review these regulations and standards might be better handled as a program since through a program the benefits from proposed projects can be coordinated more effectively especially if the benefits are interdependent. Intended interdependencies of benefits are stated in the—

    a. Program management plan

    b. Benefits management plan

    c. Benefits realization plan

    d. Project management plan

71. Assume your suggestion to your City government to combine projects into programs in the regulations and standards area has been well received. After a meeting of the City's Commissioners, they appointed you as the program manager to oversee this work. You are pleased to have this opportunity especially since it relates to your doctoral studies in program management. In fact, you believe you can use it as a case study in your dissertation. You have decided as one of your first tasks to prepare a benefits realization plan and share it with your City Manager and the Commissioners at their next meeting in three weeks. You will base this plan on the expected benefits as defined in the—

    a. Program charter
    b. Program business case
    c. Program management plan
    d. Organization's strategic plan

72. You are the program manager for a new product development program for Company AAA. This product will serve to make sure that consumers will be able to wash all types of clothing through use of your product, and therefore, they no longer will need to spend money at dry cleaning establishments. To complete your program successfully, you have identified five projects. You also will require some specialized resources that are always in demand in your organization; therefore, you meet with members of your core team and subject matter experts to—

    a. Assign roles and responsibilities
    b. Determine reporting relationships
    c. Prepare a staffing management plan
    d. Prepare a program resource plan

73. You are the program manager for a new product development program for Company AAA. This product will serve to make sure that consumers will be able to wash all types of clothing through use of your product, and therefore, they no longer will need to spend money at dry cleaning establishments. To complete your program successfully, you have identified five projects. Your core team uses an issues register to track and monitor the status of all program-level issues. This register is updated when a new issue is identified, analyzed, or resolved. This means that—

    a. The program issues register is a key tool and technique in the Manage Program Issues process
    b. Updates to the program issues register are outputs of the Manage Program Issues process
    c. The program issues register and program risk register are both inputs to the Monitor and Control Program Performance process
    d. Items on the program issues register are regular parts of the Manage Component Interfaces process

74. Your organization is embarking on a program to establish a culture of portfolio management. You have been appointed program manager because you previously worked in a company with a defined portfolio management process that was followed at all levels. The enterprise program management office (EPMO) and the CEO agree on the need for a company-wide portfolio management process with accompanying tools and techniques. Two people from the EPMO will be part of your initial core program team. These two people may be replaced by permanent staff during which one of the following processes?

    a. Initiate Team
    b. Resource Planning
    c. Manage Program Resources
    d. Human Resource Planning

75. As the program manager in your company responsible for establishing a culture of portfolio management, you were fortunate to be assigned early so you could participate in the development of the program's charter. You have been appointed program manager because you previously worked for a company with a defined portfolio management process that was followed at all levels. The enterprise program management office (EPMO) and the CEO agree on the need for a company-wide portfolio management process with accompanying tools and techniques. You have a long history of personal interest in portfolio management and have given presentations about its importance to program and project managers at several forums. Working with a small core team, you completed your program management plan and the other key subsidiary plans and also prepared a master schedule. It is now time for you to move into program execution. You should review the—

    a. Program scope statement
    b. Budget
    c. Schedule
    d. Program roadmap

76. Since you are the program manager for your company's new portfolio management system that also will interface with its program management information system, business development system, and financial management system and then you must introduce everyone in the company to follow the portfolio management process at all levels, you have major challenges. You have a long history of personal interest in portfolio management and have given presentations about its importance to program and project managers at several forums. Working with a small core team, you completed your program management plan and the other key subsidiary plans and also prepared a master schedule. As your company follows the PMI® program management standard for guidance, you know lessons learned are an output of many program management processes. However, updates to lessons learned are an output of which of the following processes?

    a. Distribute Information
    b. Close Program
    c. Approve Component Transition
    d. Report Program Performance

77. You are the program manager for a program that is using multiple suppliers. Even though you have signed partnering agreements with each supplier, you know performance problems will surface, especially with this program because more than 75 percent of the work is being done by third-party suppliers. Also, your company has not worked with five of these suppliers in the past, and two are start-up companies. Many in your organization are interested in this program and especially how the integration efforts will be accomplished given the large number of suppliers involved. Once the integration efforts are finalized, and all the testing is done, the program will transition to an operations group. This means you need to prepare a(n)—

   a. Stakeholder management strategy
   b. Operational plan
   c. Updated transition plan
   d. Updated program management plan

78. Benefits management is both a top-down and a bottom-up process. A benefits realization plan is required for programs in your organization. You will be the manager for a new program to be implemented at the beginning of the corporation's fiscal year. This program is to design the next generation refrigerator that also can serve as a dishwasher and a stove with an oven so there is only one large appliance in one's home. It will use state-of-the-art technology but will be offered at an affordable price. The new appliance is to be designed to be attractive and also not to require much space. You want to concentrate on benefits management from the start. Now, as you define this program, you should—

   a. Derive expected benefits from the business case
   b. Analyze program results
   c. Focus on organizational benefits
   d. Ensure that project managers complete required deliverables

79. You are the program manager to restructure your department within your government agency. The head of the agency informed your sponsor that she wants to change the scope of the program so you will be working to restructure the entire agency instead of just one department. The Agency Administrator felt this change would be beneficial as the Agency also has to undergo some funding cuts in the next three fiscal years. Since most everyone is involved to some extent, there is extreme resistance to change, and many key stakeholders have been going directly to the Administrator and not to you as to why their department should not be part of the reorganization. You and your team are striving to gain the support of all stakeholders, both positive and negative. You decide to—

    a. Actively use your stakeholder register
    b. Conduct a questionnaire to get everyone in the agency involved in the process
    c. Conduct interviews with the heads of each of the departments and support offices
    d. Re-evaluate your stakeholder management plan

80. Your company is a leader in the pharmaceutical industry. It has received approval from the Food and Drug Administration (FDA) for a new drug that will cure all glaucoma conditions. Although demand for the product is high, your company has many other drugs to manufacture. You are managing a process to upgrade the manufacturing process, and your CEO has given you an aggressive schedule, especially so the glaucoma drug can reach its numerous possible patients. You have five projects in this program, and you are getting ready for your second gate review on it. Your governance board is one that is extremely proactive and it also holds a number of periodic health checks on your program in between these gate reviews. This is because—

    a. They want further involvement than just a possible four meetings
    b. They want to determine if the level of risk associated with this program remains acceptable especially given the lengthy regulatory process
    c. They want to assess performance against the strategic direction of the organization
    d. They want to assess performance against expected outcomes

81. You are the legacy system conversion program manager in your company. You need to upgrade the company's business development/sales tracking system, which was developed in C++. Your governance board recognizes the importance of improving other projects in this upgrade so there is an integrated system for all applications in your company. You now have projects in your program to also upgrade the accounting/financial management system, interface them to the program management information system, and add a knowledge management system. You have a complex program. Your stakeholder management plan now is complete. As you prepared this plan, you recognized that which of the following stakeholders' interests needed special consideration—

   a. Members of the Governance Board
   b. The Chief Information Officer
   c. The Chief Financial Officer
   d. Program sponsor

82. You are the legacy system conversion program manager in your company. You need to upgrade the company's business development/sales tracking system, which was developed in C++. Your governance board recognizes the importance of improving other projects in this upgrade so there is an integrated system for all applications in your company. You now have projects in your program to also upgrade the accounting/financial management system, interface them to the program management information system, and add a knowledge management system. You have a complex program. Your stakeholder management plan now is complete. Your next step is to determine how reports and other communications will be distributed to your various stakeholders. You therefore should now prepare—

   a. A communications log
   b. A communications management plan
   c. A stakeholder register
   d. A stakeholder engagement strategy

83. You are responsible for a major systems integration program that involves converting customer relationship management software, supplier management software, human resources software, and telecom systems from legacy systems to an integrated platform. The certified project managers have prepared detailed risk management plans for each project and have maintained and updated the risk register. You prepared a program risk response plan. Because of poor performance on two of the projects and by associated vendors, you needed to implement a number of preventive actions and workarounds. Your governance board asked you to prepare a component transition request for its next meeting to assess whether these two projects should continue. This request is an output of the—

    a. Direct and Manage Program Execution process
    b. Approve Component Transition process
    c. Integrated Change Control process
    d. Monitor and Control Program Changes process

84. You are responsible for a major systems integration program that involves converting customer relationship management software, supplier management software, human resources software, and telecom systems from legacy systems to an integrated platform. The certified project managers have prepared detailed risk management plans for each project and have maintained and updated the risk register. You prepared a program risk response plan. Because of poor performance on two of the projects and by associated vendors, you needed to implement a number of preventive actions and workarounds. However, this program is long and complex, and changes are inevitable. It is important to describe the scope, limitations, expectations, and business impact of the program along with a description of each project and its resources. This process is—

    a. The purpose of the scope change control system
    b. Part of the scope statement
    c. Part of the scope management plan
    d. The purpose of the Monitor and Control Program Scope process

85. You are the program manager for a new accounting system that will affect more than 500 accounting professionals in 10 locations. You have a core team of five people, and your preliminary schedule shows that in month 13, the transition of your system to the users will begin. This aggressive schedule recently was made even more difficult as every program in your company will have a five percent budget cut; this means it will be even harder for you to get the key subject matter experts you need when you need them. You have a Governance Board for your program. It is important before you submit a recommendation to formally close the program to the Board that you—

    a. Ensure the members of the operations group are actively involved in the program from the start

    b. Provide extensive job aids to the people who will be responsible for running the program once it is completed

    c. Document your final lessons learned after you submit a performance report

    d. Review the program's transition plan

86. You are the program manager to restructure your department within your government agency. The head of the agency informed your sponsor that she wants to change the scope of the program so you will be working to restructure the entire agency instead of just one department. The Agency Administrator felt this change would be beneficial as the Agency also has to undergo some funding cuts in the next three fiscal years. Since most everyone is involved to some extent, there is extreme resistance to change, and many key stakeholders have been going directly to the Administrator and not to you as to why their department should not be part of the reorganization. Based on these discussions, you met with the Administrator today along with your program sponsor and learned she had agreed with one of the department heads that her unit would be excluded from any part of the reorganization. You have now decided it would be beneficial to—

    a. Use a stakeholder impact and issue tracking an prioritization tool

    b. Work with a mentor to update your own negotiation and influencing skills as you work with negative stakeholders on this program

    c. Conduct another stakeholder analysis since this one department is to be excluded

    d. Set up specific channels of communications

87. You have been appointed as manager for a new program in your organization. This program will receive $250,000 as an initial investment; $175,000 at the beginning of year 2; $150,000 at the beginning of year 3; and $125,000 at the beginning of year 4. The program will start with a core team of seven senior managers; three project managers will be added during year 2, and two more project managers during year 3. While you work on this program, it is essential to ensure you can—

    a. Identify and evaluate integration opportunities and needs
    b. Set up a PMO for overall support, especially in administrative requirements
    c. Focus in your planning first on a bottom-up approach and then integrate it with a top-down approach
    d. First address the program's vision and justification

88. Wanting to make sure that existing lessons learned from every project and program undertaken in your organization are actually captured and used, you have received approval from your Portfolio Selection Committee to establish a program in knowledge management for your services company. The purpose is not only to record these lessons learned in an easily accessible fashion but to also make sure they are used by future program and project managers. You have identified four projects so far that will be part of this program. You recognize for this program to have visibility among the executives of your company that the mission, vision, and strategic fit of the program must be aligned with the organization's objectives. This is done as part of the—

    a. Pre-Program Preparations phase
    b. Program Initiation phase
    c. Program Setup phase
    d. Benefits identification phase

89. You are the program manager for a new accounting system that will affect more than 500 accounting professionals in 10 locations. You have a core team of five people, and your preliminary schedule shows that in month 13, the transition of your system to the users will begin. This aggressive schedule recently was made even more difficult as every program in your company will have a five percent budget cut; this means it will be even harder for you to get the key subject matter experts you need when you need them. You have a Governance Board for your program. Possible members of your Governance Board were first identified—

    a. As a section in the governance plan
    b. At the time the business case was developed
    c. As part of the program management plan
    d. At the end of the program initiation phase

90. Rarely have hurricanes reached northern states in the United States until the past two years. People there are not equipped to deal with them and do not want to purchase hurricane shutters or hurricane-resistant glass. Instead, they want a simple approach to be able to enclose their home in the event of a hurricane that they would use one time. Therefore, the product also needs to be priced inexpensively as it will only be effective once. You are leading a program to develop this product. Your company approved its business case quickly as they recognize the product will have a high market demand. Your program has executive support, and you have a governance board that meets at least monthly to track your progress. During the last three meetings, you recognized that the Chief Financial Officer or a delegate from his office did not attend the meetings. Metrics to measure performance of stakeholder engagement activities, such as meetings, are contained in the—

a. Communications log
b. Stakeholder engagement strategy
c. Stakeholder management plan
d. Stakeholder register

91. Working on an internal program to restructure your company so it is more customer facing is a major challenge. No one ever likes reorganizations, and many people fear they will lose their jobs as a result of your program. However, it has relied on its existing customer base for its 20 year life, and a new focus is part of the company's strategic plan to attract new customers and enter new markets. As you plan your program, so far you have identified three projects, and you are to complete the reorganization in six months. It is especially important to identify the types of program resources that will be required for effective management at the program level and with the governance function. A useful tool and technique to use is—

a. Capacity planning
b. Resource assignment matrix
c. Resource pool description
d. Component analysis

92. Working on an internal program to restructure your company so it is more customer facing is a major challenge. No one ever likes reorganizations, and many people fear they will lose their jobs as a result of your program. However, it has relied on its existing customer base for its 20 year life, and a new focus is part of the company's strategic plan to attract new customers and enter new markets. As you plan your program, so far you have identified three projects, and you are to complete the reorganization in six months. While you recognize the importance of using the Monitor and Control Program Financials process to be a way to keep costs within budget, of equal importance, however, is the need to—

   a. Identify opportunities
   b. Provide information to stakeholders based on information requests
   c. Regularly update the cost management plan and the overall program management plan
   d. Recommend preventive actions

93. Your company is a leader in the pharmaceutical industry. It has received approval from the Food and Drug Administration (FDA) for a new drug that will cure all glaucoma conditions. Although demand for the product is high, your company has many other drugs to manufacture. You are managing a process to upgrade the manufacturing process, and your CEO has given you an aggressive schedule, especially so the glaucoma drug can reach its numerous possible patients. Many people who have responsibility for other drugs in your company are concerned that once your manufacturing upgrade program is complete, the production of the glaucoma drug will be given preferential treatment, and their products will not be produced in sufficient quantities. You and your team realize you have a large number of stakeholders, and many of them are negative toward your program. This means you need to foster use of—

   a. Leadership skills
   b. Management skills
   c. Strategic visioning skills
   d. Political skills

94. Your company is a leader in the pharmaceutical industry. It has received approval from the Food and Drug Administration (FDA) for a new drug that will cure all glaucoma conditions. Although demand for the product is high, your company has many other drugs to manufacture. You are managing a process to upgrade the manufacturing process, and your CEO has given you an aggressive schedule, especially so the glaucoma drug can reach its numerous possible patients. Many people who have responsibility for other drugs in your company are concerned that once your manufacturing upgrade program is complete, the production of the glaucoma drug will be given preferential treatment, and their products will not be produced in sufficient quantities. You and your team realize you have a large number of stakeholders. Of course you require a number of interpersonal skills, but the most important one is—

    a. Leadership skills
    b. Communications skills
    c. Strategic visioning skills
    d. Political skills

95. Your company is a leader in the pharmaceutical industry. It has received approval from the Food and Drug Administration (FDA) for a new drug that will cure all glaucoma conditions. Although demand for the product is high, your company has many other drugs to manufacture. You are managing a process to upgrade the manufacturing process, and your CEO has given you an aggressive schedule, especially so the glaucoma drug can reach its numerous possible patients. Many people who have responsibility for other drugs in your company are concerned that once your manufacturing upgrade program is complete, the production of the glaucoma drug will be given preferential treatment, and their products will not be produced in sufficient quantities. You and your team realize you have a large number of stakeholders; many seem to be negative toward your program. Given this situation, your best course of action should be to—

    a. Focus on customer expectations
    b. Proceed according to your program management plan
    c. Establish buy-in from all stakeholders to ensure program success
    d. Escalate this issue to your Governance Board to seek assistance in dealing with these stakeholders

96. You are the program manager for a new accounting system that will affect more than 500 accounting professionals in 10 locations. You have a core team of five people, and your preliminary schedule shows that in month 13, the transition of your system to the users will begin. You have three projects that comprise your program. This aggressive schedule recently was made even more difficult as every program in your company will have a five percent budget cut; this means it will be even harder for you to get the key subject matter experts (SME) you need when you need them. You have a Governance Board for your program. Today, you had your regularly scheduled status meeting with Project Manager A. He told you he needed a key SME earlier than anticipated because of a new technological risk that had occurred. You were able to negotiate for this SME by meeting later with Project Manager C and getting the SME reassigned for two months to Project A. This was handled appropriately by Project Manager A as he—

    a. Immediately reported the problem to you
    b. Followed the issue escalation process
    c. Realized that the SME was on Project Manager C's team and notified you accordingly
    d. Asked Human Resources where he might locate a SME before contacting you

97. You were appointed program manager early in your program's life cycle, and you are leading the development of the benefits realization plan. As a best practice, each time a new person joins your core program team, you review the benefits realization plan with this staff member. To promote buy-in and commitment, you encourage your project managers to do the same. To ensure that the benefits process is followed, you should—

    a. Conduct benefits reviews
    b. Appoint a benefits realization manager
    c. Conduct a phase-gate review
    d. Meet with the governance board periodically

98. You are meeting with your company's Program Selection Committee. Because your company has limited resources, you are selecting one of two programs to undertake. The return on investment (ROI) and payback periods for the programs are basically identical, so you are focusing on the overall benefits of the programs. The benefits of Program A are a reduction in cost, increased revenue, and improved cash management. These benefits are—

    a. Tangible
    b. Financial
    c. Indirect
    d. Intangible

99. As you work as the program manager to establish Centers of Excellence in your global company on every continent except Antarctica, you have a large number of stakeholders who are interested in your program. You also have 12 different projects and know others will be added as the program continues. Your team, therefore, is a large virtual one and you hold conference calls regularly, rotating the times in which they are held so no one is always inconvenienced. You also do a lot of traveling to the various sites. You realize you as well as your project managers must be excellent communicators on this program. These communications skills are a tool and technique in which one of the following processes?

    a. Direct and Manage Program Execution
    b. Plan Communications
    c. Distribute Information
    d. Engage Program Stakeholders

100. You are the legacy system conversion program manager in your company. You need to upgrade the company's business development/sales tracking system, which was developed in C++. Your governance board recognizes the importance of improving other projects in this upgrade so there is an integrated system for all applications in your company. You now have projects in your program to also upgrade the accounting/financial management system, interface them to the program management information system, and add a knowledge management system. You have a complex program. You feel fortunate to have a proactive governance board because the board can assist in—

    a. Managing quality across the life cycle
    b. Ensuring you have the most competent people assigned to your program
    c. Enabling you to use a benchmarking forum with other organizations that have done similar programs
    d. Providing you with direct access to the senior executives in your company as needed.

101. Assume that your organization specializes in programs to handle conferences for government agencies. Each conference tends to attract about 800 to 1,000 people throughout the country in different locations. Each conference is a separate program as it involves different agencies, subject matter, themes, and speakers. Your company handles all the logistical requirements and basically is transparent to the agencies for which it works. Most of your programs, therefore, are initiated as a result of—

    a. The company's mission statement
    b. A decision to bid for a contract
    c. Investments in new technology
    d. The desire to remain competitive in the field

102. Assume that your organization specializes in programs to handle conferences for government agencies. Each conference tends to attract about 800 to 1,000 people throughout the country in different locations. Each conference is a separate program as it involves different agencies, subject matter, themes, and speakers. Your company handles all the logistical requirements and basically is transparent to the agencies for which it works. The executive sponsor has important responsibilities in program management in each conference. At the executive level, this person has primary responsibility for providing resources and ensuring program success. The sponsor is identified—

    a. When the business case for the program is presented
    b. Before program initiation
    c. In the Program Initiation phase of the program management life cycle
    d. In the Pre-Program Preparations process

103. Assume that your organization specializes in programs to handle conferences for government agencies. Each conference tends to attract about 800 to 1,000 people throughout the country in different locations. Each conference is a separate program as it involves different agencies, subject matter, themes, and speakers. Your company handles all the logistical requirements and basically is transparent to the agencies for which it works. The executive sponsor has important responsibilities in program management in each conference. You are the program manager for the upcoming conference on portfolio management for government agency representatives. This conference is expected to attract about 200 people as each agency will send at least five people to it, many of whom will be political appointees. You realize as you plan this program, with your five identified projects in it thus far, that changes are inevitable. In your program planning, you want to include a process that states how change requests will be processed. This should be included as part of your—

    a. Integrated Change Control Plan
    b. Scope Management Plan
    c. Performance Reporting process
    d. Scope Control Plan

104. You are the legacy system conversion program manager in your company. You need to upgrade the company's business development/sales tracking system, which was developed in C++. Your governance board recognizes the importance of improving other projects in this upgrade so there is an integrated system for all applications in your company. You now have projects in your program to also upgrade the accounting/financial management system, interface them to the program management information system, and add a knowledge management system. You have a complex program. You prepared the structure for your governance board and its meeting schedules as part of the—

    a. Overall governance framework
    b. Gate review requirements established by the Enterprise Program Management Office
    c. Governance plan
    d. Program management plan

105. A program may produce different types of benefits: tangible, intangible, or both. You are making a decision as an executive sponsor about whether or not to undertake a new product development program. As you review the identified benefits, you note that a number of them are intangible. You ask the program sponsor to prioritize them to facilitate your review. This can best be done by—

    a. Structuring their delivery
    b. Showing their contribution to business objectives
    c. Defining them in terms of stakeholder expectations
    d. Understanding their dependencies

106. You are managing a complex training program in your company. It has a number of component projects plus some ongoing work especially in logistical areas. Your team consists of instructional system design specialists who support the program on a full-time basis. For each training project, you need the services of subject-matter experts (SMEs) to complement the instructional designers. Assume that you met today with the manager of Functional Unit C in your company, and she agreed to release two chemists to support Project D in your program. You now need to—

    a. Meet with Project Manager D and inform him that you have acquired the needed SMEs
    b. Transition the SMEs to the program position
    c. Determine how this assignment can benefit the SMEs in their career path
    d. Update the program resource plan

107. You are the legacy system conversion program manager in your company. You need to upgrade the company's business development/sales tracking system, which was developed in C++. Your governance board recognizes the importance of improving other projects in this upgrade so there is an integrated system for all applications in your company. You now have projects in your program to also upgrade the accounting/financial management system, interface them to the program management information system, and add a knowledge management system. You have a complex program. Thus far, you have passed gate 3 and are executing your program. Because the executing phase in the life cycle will last over a year, your governance board is holding periodic performance reviews with you and your team on a bi-monthly basis. As you conduct these reviews, a best practice to follow is to—

    a. Provide key performance indicators to attendees before the meeting is held
    b. Hold pre-meetings with each board member to better understand his or her concerns
    c. Ensure your expected benefits are in line with your original business plan
    d. Start with a high-level overview of the program

108. In managing a program, you terminated three contracts that supported your projects. One of the contractors went bankrupt, and the other two were unable to deliver as promised. To avoid similar problems in the future, your company's enterprise program management office (EPMO) plans to conduct reviews of each supplier's performance. These reviews are important because—

    a. They may be the last time for recourse for performance deficiencies
    b. They are inputs to the Close Program Procurements process
    c. They are outputs of the Close Program Procurements process
    d. Contractual terms and conditions need to be revised

109. Assume that you just finished a meeting with your Program's Governance Board. It was not a stage gate review but was a more informal health check as several of the key stakeholders were concerned that a key milestone had been missed and an incremental benefit from the program now would be delayed. They also were concerned that missing this milestone may lead to missing future milestones. Unfortunately, you are not using earned value on your program, but when you prepared your benefits realization plan, you did include a number of metrics that you and your core team have been tracking. To ensure continual realization of the intended benefits and to reassure your stakeholders and the Governance Board members that the program is not in trouble, you and your team have used which of the following techniques before taking corrective action—

    a. Delphi technique
    b. Decision trees
    c. Brainstorming
    d. Causal analysis

110. You are the program manager for a new accounting system that will affect more than 500 accounting professionals in 10 locations. You have a core team of five people and your preliminary schedule shows that in month 13, the transition of your system to the users will begin. This aggressive schedule recently was made even more difficult as every program in your company will have a five percent budget cut; this means it will be even harder for you to get the key subject matter experts you need when you need them. You have a Governance Board for your program, and you have set up a stakeholder register. You and your team are using the register to—

    a. Provide an inventory of how each type of stakeholder will be impacted the program
    b. Provide a way to make sure the key stakeholders remain engaged in the program
    c. Show how best to manage the impacts of the program on stakeholders
    d. Report and distribute program deliverables and formal and informal communications

111. You are the program manager for a new accounting system that will affect more than 500 accounting professionals in 10 locations. You have a core team of five people, and your preliminary schedule shows that in month 13, the transition of your system to the users will begin. This aggressive schedule recently was made even more difficult as every program in your company will have a five percent budget cut; this means it will be even harder for you to get the key subject matter experts you need when you need them. You have a Governance Board for your program, and you have set up a stakeholder register. To help prepare this register since this program involves organizational change you and your team found which of the following techniques to be the most useful—

    a. Brainstorming
    b. Organizational analysis
    c. Interviews
    d. Program impact analysis

112. You are the legacy system conversion program manager in your company. You need to upgrade the company's business development/sales tracking system, which was developed in C++. Your governance board recognizes the importance of improving other projects in this upgrade so there is an integrated system for all applications in your company. You now have projects in your program to also upgrade the accounting/financial management system, interface them to the program management information system, and add a knowledge management system. You have a complex program. Thus far, you have passed gate 3 and are executing your program. This means you have had two gate reviews. Additionally, you have had eight periodic performance review sessions with the board members. A best practice to follow is to—

    a. Document each decision made
    b. Prepare meeting minutes and distribute them to all stakeholders after each session
    c. Focus on ensuring your program management plan is being followed
    d. Ensure adequate oversight is being provided

113. You are the program manager to restructure your department within your government agency. The head of the agency informed your sponsor that she wants to change the scope of the program so you will be working to restructure the entire agency instead of just one department. The Agency Administrator felt this change would be beneficial as the Agency also has to undergo some funding cuts in the next three fiscal years. Since the magnitude of this program is so great and to avoid the rumor mill as much as possible, you are holding meetings every two weeks that are recorded and made available to everyone in the Agency as to your progress. You are requesting comments from people throughout the Agency after each meeting. You feel these meetings can better help you understand the urgency and probability of stakeholder-related risks so basically you are—

    a. Updating your stakeholder register
    b. Updating your communications log
    c. Striving to focus on risks as opportunities
    d. Conducting a program impact analysis

114. Working in portfolio management and helping program sponsors prepare the business case for new programs in your chemical company, you want to make sure each program supports at least one of the objectives in your company's five year strategic plan. You encourage one program sponsor to meet with the strategic planners to make sure there is alignment and also to make sure the strategic planners do not expect any major changes in the next three years, the proposed length of the sponsor's program. One best practice is to prepare a high-level roadmap and continue to use it during the program. However, a disadvantage of the roadmap is—

    a. People believe it is the program's schedule
    b. It is difficult to keep its information current and relevant
    c. It typically is not possible to balance the timing of program demands with resource availability
    d. It is hard to use it to provide senior and program managers with a view of the programs in the portfolio over time

115. Working as the program manager for Guenther, Germany's water-alleviation program, you are pleased you have such a challenging assignment. Fortunately, you have an outstanding core team of five subject matter experts and a Program Management Office to support you. So far, you have three projects in your program. As you create your program work breakdown structure (PWBS), decomposition is useful to identify program deliverables and related work. The decomposition process is complete when—

    a. Each phase of the program life cycle has been detailed
    b. The program manager has the desired level of control
    c. The work packages of the various projects in the program have been identified
    d. Verifiable products, services, or results from each project have been determined

116. Working as the program manager for Guenther, Germany's water-alleviation program, you are pleased you have such a challenging assignment. Fortunately, you have an outstanding core team of five subject matter experts and a Program Management Office to support you. So far, you have three projects in your program. Continuing to work on your water-alleviation program in Guenther, Germany, you and your team now have prepared your program's work breakdown structure. This turned out to be a far more difficult process than you imagined because in the past, you had templates you could use to assist you in preparing the PWBS. However, you and your team completed it, and now you have also prepared a WBS matrix. It is used to—

    a. Cross-reference each program work breakdown structure (PWBS) component to other PWBS components
    b. Relate the PWBS to the program organizational breakdown structure (OBS) through a common code of account identifier
    c. Use the PWBS to manage resources with a link to the Bill of Materials
    d. Provide a graphical depiction of the work elements

117. You are pleased to be the program manager for the Guenther, Germany's water alleviation program. You have assembled your core team and have a PMO. You also have met individually with your key stakeholders. You regularly communicate with your program sponsor. So far, you have three projects in your program. This program has high priority for your company and is ranked #2 on the portfolio list. Everyone is aware of its importance. Considering the various phases in the program life cycle, which one may be of unlimited duration?

    a. Execution
    b. Benefits realization
    c. Delivery of the program benefits
    d. Monitoring and controlling the program's components

118. As the program manager for the Guenther, Germany's water alleviation program, you have many challenges. Fortunately, you have assembled your core team and have a PMO. You also have met individually with your key stakeholders. You regularly communicate with your program sponsor. So far, you have three projects in your program. One challenge of course is the aggressive schedule you must meet and the high priority of this program in your company's portfolio. You also have a number of technical SMEs on your program, who seem to want to really work on technical topics in a functional environment. Also, as program manager you must work with stakeholders at all levels as well as with your team and your governance board. Your flexibility is limited by—

    a. Communication channels
    b. Constraints
    c. Assumptions
    d. Benefits analysis

119. For Guenther, Germany's water-alleviation program, you have many challenges. Fortunately, you have assembled your core team and have a PMO. You also have met individually with your key stakeholders. You regularly communicate with your program sponsor. So far, you have three projects in your program. Your core team uses earned value at the program package level. Your cost performance index (CPI) is at 0.67, although the schedule performance index (SPI) is at 0.88. Your team recognizes the cost overrun and the fact that you are only 15 percent into the program. The team revises the Estimate to Complete, and you present the revision to your governance board. The Estimate to Complete is—

    a. A forecast
    b. A trend
    c. Atypical
    d. An inappropriate technique at this time

120. You have been managing Guenther, Germany's water alleviation program for three years. Fortunately, you have had an outstanding your core team and have a PMO. Your project managers have diligently completed their projects, and their deliverables have been accepted by the City. Now, the program is officially complete, as all deliverables have been accepted by the City. Your next step is to—

   a. Prepare your closure report
   b. Archive your program records
   c. Meet with the customer for a closure review
   d. Obtain a signed final acceptance from the customer

121. You are the director of your telecommunications company's enterprise project management office (PMO). Your company has more than 200 projects under way, and you are considering managing some of them as a program. It took about six months to even determine how many projects were in process as many people felt if they described every project they worked on, their "pet" project that they felt would really benefit the company might be canceled. Obtaining the trust of the project professionals was a major challenge, but you believe you have an inventory now of all the project work. As you move into program management, which of the following is best suited to manage as a program?

   a. Conducting a training class in program management
   b. Providing product support to a recently introduced cellular phone
   c. Developing the next-generation cellular phone and related products
   d. Preparing a marketing campaign to introduce the next phone when it is developed

122. In your role as program manager for your country's food safety department to ensure the safety of imported food in your country, you are facing a number of challenges. It seems as if more imported food is arriving rather than producing the food domestically. Many of the food products are totally new to your country. You lack the needed number of inspectors who have expertise in some of the exotic food that now is being imported, and you are implementing a Hazard Analysis Critical Control Program approach as part of this important program. You realized you needed a governance board to assist in ensuring your program continued to meet the Department's strategic objectives. As you prepared your governance plan, the main foundation for its structure and organization was provided by—

   a. The strategic directive for the program
   b. The program's executive sponsor
   c. The program's priority in the Department's portfolio
   d. The Department's organizational chart

123. You are managing a program to develop a new source of energy to use in the tropics when solar power is not available. Working with your core program team and your governance board, you identify a number of component projects. However, several other key projects are under way in your company, and resources will be difficult to acquire for a new program. In determining whether you will use internal or external resources, you should consider—

    a. When the resources will be needed
    b. Your ability to negotiate with functional managers for the needed staff
    c. Previous work by the staff as a successful team
    d. The need to advertise for the open positions

124. You are managing a program to develop a new source of energy to use in the tropics when solar power is not available. Working with your core program team and your governance board, you identify a number of component projects. You also have identified some non-project activities. Analysis of program costs must be performed, although some overlook the need to consider the non-program/non-project cost activities. You are, however, analyzing them on your program as you believe doing so is a best practice for program and project managers. Accordingly, they—

    a. Should be tracked outside the program's budget
    b. Are a tool and technique of the Monitor and Control Program Financials process
    c. Are part of earned value management as a tool and technique in the Monitor and Control Program Financials process
    d. Are handled by the performing organization at the portfolio level

125. Assume you have sponsored a program to develop a new stent for coronary patients that is based on new laser technology and that will only take 30 minutes from the time the patient actually enters the hospital. Then, the patient will be able to be discharged and resume normal activities as if nothing happened. The patient will not experience any side effects from this new approach. You have obtained approval from your Executive Committee to develop this program in more detail so you are now in the initiating process. Your first step is to—

    a. Authorize the program
    b. Authorize the project
    c. Initiate the program
    d. Define the program

126. Assume you have sponsored a program to develop a new stent for coronary patients that is based on new laser technology and that will only take 30 minutes from the time the patient actually enters the hospital. Then, the patient will be able to be discharged and resume normal activities as if nothing happened. The patient will not experience any side effects from this new approach. Your sponsor selected you to manage this key program to your company. As a project manager, when you prepared your schedule, you focused on identifying activities on your critical path and managing them aggressively. You have been promoted to program manager. Your focus now is on—

    a. Estimating program activity duration
    b. Using a critical chain to incorporate buffers and manage drum resources that affect your component projects
    c. Identifying interdependences among the constituent projects
    d. Performing "what if" analyses to ensure that the key stakeholders' expectations for program deliverables are met

127. Recently, a member of your core team on your program for the next generation air traffic control system in your country obtained his Risk Management Professional credential from the Project Management Institute. While you and your core team spent time early in the program preparing a risk management plan, which was approved by your Governance Board, and you have been maintaining a program risk register, this core team member felt you and the other team members needed to perform another in depth session identifying risks given that the program had slightly changed direction during the past year and had added one more project than planned. Also, the Administrator of your government agency resigned to take a position in industry, and the new Administrator is more risk adverse, especially where new technology is involved. You have a choice of different technologies to employ. As you considered each one in terms of possible risks, you and your team used which of the following techniques to best make a recommendation to the Administrator and the core team in terms of overall program benefits—

    a. Sensitivity analysis
    b. Modeling through Monte Carlo simulation
    c. Decision-tree analysis
    d. Risk urgency analysis

128. In developing your benefit realization plan for this air traffic control upgrade system, you and your core team set it up in order that you would have specific metrics in place to help monitor the actual realization of the benefits throughout the program. The plan includes both tangible and intangible benefits of this major program. While the tangible benefits are easy to monitor, you now are finding the intangible benefits to be a challenge. One approach that has been useful to you so far is to use—

    a. Business value measurement
    b. Total cost of ownership
    c. Cost of quality
    d. Trend analysis

129. In your role as program manager for your country's food safety department to ensure the safety of imported food in your country, you are facing a number of challenges. It seems as if more imported food is arriving rather than producing the food domestically. Many of the food products are totally new to your country. You lack the needed number of inspectors who have expertise in some of the exotic food that now is being imported, and you are implementing a Hazard Analysis Critical Control Program approach as part of this important program. You realized you needed a governance board to assist in ensuring your program continued to meet the Department's strategic objectives. Your sponsor agreed and assisted you in preparing a governance plan and also obtained commitments from senior level executives in the Department to be board members. As you worked on your plan, you realized a key activity that occurs within governance is—

    a. Resource management
    b. Issue management
    c. Resource identification
    d. Transition planning

130. You are a member of your company's Program Selection Committee, which is deciding which program to pursue in consideration of the company's limited resources. Your company prides itself on time to market as an attribute that distinguishes it from its competitors in the automobile parts field. Each program has prepared a business case addressing its strategy, organization, process, metrics and tools, and culture. Proposed Program A will eliminate features if necessary in a trade-off situation; Proposed Program B will delay its schedule if necessary; Proposed Program C has a flexible structure to ensure innovative features at a minimum cost; and Proposed Program D will focus on technical, cost, and schedule in its metrics. Which program should be selected?

    a. Program A
    b. Program B
    c. Program C
    d. Program D

131. Assume you are managing a program in which individuals can purchase helicopters for personal transit to locations within a 50-mile radius of their homes. The objective is to use the helicopters to relieve traffic congestion as now to drive 50 miles as it generally takes at least two hours and possibly four hours to reach one's destination. You have worked on your program charter, and it has been approved. Now, you are working on your program's cost estimate. You traditionally have disliked estimating because you know almost every estimate turns out not to be accurate even if you have outstanding historical information to help you in this process and organizational templates. You just met with each of the project managers on this program and received individual estimates for their projects based on their WBS work packages. Your next step is to—

    a. Publish this cost estimate
    b. Meet with the key program stakeholders to review the estimates, ensure that nothing has been omitted, and obtain buy-in
    c. Prepare program and component cost estimates
    d. Work with the program manager to finalize the estimate to be submitted to the governance board

132. In your role as program manager for your country's food safety department to ensure the safety of imported food in your country, you are facing a number of challenges. It seems as if more imported food is arriving rather than producing the food domestically. Many of the food products are totally new to your country. You lack the needed number of inspectors who have expertise in some of the exotic food that now is being imported, and you are implementing a Hazard Analysis Critical Control Program approach as part of this important program. You realized you needed a governance board to assist in ensuring your program continued to meet the Department's strategic objectives. Your sponsor agreed and assisted you in preparing a governance plan and also obtained commitments from senior level executives in the Department to be board members. You had your first gate review, and the board approved your request to move to gate two in the review process. Minutes from the gate-review meeting are useful to—

    a. Highlight any risks
    b. Uncover alternatives as problems are identified
    c. Show any intermittent and inevitable failures are documented for future lessons learned
    d. Highlight effectiveness organizational processes and procedures

133. You are managing a program to build your country's new embassy, consulate, residences, and other facilities in the Republic of Sarsmania. It will be the largest construction project on the Isthmus of Rak, requiring more than 50 subcontractors working on 20 projects. To select the best subcontractors, the selection process criteria must be defined—

    a. At the program level
    b. At the project level
    c. By professionals in the construction business
    d. By local Sarsmanian officials

134. Managing a program to improve the services of your city government to elderly people, you have six projects in progress. Your program is to be completed in two years. You may have one or two additional projects as you are just in the first six months of this program. Project Manager B met with you today and requested a change to the scope of her project. She noted that this scope change also affected Projects A and E, which is why she is escalating it to you. The next step should be to—

    a. Convene a meeting of all six project managers to discuss the ramifications of this change
    b. Analyze the change request
    c. Ask a member of your core team to analyze the change request and determine its impact in terms of overall program benefits
    d. Meet with your Program Board to inform them of this change and receive their authorization to implement it

135. Rarely have hurricanes reached northern states in the United States until the past two years. People there are not equipped to deal with them and do not want to purchase hurricane shutters or hurricane-resistant glass. Instead, they want a simple approach to be able to enclose their home in the event of a hurricane that they would use one time. Therefore, the product also needs to be priced inexpensively as it will only be effective once. You are leading a program to develop this product. Your company approved its business case quickly as they recognize the product will have a high market demand. As you are the program manager, you want to keep all of your stakeholders apprised of your process on this program so you and your small team conducted a stakeholder analysis and prepared a stakeholder register. As you prepared this register, you wanted to have a detailed understanding of the impact of the program on stakeholders so therefore you used—

    a. Interviews
    b. Focus groups
    c. Questionnaires
    d. Organizational analysis

136. Rarely have hurricanes reached northern states in the United States until the past two years. People there are not equipped to deal with them and do not want to purchase hurricane shutters or hurricane-resistant glass. Instead, they want a simple approach to be able to enclose their home in the event of a hurricane that they would use one time. Therefore, the product also needs to be priced inexpensively as it will only be effective once. You are leading a program to develop this product. Your company approved its business case quickly as they recognize the product will have a high market demand. As you are the program manager you want to have available a comprehensive summary of how each stakeholder and stakeholder group will be impacted by this program so you prepare a—

    a. Stakeholder management plan
    b. Stakeholder register
    c. Stakeholder inventory
    d. Stakeholder management strategy

137. You are a member of your insurance company's Program Selection Committee, which is considering a number of possible programs to pursue. Each one has identified benefits that will support your company's overall strategic plan. Program A is estimated to cost $100,000 to implement and will have annual net cash inflows of $25,000; Program B is estimated to cost $250,000 to implement, with annual net cash inflows of $75,000; Program C is estimated to cost $300,000 to implement, with annual net cash inflows of $80,000; and Program D is estimated to cost $500,000 to implement, with annual net cash inflows of $225,000. You should recommend that your company select—

    a. Program A
    b. Program B
    c. Program C
    d. Program D

138. You are managing a program, BBB, for your manufacturing firm. You have decided that since you have five projects in your program (three were under way before the program officially began) that it makes sense to have an indefinite quantity contract to support additional resources that all five projects may require during the life cycle of the program rather than having each project have a separate contract for resource acquisition. A member of your core team will focus on administering this contract at the program level. The focus at the program level is on contracts such as this one that span the program domain and that—

    a. Involve high-risk items
    b. Have one provider that supports several projects
    c. Have service level agreements
    d. Involve contact with external organizations, such as the media, consumer groups, and advocacy organizations

139. You have just received approval from your Executive Team to begin to develop the next generation of stealth shield aircraft. You prepared a business case, which the Executive Team accepted, and it showed you could achieve a payback on your investment in this new program within three years. Before you received approval, you met individually with the various members of the Executive Team to address any concerns they may have and to be able to successfully address them during the Team's meeting. You received approval to begin to initiate this program. Now, you are preparing order-of-magnitude estimates of cost and—

    a. Resources
    b. Scope
    c. Risk
    d. Benefits

140. You have been the program manager for an aerospace company on its stealth shield aircraft program now for five years and officially closed the program. However, your product support team monitors the product from a reliability and availability-for-use perspective and compares it with the expected performance, which was predicted when the product was developed. The team cites a need to improve reliability and uncovers various anomalies in the software system. Your best approach in this situation is to—

    a. Use project management to perform the upgrade
    b. Contact the client and all stakeholders immediately
    c. Support this new problem independently of the program through an operations function in the company
    d. Relinquish the product support function to the client

141. You are the manager for a wind-energy program that will last for eight years. You identify a number of component projects and expect to add others as the program proceeds, especially since this program will last such a long time. Although you have fully staffed your program team, you realize that some of your core team members and project managers will leave the organization or your program for other opportunities. These activities are part of which one of the following processes?

    a. Develop Program Team
    b. Develop Program Infrastructure
    c. Manage Program Resources
    d. Manage Program Team

142. You are the program manager to restructure your department within your government agency. The head of the agency informed your sponsor that she wants to change the scope of the program so you will be working to restructure the entire agency instead of just one department. The Agency Administrator felt this change would be beneficial as the Agency also has to undergo some funding cuts in the next three fiscal years. Since the magnitude of this program is so great and to avoid the rumor mill as much as possible, you are holding meetings every two weeks that are recorded and made available to everyone in the Agency as to your progress. These meetings then may need to update the—

    a. Stakeholder management strategy
    b. Stakeholder register
    c. Stakeholder analysis
    d. Stakeholder inventory

143. You are a member of your energy services company's Program Selection Committee, which is considering a number of possible programs to pursue. Each one has identified benefits that will support your company's overall strategic plan. You have the following data on four possible programs. You may select only one because of resource limitations.

Program A NPV at	Program B NPV at	Program C NPV at	Program D NPV at
5% = 3,524	5% = 2,201	5% = 6,400	5% = 3,055
10% = 2,901	10% = 2,254	10% = 3,275	10% = 2,857
15% = 1,563	15% = 1,632	15% = 1,679	15% = 1,125

Note: NPV = net present value.

You should recommend that your company select—

a. Program A
b. Program B
c. Program C
d. Program D

144. Assume you are the program manager to implement enterprise resource planning software in all the agencies in your province. This program would be difficult if it were limited to only one agency, but it is especially hard because you have 17 agencies in the process, and each one has its own legacy system that it uses. You will have to have a separate project for each agency as well as projects for training, implementation, and maintenance. This program thus will span several years and budget cycles. Obviously, you require a program financial plan as part of the program management plan. Among other things, it should address—

a. Baseline budget
b. Basis of estimates
c. Criteria for the program package plans
d. Proposed return on investment

145. Assume you are the program manager to implement enterprise resource planning software in all the agencies in your province. This program would be difficult if it were limited to only one agency, but it is especially hard because you have 17 agencies in the process, and each one has its own legacy system that it uses. You will have to have a separate project for each agency as well as projects for training, implementation, and maintenance. This program thus will span several years and budget cycles. You prepare a quality management plan to describe how the program's quality assurance and quality control processes will be handled. To ensure that each project manager follows a similar approach, you should use which one of the following tools and techniques?

    a. Standard templates
    b. Flowcharts
    c. Checklists
    d. Cost-benefit analysis

146. Assume you are the program manager to implement enterprise resource planning software in all the agencies in your province. This program would be difficult if it were limited to only one agency, but it is especially hard because you have 17 agencies in the process, and each one has its own legacy system that it uses. You will have to have a separate project for each agency as well as projects for training, implementation, and maintenance. This program thus will span several years and budget cycles. You need Six Sigma Black Belt experts to support your program. Two people in your company have this credential, but they are always busy. The executive director of your program governance board suggests that you explore local consulting firms. The best document to use to identify potential sellers is the—

    a. Request for information (RFI)
    b. Invitation to bid
    c. Contract terms and conditions
    d. Contract statement of work

147. Introducing program management to your electric company has been a challenge but is finally being embraced as executives to team members now are seeing that using programs can produce more benefits to the company and its customers than if projects were managed in a standalone way. One approach that has been useful to you in your role of leading this culture change in the electric company has been to prepare a benefits realization plan and to get it signed off by your sponsor, members of the Governance Board, and other key stakeholders. Your company also uses the balanced scorecard approach, and your benefits realization plan considered it when you developed it so the benefits are aligned to the scorecard. One benefit that is often overlooked is—

    a. Cost of quality
    b. New income
    c. Competitive advantage
    d. Risk avoidance

148. One of the first programs you managed at your electric company, DDD, was for a city in Draeger, New York. The purpose was to reduce the numerous power outages so that if a power outage occurred, residents in Draeger would only lose power momentarily until a backup system could be deployed to provide time for on-site personnel to arrive at the location and diagnose the problem and provide corrective action. When you prepared your benefits realization plan for this program early on, one of the items you included in it was—

    a. Review sessions to be held on a periodic basis by citizens of Draeger
    b. Methods to maximize citizen satisfaction in the program delivery
    c. Ways to ensure all stages of the program are managed in a way to satisfy the use of the program's outputs
    d. Overall business requirements, including scope and limitations

149. Since programs are established to attain more benefits than if the benefits were managed in a standalone fashion, identifying benefits as the business case for the program is prepared is essential. However, benefits management is difficult and often is overlooked. It also tends to require people with different types of skills and competencies. Once benefits are identified, they must be measured, tracked, and their results communicated. To do so, people require skills and competencies in—

    a. Marketing
    b. Trend analysis
    c. Scenario analysis
    d. Business strategy

150. Your organization receives an award for the construction of a new courthouse complex in the state capital of State A. Your company is located in State B, approximately 1,000 miles away, and has never worked in State A. You plan to use a number of contractors and to hire local people to support the program team. From time to time, you will need cranes. To facilitate acquiring these cranes, you should—

    a. Purchase the cranes
    b. Develop a qualified seller list
    c. Hold a bidders conference
    d. Issue a request for proposals (RFP)

151. Your organization receives an award for the construction of a new courthouse complex in the state capital of State A. Your company is located in State B, approximately 1,000 miles away, and has never worked in State A. You plan to use a number of contractors and to hire local people to support the program team. From time to time, you will need cranes. However, you always have some type of risks whenever you use contactors. Therefore, it is important as a best practice to—

    a. Only use contractors on the qualified seller list
    b. Perform a site visit to each contractor's headquarters to demonstrate to its leaders the importance of your program
    c. Have each contractor prepare a monthly performance report
    d. Manage risk in accordance with the risk management plan

152. Assume this is the first time you are managing a program. You have had success in your company in project management, and you are on a career path that now leads to program management. You are pleased to on track to future promotions and opportunities in your manufacturing company. On your program, you want to apply some of the successful best practices you used on your projects, recognizing the differences between programs and projects and their greater complexity. However, since you have been in project management for so long now in this company (17 years), you also know that—

    a. You need to prepare a comprehensive WBS for the program that includes the work of the projects
    b. You want to build your program schedule only after all the project schedules are complete
    c. You recognize the importance of qualifying and quantifying all possible risks
    d. You realize project stakeholders are also program stakeholders

153. You are managing a program that comprises new systems application development and maintenance activities. These applications are critical to your company, CDE, as they involve access to proprietary data. The systems must be available to your clients on a 24/7/365 basis. Much of the work on you program will be outsourced as you have an aggressive schedule to meet; fortunately CDE has a qualified vendor list to simplify the acquisition process. This program has high visibility in CDE and is a major change to the organization. Therefore, CDE's CEO decided to serve as the executive director of the program and chairs each meeting of your program's governance board. You are getting ready for a stage gate meeting to move into phase 3 in your gate review process. Before you approach the governance board for a final decision, you should—

   a. Set up a process to meet with members of each governance board's staff for a pre-meeting
   b. Review your program issues register
   c. Follow the Monitor and Control Program's change process
   d. Follow the distribute information process

154. You are managing a program that comprises new systems application development and maintenance activities. These applications are critical to your company, CDE, as they involve access to proprietary data. The systems must be available to your clients on a 24/7/365 basis. Much of the work on you program will be outsourced as you have an aggressive schedule to meet; fortunately CDE has a qualified vendor list to simplify the acquisition process. This program has high visibility in CDE, and is a major change to the organization. Therefore, CDE's CEO decided to serve as the executive director of the program and chairs each meeting of your program's governance board. One way to serve as a check and balance on the governance board's decision process is to—

   a. Have a member of the board who also serves as a member of the organization's Portfolio Management Board to ensure the program is in alignment with strategic objectives
   b. Use audit reports
   c. Use expert judgment
   d. Have a change management specialist as a board member

155. In determining whether it is better to use program management or project management, the culture of the organization should be considered. Your organization is considering implementation of program management, and you are leading a team to recommend this approach to your CEO and other members of the executive team. One of your arguments for the change is that the organization's culture has transitioned so that it is now characterized by—

   a. A specialist level of business expertise
   b. A strong connection between execution output and strategic objectives
   c. A lower dependency between cross-discipline specialties in the organization
   d. Less need for a time-to-money improvement

156. You are managing a program that comprises new systems application development and maintenance activities. These applications are critical to your company, CDE, as they involve access to proprietary data. The systems must be available to your clients on a 24/7/365 basis. Much of the work on you program will be outsourced as you have an aggressive schedule to meet; fortunately CDE has a qualified vendor list to simplify the acquisition process. This program has high visibility in CDE, and is a major change to the organization. Therefore, CDE's CEO decided to serve as the executive director of the program and chairs each meeting of your program's governance board. Before Board meetings are held to review program performance, your board members have asked you to submit—

   a. Benefit realization reports
   b. Estimate to complete data
   c. To-complete performance index data
   d. Financial reports

157. Now that you have moved into this program management role in your manufacturing company, you realize your work really involves active involvement with stakeholders at a variety of levels. It is also compounded because on your program you have external stakeholders involved and need to spend time communicating with them. It seems as if each time you pass a stage gate review, the number of stakeholders increases, or people who lacked interest in the program now are interested. Therefore, the primary skill to best manage stakeholders—

   a. Negotiation
   b. Conflict management
   c. Communications
   d. Influencing

158. One of the project managers in your program has told you that although he did a thorough job of risk management planning, a new risk has emerged that has major negative ramifications for the project. This risk could also affect another project in the program, as it involves a lack of critical resources. Another project manager tells you that he will need this same resource on his project, although he did not consider it during resource planning. In this situation, you should—

    a. Implement your contingency reserve to hire needed resources to supportthese projects
    b. Propose a solution to these risks escalated by the project managers
    c. Ask each project manager to revise his risk register to add these risks and to use a workaround
    d. Revise your program work breakdown structure (PWBS) accordingly, because this risk shows that a key planning package is missing

159. You are a member of your organization's Program Selection Committee. The company's strategic plan includes five major goals, which are all weighted equally. Goal 1 is to fall within the time-to-market window; goal 2 is to reduce operational costs; goal 3 is to differentiate the products from others on the market; goal 4 is to deliver the highest-quality product; and goal 5 is to promote economic sustainability. At the next committee meeting, you will consider four programs and recommend one. Program A partially supports goal 1, fully supports goals 2–4, and does not support goal 5. Program B fully supports goals 1, 3, 4, and 5, but does not support goal 2. Program C fully supports goals 1 and 2, partially supports goals 3 and 4, but does not support goal 5. Program D partially supports goals 1, 2, and 5, and fully supports goals 3 and 4. With this information, which program will you recommend?

    a. Program A
    b. Program B
    c. Program C
    d. Program D

160. You are managing a complex program to develop the next-generation submarine. It is planned to replace the existing non-nuclear submarines in your country with nuclear weapons. It is estimated to take about nine years to complete as you will be using new technology now not available in your country. The program includes a number of projects, and you plan to use subcontractors extensively. You also plan contracts for services or for insurance to protect the program. For these contracts, you need to—

a. Use qualified seller lists
b. Document the relevant parties' responsibilities regarding risk
c. Prepare a contract administration plan
d. Prepare component cost estimates

161. You are managing a program that comprises new systems application development and maintenance activities. These applications are critical to your company, CDE, as they involve access to proprietary data. The systems must be available to your clients on a 24/7/365 basis. Much of the work on you program will be outsourced as you have an aggressive schedule to meet; fortunately CDE has a qualified vendor list to simplify the acquisition process. This program has high visibility in CDE, and is a major change to the organization. Therefore, CDE's CEO decided to serve as the executive director of the program and chairs each meeting of your program's governance board. Governance oversight needs to be an internal-looking practice in order to—

a. Ensure budgetary issues can be discussed
b. Make sure proprietary information is not disclosed inadvertently
c. Promote continuous improvement
d. Protect intellectual property

162. Your organization recently conducted an Organizational Project Management Maturity Assessment (*OPM3*). The assessment results and the improvement plan showed much work needed to be done in the area of portfolio management. It was especially apparent that many projects, and almost every program, lacked a defined business case that had been prepared by the sponsor and then approved and authorized by leadership. After receiving the reports from the *OPM3* assessor, you held a focus group of program sponsors to determine why business cases were not regularly prepared. It turned out many of the people in the focus group lacked an understanding of the benefits of preparing one. You explained that the primary benefit is to—

a. Establish alignment with strategic goals
b. Provide a perspective on how best to execute the program
c. Determine how the program will help the organization meet its business and strategic goals
d. Make the portfolio process more effective

163. Your organization announces that funds in all areas will be cut by 10 percent. Even though you are still in the planning stages and your program is a high priority for your company, your program is not exempt from the budget cuts. Management is interested in your program because it is required for the company's continued viability in the production of sport utility vehicles. Management has also mandated certain delivery dates that will be hard to meet with the budget cuts. As you decide which program components should be handled internally and which should be outsourced, you consider the—

   a. Product description
   b. Program scope statement
   c. Program budget allocations
   d. Risk management plan

164. Assume that your program for Draeger, New York is in its final stages. The purpose was to reduce the numerous power outages so that if a power outage occurred, residents in Draeger would only lose power momentarily until a backup system could be deployed to provide time for on-site personnel to arrive at the location and diagnose the problem and provide corrective action. Testing has been done, and recently, there was a power outage in one part of the City. The new power station's backup capability was available in less than two minutes. Few citizens even noticed that an outage had occurred. Technicians then arrived, and corrected the problem. It is now time to close this program and transition it to ongoing operations. Before doing so, a best practice is to—

   a. Review the program's scope statement
   b. Conduct a customer satisfaction survey
   c. Review the quality assurance plan
   d. Review the benefits realization plan

165. In determining whether to pursue a program, it is important to assess goals and objectives. In your new product development organization, of the triple constraint, quality and scope are the dominant. This does not imply the schedule and budget are not important, but given that the programs must achieve regulatory approval, quality dominates in the company. Quality goals that are too low may lead to customer and end-user dissatisfaction, whereas goals that are too high may result in a high cost to the business. Therefore, it is important to consider—

   a. Market needs and expectations
   b. The value proposition
   c. Cash-flow management
   d. Risk analysis and assessment

166. In determining whether to pursue a program, it is important to assess goals and objectives. In your new product development organization, of the triple constraint, quality and scope are the dominant. This does not imply the schedule and budget are not important, but given that the programs must achieve regulatory approval, quality dominates in the company. You have been appointed as the program manager for the next generation of cellular phones, with the code name of Scott. You will use a combination of internal and external resources to develop this phone. As part of your procurement management plan for this new product development program, you have explicitly stated the actions that you and your program team can take on its own and those that require involvement by or should be deferred to the Procurement or Contracting Department. As you prepare your procurement management plan, you need to—

    a. Review your program charter
    b. Review your resource management plan
    c. Obtain a delegation of procurement authority
    d. Review your stakeholder analysis chart

167. You are Company A's program manager for the development of an online banking system for your community bank. One of its objectives is to make sure all transactions are secure. Many people have said they will not use the online system in public WiFi areas and only will use it from secure locations in your home. You have a large team supporting you as program manager, and you have four projects thus far. Two of the project managers are new to your company and lack familiarity with the company's standard program management procedures. Because time and quality are of the essence in this program, you are need to make sure these two project managers understand what must be done to comply with the various procedures. Your best approach to do so is through—

    a. One-on-one meetings each day
    b. Developing an on-line training system to show all the various procedures to follow
    c. Using mentoring
    d. Using skills in creative thinking

168. You are Company A's program manager for the development of an online banking system for your community bank. One of its objectives is to make sure all transactions are secure. Many people have said they will not use the online system in public WiFi areas and only will use it from secure locations in your home. You have a large team supporting you as program manager, and you have four projects thus far. Two of the project managers are new to your company and lack familiarity with the company's standard program management procedures. You have set up a change management plan as you know programs involve change and with this program and its four projects, changes will occur. You especially want to use it to help control—

    a. Benefits
    b. Issues
    c. Quality
    d. Human resources

169. Assume you are sponsoring a proposed program. You have identified tangible benefits such as a one year payback period, a high return on investment, and an increase in productivity by 25 percent. Some of the intangible benefits that you have identified include an increase in employee morale with retention of intellectual property. You also believe it will contribute to knowledge sharing. You are getting ready to present your business case to the Portfolio Review Board. Before doing so, you want to make sure it has been completed properly so you first should—

    a. Present a cost/benefit analysis
    b. Describe the business opportunity and product, service, or result that you are proposing
    c. Identify the Key Performance Indicators
    d. Describe the high-level risks if the program is approved

170. Rarely have hurricanes reached northern states in the United States until the past two years. People there are not equipped to deal with them and do not want to purchase hurricane shutters or hurricane-resistant glass. Instead, they want a simple approach to be able to enclose their home in the event of a hurricane that they would use one time. Therefore, the product also needs to be priced inexpensively as it will only be effective once. You are leading a program to develop this product. Your company approved its business case quickly as they recognize the product will have a high market demand. You are pleased to be the program manager, and you will have a governance board to oversee the program and to approve its progress in the company's stage gate process. You are determining specific governance roles and responsibilities and to do so, you need to answer a number of questions such as—

   a. Who will ensure architectural principles are not violated?
   b. Who will ensure the level of risks remains acceptable to the organization?
   c. Who will ensure that a program management information system is established?
   d. Who will ensure the program supports the company's strategic plan?

Answer Sheet for Practice Test 2

1.	a	b	c	d	20.	a	b	c	d
2.	a	b	c	d	21.	a	b	c	d
3.	a	b	c	d	22.	a	b	c	d
4.	a	b	c	d	23.	a	b	c	d
5.	a	b	c	d	24.	a	b	c	d
6.	a	b	c	d	25.	a	b	c	d
7.	a	b	c	d	26.	a	b	c	d
8.	a	b	c	d	27.	a	b	c	d
9.	a	b	c	d	28.	a	b	c	d
10.	a	b	c	d	29.	a	b	c	d
11.	a	b	c	d	30.	a	b	c	d
12.	a	b	c	d	31.	a	b	c	d
13.	a	b	c	d	32.	a	b	c	d
14.	a	b	c	d	33.	a	b	c	d
15.	a	b	c	d	34.	a	b	c	d
16.	a	b	c	d	35.	a	b	c	d
17.	a	b	c	d	36.	a	b	c	d
18.	a	b	c	d	37.	a	b	c	d
19.	a	b	c	d	38.	a	b	c	d

39.	a	b	c	d
40.	a	b	c	d
41.	a	b	c	d
42.	a	b	c	d
43.	a	b	c	d
44.	a	b	c	d
45.	a	b	c	d
46.	a	b	c	d
47.	a	b	c	d
48.	a	b	c	d
49.	a	b	c	d
50.	a	b	c	d
51.	a	b	c	d
52.	a	b	c	d
53.	a	b	c	d
54.	a	b	c	d
55.	a	b	c	d
56.	a	b	c	d
57.	a	b	c	d
58.	a	b	c	d
59.	a	b	c	d
60.	a	b	c	d

61.	a	b	c	d
62.	a	b	c	d
63.	a	b	c	d
64.	a	b	c	d
65.	a	b	c	d
66.	a	b	c	d
67.	a	b	c	d
68.	a	b	c	d
69.	a	b	c	d
70.	a	b	c	d
71.	a	b	c	d
72.	a	b	c	d
73.	a	b	c	d
74.	a	b	c	d
75.	a	b	c	d
76.	a	b	c	d
77.	a	b	c	d
78.	a	b	c	d
79.	a	b	c	d
80.	a	b	c	d
81.	a	b	c	d
82.	a	b	c	d

83.	a	b	c	d		105.	a	b	c	d
84.	a	b	c	d		106.	a	b	c	d
85.	a	b	c	d		107.	a	b	c	d
86.	a	b	c	d		108.	a	b	c	d
87.	a	b	c	d		109.	a	b	c	d
88.	a	b	c	d		110.	a	b	c	d
89.	a	b	c	d		111.	a	b	c	d
90.	a	b	c	d		112.	a	b	c	d
91.	a	b	c	d		113.	a	b	c	d
92.	a	b	c	d		114.	a	b	c	d
93.	a	b	c	d		115.	a	b	c	d
94.	a	b	c	d		116.	a	b	c	d
95.	a	b	c	d		117.	a	b	c	d
96.	a	b	c	d		118.	a	b	c	d
97.	a	b	c	d		119.	a	b	c	d
98.	a	b	c	d		120.	a	b	c	d
99.	a	b	c	d		121.	a	b	c	d
100.	a	b	c	d		122.	a	b	c	d
101.	a	b	c	d		123.	a	b	c	d
102.	a	b	c	d		124.	a	b	c	d
103.	a	b	c	d		125.	a	b	c	d
104.	a	b	c	d		126.	a	b	c	d

127.	a	b	c	d
128.	a	b	c	d
129.	a	b	c	d
130.	a	b	c	d
131.	a	b	c	d
132.	a	b	c	d
133.	a	b	c	d
134.	a	b	c	d
135.	a	b	c	d
136.	a	b	c	d
137.	a	b	c	d
138.	a	b	c	d
139.	a	b	c	d
140.	a	b	c	d
141.	a	b	c	d
142.	a	b	c	d
143.	a	b	c	d
144.	a	b	c	d
145.	a	b	c	d
146.	a	b	c	d
147.	a	b	c	d
148.	a	b	c	d

149.	a	b	c	d
150.	a	b	c	d
151.	a	b	c	d
152.	a	b	c	d
153.	a	b	c	d
154.	a	b	c	d
155.	a	b	c	d
156.	a	b	c	d
157.	a	b	c	d
158.	a	b	c	d
159.	a	b	c	d
160.	a	b	c	d
161.	a	b	c	d
162.	a	b	c	d
163.	a	b	c	d
164.	a	b	c	d
165.	a	b	c	d
166.	a	b	c	d
167.	a	b	c	d
168.	a	b	c	d
169.	a	b	c	d
170.	a	b	c	d

Answer Key for Practice Test 2

1. b. Benefits realization report

   The benefits realization report is an output of the Manage Program Benefits process. It compares the benefits realization plan against the actual benefits realized.

   PMI®, *The Standard for Program Management*, 2008, 266

2. d. Strategic visioning

   Program managers require a combination of knowledge, skills, and competencies. Strategic visioning and planning are two critical skills that are required to align program goals and benefits with the organization's long-term goals. The program manager also must align individual project plans with the program goals and benefits.

   PMI®, *The Standard for Program Management*, 2008, 12–13

3. b. Delivery of Program Benefits

   The program manages and accrues benefits during the Delivery of Program Benefits phase. This is the longest phase in the life cycle of the program, as benefits are progressively delivered, and it ends only when all planned benefits have been achieved, delivered, and accepted, or when a decision has been made to terminate the program.

   PMI®, *The Standard for Program Management*, 2008, 28

4. b. Note stakeholder considerations in your program charter

   It is highly appropriate to perform market research to identify any potential stakeholders who may have an interest in or influence over your program and its component projects. The program charter should describe stakeholder considerations, including an initial strategy to effectively manage them.

   PMI®, *The Standard for Program Management*, 2008, 24

5. b. Flow to the Distribute Information process

   It is common to receive numerous requests for program information from both internal and external stakeholders. Many of these requests are an output of program management processes; they should flow to the Distribute Information process, which creates appropriate responses as outputs.

   PMI®, *The Standard for Program Management*, 2008, 39

6. a. Determine any program management processes that must be revisited

   Changes affect various program-level processes. The program manager should prepare a list of all the program management processes that will need to be carried out, such as updates to the program work breakdown structure or revisions to the risk register.

   PMI®, *The Standard for Program Management*, 2008, 64

7. a. Formalize benefits at the portfolio level

   The purpose of benefits management is to define and formalize the program's expected benefits. If a portfolio management system is established, then the benefits are typically formalized at the portfolio level and then delegated to the program for execution.

   PMI®, *The Standard for Program Management*, 2008, 9

8. b. Define a common life-cycle model for the various projects

   Although different projects could use different life cycles, a standard project life-cycle model will create a common language and a frame of reference for the program's stakeholders. A common life cycle can also facilitate reporting, monitoring, and control of the status of each project in a program.

   PMI®, *The Standard for Program Management*, 2008, 19

9. c. Program management plan

   The program management plan is an input to the Close Program process. It is important to review it along with every subsidiary program plan to ensure that requirements have been met, final updates have been made, and any outstanding or active projects are brought to an orderly close.

   PMI®, *The Standard for Program Management*, 2008, 99

10. d. Establishing program direction

    Substantive leadership skills are required to manage multiple project teams in the program life cycle. Program leadership entails establishing program direction, identifying interdependencies, communicating requirements, tracking progress, making decisions, and resolving conflicts and issues, among other important tasks.

    PMI®, *The Standard for Program Management*, 2008, 13

11. a. Provide guidelines for project-level stakeholder management

   While the stakeholder management plan documents how stakeholders will be identified, managed, engaged, and managed during the life of the program, the program manager also provides guidelines for component stakeholder management to the individual projects that are part of the program.

   PMI®, *The Standard for Program Management*, 2008, 231

12. c. Program Closing phase

   During phase five of the program life cycle (the Program Closing phase), all program work has been completed and program benefits are accruing. A key activity in this phase is for the program manager to review the status of the benefits with stakeholders.

   PMI®, *The Standard for Program Management*, 2008, 30

13. a. Delivery of Program Benefits phase

   As program manager, you establish a program control framework during the Program Setup phase of the program life cycle. During the Delivery of Program Benefits phase, the program management team reviews change requests that affect program activities and authorizes additional work as appropriate.

   PMI®, *The Standard for Program Management*, 2008, 29

14. d. Focus on areas rather than specific points to ensure the overall program is successful

   In addition to phase-gate reviews, governance boards tend to have less formal 'periodic health check' sessions to assess performance against expected outcomes and the need to realize and sustain program benefits in the long term. These reviews among other things focus on areas rather than specific points to make sure the program will be successful.

   PMI®, *The Standard for Program Management*, 2008, 251

15. b. Benefits analysis and planning phase

   During the Program Initiation phase, in the benefits life cycle, the components are derived and prioritized as the foundation of the program continues to develop, and a detailed road map is prepared. The benefits analysis and planning phase is where prioritization is done.

   PMI®, *The Standard for Program Management*, 2008, 20

16. b. Reducing risks

    Reducing risk is essential as a business case driver for financial control and compliance with external requirements such as corporate reporting and mandatory audits.

    PMI. *Program Management Professional* (PgMP)® *Examination Content Outline*, 2011, 6

    David Williams and Tim Parr, *Enterprise Program Management Delivering Value*, 2006, 124

17. a. Program management office (PMO)

    The program management office (PMO) is a key stakeholder on programs. It provides support to individual program teams or program managers by dealing with administrative issues centrally, and it defines and manages program-related governance processes, procedures, templates, and so on.

    PMI®, *The Standard for Program Management*, 2008, 235

18. d. Governance plan

    Component initiation criteria are part of the program's governance plan, and the initial gate review for a component is at its initiation. Clear criteria are required to ensure the components are executed at the right time.

    PMI®, *The Standard for Program Management*, 2008, 250

19. c. Risk management consolidation

    Program-level planning processes are key results of the Program Setup phase of the life cycle. One key process is risk management consolidation—that is, considering the risks of the various components of the program to address a key question in the program management plan: What are the risks and issues?

    PMI®, *The Standard for Program Management*, 2008, 27

20. c. Delivery of Program Benefits phase

    Phase four of the program life cycle (the Delivery of Program Benefits phase) involves initiating the various projects of the program and coordinating deliverables to achieve incremental benefits. Because the program management team is responsible for overall management of the projects in a coordinated and consistent way, the team must ensure that project managers adhere to established methodologies.

    PMI®, *The Standard for Program Management*, 2008, 28

21. c. Convene a meeting of your Governance Board

    Program governance activities are conducted throughout the program life cycle. One purpose is to establish and enforce policies addressing managing program change. The Governance Board should be consulted about this major change and how best to handle it.

    PMI®, *The Standard for Program Management*, 2008, 243–244

22. a. Benefits delivery

    Benefits delivery is one measure of a program's success, along with the degree to which the program satisfies the needs for which it was undertaken.

    PMI®, *The Standard for Program Management*, 2008, 11

23. b. Evaluate your proposed program's alignment to the strategic plan by consulting with organizational leaders

    A best practice is to evaluate the organization's capability to take on a new program by consulting with organizational leaders to develop, validate, and assess the program objectives, its priority, feasibility, readiness, and alignment to strategic goals. This in turn will assist in identifying stakeholders and gaining their support before the business case is presented.

    PMI. *The Standard for Program Management Second Edition,* 2008, 23

    PMI. *Program Management Professional* (PgMP)® *Examination Content Outline,* 2011, 6

24. a. Executive sponsor

    The executive sponsor is the individual who is responsible for providing program resources and ensuring program success. He or she is typically a senior manager who defines the direction of the organization and its investment decisions.

    PMI. *The Standard for Program Management Second Edition,* 2008, 245

25. a. May be extended as some projects transition or others begin

    Some projects may produce benefits that can be realized immediately, whereas others may deliver capabilities that must be integrated with those of other projects to realize benefits. The program life cycle may be extended as some projects transition and others begin.

    PMI®, *The Standard for Program Management*, 2008, 19 and 28

26. b. An appropriate governance structure in place

    The governance structure ensures the program's goals and objectives are aligned with the strategic goals. This program's original governance structure may no longer be appropriate given the dramatic change to the program. Different people may now be needed as members of the governance board, including that of the executive sponsor.

    PMI®, *The Standard for Program Management*, 2008, 243–245

27. a. A constraint

    Constraints limit the options of the program management team. A fixed, imposed date is an example of a schedule constraint.

    PMI®, *The Standard for Program Management*, 2008, 38

28. c. Input to the Monitor and Control Program Changes and Distribute Information processes

    The change request log is used to record, describe, or denote change requests. Any approved changes are accurately recorded in the log.

    PMI®, *The Standard for Program Management*, 2008, 149, 268–269

29. d. Contract closure procedure

    The contract closure procedure is a tool and technique in the Close Program Procurements process. It outlines the requirements for formally closing and/or terminating contractual agreements, including verification criteria to prevent the organization from contract breach. It ensures that all conditions are met and addresses any follow-on activities such as warranties and remedies.

    PMI®, *The Standard for Program Management*, 2008, 205

30. b. The program charter

    The program charter is the key output of the Program Initiation phase, as it defines the program's high-level scope, strategic fit, outcomes, vision, constraints, and assumptions, among other things.

    PMI®, *The Standard for Program Management*, 2008, 24

31. b. Political

    Program managers require technical skills, time management abilities, and program management people skills, including political skills.

    PMI®, *The Standard for Program Management*, 2008, 12

32. b. Benefits

The purpose of the Closing Process Group is to formalize acceptance of the program's product, service, or results to bring the program (or program component) to completion. One purpose is to demonstrate and confirm that all program benefits have been delivered.

PMI®, *The Standard for Program Management*, 2008, 66

33. a. Representatives from each business unit in the organization would participate in the program

Such internal programs serve as a catalyst for change. Participation across the various business units is desirable so that resources can be shared. Furthermore, while the maturity assessment itself is typically conducted rather quickly, it takes time to implement the various recommendations, each of which is a specific project that depends on other projects to create a set of benefits.

PMI®, *The Standard for Program Management*, 2008, 23

34. a. Program architecture baseline

In the Manage Component Interfaces process, the program architecture baseline is an input because it is the set of program components that outlines their characteristics, capabilities, deliverables, timing, and interfaces and how the components contribute to program benefits.

PMI®, *The Standard for Program Management*, 2008, 114 and 120

35. d. Program Sponsor

The program sponsor is the person or group who champions the program's initiative, is responsible for providing the resources, and is ultimately responsible for delivering the program's benefits.

PMI®, *The Standard for Program Management*, 2008, 235

36. a. Conduct inspections and audits

Inspections and audits are tools and techniques in the Administer Program Procurements process. Audits confirm that sellers have delivered their contractual obligations and that the statement of work was achieved. Both inspections and audits must also focus on contract conformance issues.

PMI®, *The Standard for Program Management*, 2008, 202

37. c. Important interfaces are managed

   One important factor in the governance framework for a program is to ensure that important interfaces are managed carefully to minimize conflicts at the program level and between components. It is recognized that programs may overlap a number of enterprises, including suppliers.

   PMI®, *The Standard for Program Management*, 2008, 245

38. c. Update your program plans as required

   Budget cuts, the organization's fiscal year, and the budget planning cycle may affect programs and projects. If they affect your program, as program manager, you have the responsibility to revisit and update program plans as necessary. This is particularly the case as noted in the Monitor and Control Program Financials process.

   PMI®, *The Standard for Program Management*, 2008, 226

39. c. Program management office (PMO)

   For most programs, the program management office (PMO) is the core of the program infrastructure. The program infrastructure is an output of the Develop Program Infrastructure process and defines the required support structure, capabilities, and resources.

   PMI®, *The Standard for Program Management*, 2008, 86

40. d. Input to the Provide Governance Oversight process

   Program performance reports are an input to the Provide Program Governance process. Examples of these reports are status reports, financial reports, and resource deviation reports.

   PMI®, *The Standard for Program Management*, 2008, 261

41. c. Charter

   Building on the high-level plan from the pre-program preparation phase, the program charter then consolidates all available information about the program. Within the charter, the justification describes the importance of the program and what it is to achieve, and the vision describes the end state and the benefit to the organization.

   PMI®, *The Standard for Program Management*, 2008, 23–24

42. c. Standard measurement criteria

   On each program, standard measurement criteria for success must be defined for all consistent projects. This is done by analysis of stakeholder expectations and requirements across the projects in order to manage and control the program.

   PMI. *Program Management Professional* (PgMP)® *Examination Content Outline*, 2011, 8

43. a. Historical information

   Previous programs are good sources of lessons learned and best practices. This is especially important if the work is primarily performed by a virtual team or involves multicultural interactions. Common knowledge assets are sources of useful information in these situations.

   PMI®, *The Standard for Program Management*, 2008, 38

44. c. Benefits analysis and planning phase

   Benefits are mapped into the program plan during the benefits analysis and planning phase, as the program management and technical infrastructure are established. Because the program plan is developed during the Program Setup phase, it is appropriate to map the benefits into the plan when the infrastructure is established.

   PMI®, *The Standard for Program Management*, 2008, 21

45. d. Shows the type of stakeholder who defines the command, control loops, and communication mechanisms

   Mapping is a useful stakeholder identification technique to analyze stakeholders and map them into various categories. It can show the type of stakeholder against an area of interest; the type of interaction required based on the stakeholder's influence and level of importance; the ability of the stakeholder to influence versus the impact the program will have on the stakeholder; and the type of stakeholder who defines command, control loops, and communication mechanisms.

   PMI®, *The Standard for Program Management*, 2008, 231

46. c. Gain an understanding of CDE's culture, attitudes, and communications requirements

    The purpose of the stakeholder analysis is to understand the organization's culture as well as the needs and expectations of program stakeholders. The first step is to use stakeholder interviews, focus groups, and surveys/questionnaires to help in understanding the organizational culture, stakeholder attitudes toward the program, and communications requirements.

    PMI®, *The Standard for Program Management*, 2008, 230

47 b. A process asset library

    Organizational process assets (asset libraries) are key inputs to many program management processes. They may include the organization's knowledge bases, may exist in paper or electronic format, and may include process-related plans, policies, procedures, and guidelines institutionalized by the organization.

    PMI®, *The Standard for Program Management*, 2008, 38

48. c. High-level plan

    The next step is to develop a high-level plan to show that you understand why the program was selected, what its objectives are, and how its objectives align with the organization's objectives.

    PMI®, *The Standard for Program Management*, 2008, 23

49. a. Ongoing operations

    Even after the program life cycle ends, benefits management allows the organization to realize and sustain the benefits from its investment. The program manager ensures that this is accomplished within the framework of ongoing operations in the organization.

    PMI®, *The Standard for Program Management*, 2008, 31–32

50. b. Determine how receptive the stakeholder is to communications from the program

    Although all are part of the steps in the stakeholder analysis process, the last one is to determine how receptive the stakeholder is to receiving information about the program. The communications management plan needs to consider specific requirements of each stakeholder for information needs including when they need information about the program.

    PMI®, *The Standard for Program Management*, 2008, 230

51. d. Follow the issue escalation process

   The issue escalation process should be used in this situation to escalate this issue to your governance board and involve them in the decision-making process as stated in your governance plan.

   PMI®, *The Standard for Program Management*, 2008, 251

52. a. Issues analysis

   Issues analysis is a tool and technique in the Manage Program Issues process. Such an analysis assesses the impact and severity of the issue, its root cause, and possible remedies.

   PMI®, *The Standard for Program Management*, 2008, 96–97

53. d. Benefits realization

   The benefits realization phase tracks to the Delivery of Program Benefits phase, when the major work of the program is under way. This phase ends when the planned benefits are achieved or when the program is terminated for some reason. The benefits register is maintained during this phase.

   PMI®, *The Standard for Program Management*, 2008, 20

54. b. Leave a legacy of operational benefits sustainment

   One purpose of the Closing Process Group is to leave in place a legacy of operational benefits sustainment, thus deriving optimal value from the work accomplished by the program.

   PMI®, *The Standard for Program Management*, 2008, 67

55. b. Total available resources

   Resources—funding, equipment, and people—are limited in all organizations. In selecting a program, it is necessary to consider the total available resources that will be required to successfully implement it.

   PMI®, *The Standard for Program Management*, 2008, 23

56. b. Set forth in your audit plan

   The audit plan describes the objectives and timing for audits; external and internal audits can be conducted at regular and predefined intervals.

   PMI®, *The Standard for Program Management*, 2008, 251

57. c. Program director

    The stakeholder register lists the key stakeholders and their roles and responsibilities to help determine communications requirements. The program director is the individual with the executive ownership of the program.

    PMI®, *The Standard for Program Management*, 2008, 234

58. b. Delivering benefits

    The purpose of phase four is to initiate program components and manage the development of program benefits that were identified during the initial program phases.

    PMI®, *The Standard for Program Management*, 2008, 28

59. b. Suppliers are now a major stakeholder

    In this situation, suppliers are a major stakeholder especially because of the changing policies and procedures in your organization. They require communications about this change and will need interaction with the program manager and his or her team so they do not become negative stakeholders.

    PMI®, *The Standard for Program Management*, 2008, 235

60. a. Tolerances

    Tolerances are a tool and technique in the Develop Program Management Plan process. They are ranges set for various aspects of the program such as time, cost, and scope. Without defined tolerances, the potential exists for conflicts over boundaries of authority.

    PMI®, *The Standard for Program Management*, 2008, 82

61. c. Update the program-level documentation and records

    The Manage Component Interfaces process is ongoing throughout the program. Transparent management of interfaces is critical for scope adherence. It may trigger a need to redeploy resources as projects are authorized. This is managed at the program level. Outputs from other processes and program-level documentation and records dealing with affected projects must be updated to reflect their new status.

    PMI®, *The Standard for Program Management*, 2008, 119

62. b. Prepare a change request

    To ensure that stakeholder expectations are in line with program activities and deliverables as issues are identified, analyzed, and resolved, it may be necessary to change the program scope. The first step is to prepare a change request, which is an output of the Manage Program Issues process.

    PMI®, *The Standard for Program Management*, 2008, 97

63. d. Update your risk management plan

    It is important to evaluate the risks stakeholders identify, including sponsors, and then incorporate them in the risk management plan.

    PMI. *Program Management Professional* (PgMP)® *Examination Content Outline*, 2011, 14

64. b. There are broad interdependencies between these projects

    Program stakeholder management expands beyond project stakeholder management as it considers additional levels of stakeholders because of the broader interdependencies between projects, the larger scope, and the impacts beyond the executing organization.

    PMI®, *The Standard for Program Management*, 2008, 227

65. d. Program team

    The program team is responsible for developing program-level benefits and managing the components in a repeatable, consistent, and coordinated manner to achieve results that would not be possible if they were managed individually.

    PMI®, *The Standard for Program Management*, 2008, 28

66. a. Expected benefits are in line with the original business plan

    The gate review assesses the program with respect to a number of quality and strategic-related criteria including whether the expected benefits are in line with the original business plan.

    PMI®, *The Standard for Program Management*, 2008, 250

67. c. Organizational analysis

     Analysis of people in the organization involved in the program and their formal and informal roles is a valuable technique for revealing stakeholders with a significant but not obvious role in the program. External organizations with a strong interest in the program also are analyzed. The inventory then shows how each stakeholder and stakeholder group will be impacted by the program, their likely responses, identified issues, and planned mitigation approaches.

     PMI®, *The Standard for Program Management*, 2008, 233, 235

68. c. Program Initiation phase

     During the Program Initiation phase, the program components are defined. This phase may also include a high-level plan for all components.

     PMI®, *The Standard for Program Management*, 2008, 24

69. a. Programs and projects in the portfolio are focused on delivering lasting results and benefits

     Portfolio management involves the process of creating, managing, and evaluating a portfolio of strategic initiatives focused on delivering lasting results and benefits. The objective is to manage the portfolio along with the evolution of the business strategy to obtain maximum value.

     PMI. *Program Management Professional* (PgMP)® *Examination Content Outline*, 2011, 6

     PMI. *The Standard for Program Management*, 2008, 9

     David Williams and Tim Parr, *Enterprise Program Management Delivering Value*, 2006, 19

70. c. Benefits realization plan

     The benefits realization plan identifies the business benefits and documents the plan to realize them. It includes intended interdependencies of benefits being delivered by the various projects in the program. It identifies organizational processes and systems required, changes to these processes and systems, and how and when the transition to the new arrangements will occur.

     PMI®, *The Standard for Program Management*, 2008, 109

71. b. Program business case

     The benefits realization plan is a part of Program Initiation. Expected benefits are defined in the business case for the program, and the benefits realization plan is based on this information.

     PMI®, *The Standard for Program Management*, 2008, 31

72. d. Prepare a program resource plan

A program resource plan is an output of the Develop Program Infrastructure process. It describes the required program resources such as personnel, equipment, facilities, and finances.

PMI®, *The Standard for Program Management*, 2008, 86

73. b. Updates to the program issues register are outputs of the Manage Program Issues process

Although the program issue register is an input to the Manage Program Issues process and all issues are recorded in it, updates to it are outputs of this process.

PMI®, *The Standard for Program Management*, 2008, 96–98

74. c. Manage Program Resources

Many organizations set up a team for program initiation or program start-up and then replace this team with permanent staff later in the program. The Manage Program Resources process tracks the use of program resources throughout the program life cycle, thereby enabling adaptation of such resources as circumstances warrant.

PMI®, *The Standard for Program Management*, 2008, 91

75. d. Program roadmap

The program roadmap is an input in the Direct and Manage Program Execution process because it is used to determine when new components should be initiated and made part of the program.

PMI®, *The Standard for Program Management*, 2008, 89

76. a. Distribute Information

Lessons learned updates are an output of the Distribute Information process and may include specific outputs of lessons learned activities, such as updates to the lessons learned repository; knowledge management databases; corporate policies, procedures, and processes; and risk management plan.

PMI®, *The Standard for Program Management*, 2008, 151–152

77. a. Stakeholder management strategy

   The stakeholder management strategy captures mitigation approaches as stakeholders are identified and helps to manage the impacts of the program on stakeholders. This means that comprehensive training may be needed to those who now will be involved with the program now that it is complete, job aids may be needed to work with the new systems, and the operations and product support personnel will need intensive communication and involvement in the program to assume responsibility at the right time.

   PMI®, *The Standard for Program Management*, 2008, 236

78. a. Derive expected benefits from the business case

   Program managers must focus on benefits realization and benefits management. The first step is to derive expected benefits from the business case for the program because programs are initiated to create benefits that transcend those of a single project.

   PMI®, *The Standard for Program Management*, 2008, 30–31

79. b. Conduct a questionnaire to get everyone in the agency involved in the process

   Given the magnitude of this program in that it affects almost everyone in the agency to some extent, the questionnaire is a key approach to solicit feedback from stakeholders and provides the opportunity to get greater input than that possible with other approaches.

   PMI®, *The Standard for Program Management*, 2008, 234

80. d. They want to assess performance against expected outcomes

   Phase-gate reviews are not a substitute to periodic performance reviews, which are used to asses performance against expected outcomes and against the need to realize and sustain program benefits into the long term.

   PMI®, *The Standard for Program Management*, 2008, 251

81. d. Program sponsor

   The program sponsor identification is an input to the Plan Program Stakeholder Management process. Since he or she is providing resources for the program and makes the final decision as to when to close the program, his or her interests are especially important in this process, and he or she is a key primary stakeholder.

   PMI®, *The Standard for Program Management*, 2008, 230

82. c. A stakeholder register

    The stakeholder register is the primary input for the distribution of program reports and other communications as it shows the key stakeholders and their roles and responsibilities on the program.

    PMI®, *The Standard for Program Management*, 2008, 231, 234–235

83. a. Direct and Manage Program Execution process

    The Direct and Manage Program Execution process is responsible for delivery of the program's benefits. Component transition requests are an output as a formal request that is sent to governance for gate transition approval.

    PMI®, *The Standard for Program Management*, 2008, 90

84. b. Part of the scope statement

    The program scope statement is an input to the Monitor and Control Program Scope process. In addition, it addresses organizational needs and requirements; initial, high-level product requirements; the vision of the solution; and assumptions and constraints.

    PMI®, *The Standard for Program Management*, 2008, 106 and 122

85. d. Review the program's transition plan

    Before submitting the closure recommendation, the program transition plan should be reviewed as it outlines the steps to move the program from a development state to an operational state pending approval that the program has satisfied all of its requirements.

    PMI®, *The Standard for Program Management*, 2008, 83

86. a. Use a stakeholder impact and issue tracking and prioritization tool

    Stakeholder issues and concerns should be tracked to closure. Using a tool to document, prioritize, and track these issue and stakeholder interests can help ensure the stakeholder concerns are properly addressed.

    PMI®, *The Standard for Program Management*, 2008, 238

87. a. Identify and evaluate integration opportunities and needs

In strategic program management, once organizational leadership for the program has been obtained and the authorization to initiate the program is received, it then is necessary to identify and evaluate integration opportunities and needs. These range from human capital, human resource requirements and skills sets, to facilities, finance, assets, processes, and systems within the program and its operational activities to align and integrate benefits across the organization.

PMI. The Standard for Program Management Second Edition, 2008, 23

PMI. *Program Management Professional* (PgMP)® *Examination Content Outline*, 2011, 6

88. b. Program Initiation phase

A statement of the program's mission, vision, and strategic fit is included as part of the program charter, which is developed in the Program Initiation phase. The charter provides the authority to move forward to Program Setup or to Planning in the life cycle from the *Examination Content Outline.*

PMI®, *The Standard for Program Management*, 2008, 24

89. d. At the end of the program initiation phase

Among other things, at the end of the program initiation phase, potential members of the governance board are identified as well as the key decision makers and stakeholders in the program and their expectations and interests.

PMI®, *The Standard for Program Management*, 2008, 25

90. c. Stakeholder management plan

Working to actively engage stakeholders, metrics are needed to measure performance of stakeholder engagement activities, such as meeting attendance and communication plan delivery. These metrics are part of the stakeholder management plan as it describes among other things how to effectively engage stakeholders in the program.

PMI®, *The Standard for Program Management*, 2008, 237

91. a. Capacity planning

    The program resource plan is prepared in the Develop Program Infrastructure process. Capacity planning is used to assess needed resources such as staff, information, expertise, funds, facilities, and production capabilities. Limitations in these resources must be addressed if the program is to be successful.

    PMI®, *The Standard for Program Management*, 2008, 85

92. a. Identify opportunities

    During the Monitor and Control Program Financials process, the program manager may identify opportunities to return funding from the program to the enterprise. Such opportunities can provide benefits to both the program and the enterprise.

    PMI®, *The Standard for Program Management*, 2008, 226

93. d. Political skills

    While a number of key interpersonal skills are needed in program management, political relationship must be observed and fostered within a program. Understanding the political climate and temperature of the program is important in achieving a positive relationship.

    PMI®, *The Standard for Program Management*, 2008, 14

94. b. Communications skills

    Although program management requires a special blend of technical skills, time management, and a sound foundation of people skills, including political skills, communications is the most important competence. The program manager requires strong communications skills to deal with all the stakeholders—team members, sponsors, executives, functional managers, customers, vendors, the public, and other stakeholders.

    PMI®, *The Standard for Program Management*, 2008, 12

95. c. Establish buy-in from all stakeholders to ensure program success

    All the interests of stakeholders are important ones. As the program manager working with stakeholders involves a great deal of time and effort to communicate program goals, manage their expectations, and establish buy-in to ensure success of the program.

    PMI®, *The Standard for Program Management*, 2008, 12

96. b. Followed the issue escalation process

    The issue escalation process, developed in the plan and establish governance structure, operates at two levels, one of which is between project teams and the program management team.

    PMI®, *The Standard for Program Management*, 2008, 251

97 a. Conduct benefits reviews

    A benefits review is a tool and technique in the Manage Program Benefits process. These reviews verify that the delivery of program benefits has not been compromised by decisions made during program execution and reassures stakeholders that all is going well with program components.

    PMI®, *The Standard for Program Management*, 2008, 264–265

98. a. Tangible

    Benefits tend to be either tangible or intangible. Tangible benefits may be either financial or nonfinancial, but they can be quantified.

    PMI®, The Standard for Program Management, 2008, 23

    Williams and Parr, *Enterprise Program Management Delivering Value*, 2006, 174

99. c. Distribute Information

    Communication skills are part of overall general management skills and are required by program managers. They are a tool and technique in the Distribute Information process.

    PMI®, *The Standard for Program Management*, 2008, 150

100. a. Managing quality across the life cycle

    Programs are too complex to be managed by a single individual, which is why governance is critical to success. Program governance assists in managing risks, stakeholders, benefits, resources, and quality across the life cycle.

    PMI®, *The Standard for Program Management*, 2008, 21

101. b. A decision to bid for a contract

    Programs are initiated for several reasons, including in response to the organization's strategic plan, to fulfill an initiative in a portfolio, or as a result of a bid on a contract by an external company.

    PMI®, *The Standard for Program Management*, 2008, 42

102. c. In the Program Initiation phase of the program management life cycle

The sponsor and the program manager are appointed as a result of the Program Initiation phase of the program life cycle.

PMI®, *The Standard for Program Management*, 2008, 25

103. b. Scope management plan

The scope management plan is a subsidiary plan to the program management plan. It describes how scope changes are identified, processed, and integrated in the program. It also describes scope management.

PMI®, *The Standard for Program Management*, 2008, 106

104. c. Governance plan

The governance plan contains several sections, which include its structure and meeting schedules and then becomes part of the program management plan. This section includes outputs of governance planning activities, including schedules of governance activities and meetings, such as health checks, gate reviews, and audits.

PMI®, *The Standard for Program Management*, 2008, 250

105. b. Showing their contribution to business objectives

Intangible benefits are difficult to quantify, although many contribute in a meaningful way to tangible benefits. Their contribution to business objectives must be assessed and the objectives must be stated in the most specific and measurable way possible.

PMI®, *The Standard for Program Management*, 2008, 23

Williams and Parr, *Enterprise Program Management Delivering Value*, 2006, 174

106. d. Update the program resource plan

Staffing internally involves identifying existing personnel qualified for the positions, negotiating for their services with their management, and then transitioning them to the program position. Changes in assignment of program staff are reflected in updates to the program resource plan.

PMI®, *The Standard for Program Management*, 2008, 93

107. d. Start with a high-level overview of the program

Periodic performance reviews should start with a high-level overview of the program and then drill down more deeply as needed. This approach is recommended to make sure all the members of the board understand the purpose of the program, especially if they may be new to the board or serving as a substitute for a board member, and to ensure there is common understanding of the overall purpose of the program.

PMI®, *The Standard for Program Management*, 2008, 251

108. a. They may be the last time for recourse for performance deficiencies

Supplier performance reviews are a tool and technique in the Close Program Procurements process. They may be the last opportunity for recourse to address performance deficiencies with suppliers.

PMI®, *The Standard for Program Management*, 2008, 205

109. d. Causal analysis

Causal analysis is a technique that is used to provide the real reason why something has happened in order to then take corrective action for focused change activity. It emphasizes the root cause and often cause-and-effect diagrams are used.

PMI. *Program Management Professional* (PgMP)® *Examination Content Outline*, 2011, 13

110. d. Report and distribute program deliverables and formal and informal communications

The stakeholder register is used throughout the program as it lists all the stakeholders and is used for reporting, distributing program deliverables, and formal and informal communications. It is the primary output of the Identify Program Stakeholders process.

PMI®, *The Standard for Program Management*, 2008, 234

111. c. Interviews

Interviews are a useful tool to help prepare the stakeholder register especially in programs such as this one which involve organizational process changes. Open-ended questions are recommended.

PMI®, *The Standard for Program Management*, 2008, 234

112 a. Document each decision made

Governance meetings including minutes, action item logs, or other forms of decision records should be documented in a decision register, which then becomes useful in the program and organization's knowledge management system.

PMI®, *The Standard for Program Management*, 2008, 262

113. d. Conducting a program impact analysis

The program impact analysis is used to focus on stakeholder issues and concerns that are likely to affect program costs, schedules, and priorities. These impact analysis tools can help program managers understand the urgency and probability of stakeholder-related risks.

PMI®, *The Standard for Program Management*, 2008, 238

114. a. People believe it is the program's schedule

A high-level program roadmap or framework can set a baseline for program definition, planning, and execution. It is dynamic and is prepared or updated along with the portfolio management process. A disadvantage to it is that developing and updating the road map requires discipline that many organizations lack to keep its information current and relevant

PMI®, *The Standard for Program Management*, 2008, 25 and 78

Milosevic, Dragan Z., Martinelli, Russ J., and Waddell, James M., *Program Management for Improved Business Results*, 2007, 295–296

PMI. *Program Management Professional* (PgMP)® *Examination Content Outline*, 2011, 6

115. b. The program manager has the desired level of control

The program work breakdown structure (PWBS) does not replace the work breakdown structure (WBS) on each of the program's projects. From a program perspective, the PWBS should be decomposed to the level of control that the program manager requires, which typically corresponds to the first one or two levels of the WBS of the component projects.

PMI®, *The Standard for Program Management*, 2008, 114

116. d. Provide a graphical depiction of the work elements

The work breakdown structure (WBS) matrix is an output of the Develop Program WBS process. It is a graphical depiction of a deliverable or product-oriented grouping of work elements that is used to organize and subdivide the total work scope of the program.

PMI®, *The Standard for Program Management*, 2008, 117

117. c. Delivery of the program benefits

The delivery of the program benefits phase is iterative and can be of unlimited duration. Each activity in this phase is repeated as often as needed, and the benefits accrue in a cumulative fashion. It ends only when the planned benefits have been achieved, delivered, and active or when the program is terminated.

PMI®, *The Standard for Program Management*, 2008, 28–29

118. b. Constraints

Constraints are factors that limit the program team's options; typically, they affect schedule, cost, resources, or program deliverables. They are an input common to many program management processes and may restrict action.

PMI®, *The Standard for Program Management*, 2008, 38

119. a. A forecast

The Estimate to Complete is a forecasting technique; it is an estimate to complete the remaining work for an activity, program package, or control account. Such forecasting techniques are used in the Monitor and Control Program Financials process.

PMI®, *The Standard for Program Management*, 2008, 225

120. c. Meet with the customer for a closure review

It is important to obtain formal acceptance of the program through a review with the sponsor or customer. It is time to review the program scope and closure documents of project and non-project activities. The sponsor or customer should sign off on each of these activities to verify completion of deliverables against requirements and should acknowledge final acceptance by signing the closure documents.

PMI®, *The Standard for Program Management*, 2008, 98

121. c. Developing the next-generation cellular phone and related products

The development of the next-generation cellular phone and related products is best suited to be managed as a program. It will include numerous projects that should be managed in a coordinated way to obtain greater benefits and control than would be possible if they were managed individually.

PMI®, *The Standard for Program Management*, 2008, 5

122. d. The Department's organizational chart

Organization charts indicate authority levels in the organization and scope of control. Feedback and authorization need to be received as quickly and clearly as possible so as to not impede program progress; therefore, the organization chart is the main foundation for the structure and organization of the governance plan.

PMI®, *The Standard for Program Management*, 2008, 248

123. a. When the resources will be needed

Resource availability is an input to the Manage Program Resources process. It indicates availability of the personnel, assets, materials, or capital resources that are required to accomplish program goals and deliverables.

PMI®, *The Standard for Program Management*, 2008, 92

124. b. Are a tool and technique of the Monitor and Control Program Financials process

In the Monitor and Control Program Financials process, analysis of the actual cost for non-program or non-project activities is an input. These costs, such as ones associated with program management and infrastructure, must be monitored and controlled because they are part of the program.

PMI®, *The Standard for Program Management*, 2008, 225

125. c. Initiate the program

A number of activities may be performed before initiating a program. However, the first step in the Initiating Process Group is to actually initiate the program, because it provides a process to help define the program's scope and benefits expectations.

PMI®, *The Standard for Program Management*, 2008, 42–43

126. c. Identifying interdependences among the constituent projects

As a program manager, you must ensure that the independencies among the constituent projects are reflected and managed in the program schedule, whereas the project manager concentrates on detailed activities in the project schedule. Internal and external dependencies are a key input to this process. The program schedule includes component milestones that represent an output to the program or share an interdependency with other components.

PMI®, *The Standard for Program Management*, 2008, 11–12 and 130

127. c. Decision-tree analysis

Decision-tree analysis is used to assist in choosing available alternatives when some future scenarios or outcomes are uncertain. It helps organizations identify the relative values of alternate actions. In program management it is a technique that is helpful in analyzing and updating the benefit realization plan and sustainment plans for uncertainty, risk identification, risk mitigation, and risk opportunity.

PMI. *Program Management Professional* (PgMP)® *Examination Content Outline*, 2011, 13

128. a. Business value measurement

Business value measurement is useful in overall benefit measurement but especially in measuring intangible benefits. This approach tests the intangible benefits against business strategies and objectives continually to ensure they are robust, relevant, and in some way measureable 3en if against an artificial scale aligned to a business objective.

PMI. *Program Management Professional* (PgMP)® *Examination Content Outline*, 2011, 13

Williams, D. and Parr, T., *Enterprise Programme Management*, 2006, 179

129. b. Issue management

Issue escalation is an activity that occurs within governance. Skillfully tracking, managing, and resolving program-level and inter-component issues helps enable effective governance.

PMI®, *The Standard for Program Management*, 2008, 248

130. a. Program A

     Program A will drop features if necessary in a trade-off situation. It is schedule-driven and supports the time-to-market attribute of the company, thus aligning itself with the organization's culture and environment.

     Milosevic, Martinelli, and Waddell, *Program Management for Improved Business Results*, 2007, 75–76

     PMI. *Program Management Professional* (PgMP)® *Examination Content Outline*, 2011, 6

131. c. Prepare program and component cost estimates

     Program and component cost estimates are the outputs of the Estimate Program Costs process. The program cost estimate is typically prepared in stages and becomes more detailed as additional information becomes available.

     PMI®, *The Standard for Program Management*, 2008, 220

132. a. Highlight any risks

     The decision record and meeting minutes from the gate review also highlights any risks as the component program completes one phase and moves to the next phase. Risks can be categorized as high, medium, and manageable ones. Often phase transition may proceed even through a number of high risks have been identified.

     PMI®, *The Standard for Program Management*, 2008, 262

133. a. At the program level

     To achieve consistency at the program level across all construction activities, the subcontractor selection process should be defined at the program level.

     PMI®, *The Standard for Program Management*, 2008, 198

134. b. Analyze the change request

     The Monitor and Control Program Scope process involves managing the scope as the program is executed to ensure successful completion. Each potential change needs to be analyzed, and impacts need to be identified.

     PMI®, *The Standard for Program Management*, 2008, 121

135. b. Focus groups

Focus groups are useful to provide a deeper understanding of the program impacts than can be done through individual interviews or a questionnaire; they provide feedback from groups of stakeholders regarding their attitude toward the program and approaches for communications and impact mitigation.

PMI®, *The Standard for Program Management*, 2008, 234

136. c. Stakeholder inventory

The Stakeholder Inventory provides a comprehensive summary of how each stakeholder and stakeholder group will be impacted by the program, an assessment of the likely stakeholder responses, identified issues, and planned mitigation approaches.

PMI®, *The Standard for Program Management*, 2008, 235

137. d. Program D

The payback period can be determined by dividing the initial fixed investment in the program by the estimated annual net cash inflows. In this example, the payback period for Program D is 2.2 years, and it should be selected.

PMI. *Program Management Professional* (PgMP)® *Examination Content Outline*, April 2011 6

Milosevic, Martinelli, and Waddell, *Program Management for Improved Business Results*, 2011, 21 and 42

138. c. Have service level agreements

The Administer Program Procurements process involves program-level contracts. In some cases, service level agreements (SLAs) are used in place of formal contracts for delivery of ongoing services.

PMI®, *The Standard for Program Management*, 2008, 198

139. b. Scope

Typically, order-of-magnitude estimates are prepared for cost, scope, and effort. These estimates may be called feasibility studies or may be part of feasibility studies that are completed before the program officially begins.

PMI®, *The Standard for Program Management*, 2008, 42

140. a. Use project management to perform the upgrade

    Delivered benefits must be sustained when the program is over. It may be necessary to assure that ongoing product support adds value by managing the post-production life cycle. Project management is often used to deliver upgrades to the product during its life cycle.

    PMI®, *The Standard for Program Management*, 2008, 31

141. c. Manage Program Resources

    During program execution, this process allows for the adjustment and reallocation of resources to meet the needs of the individual projects and related non-project work.

    PMI®, *The Standard for Program Management*, 2008, 57 and 91

142. a. Stakeholder management strategy

    Stakeholder meetings serve two main purposes: communicating program status and hearing issues and concerns of the stakeholders. These issues and concerns then are captured in the stakeholder issue inventory and lead to an update of the stakeholder management strategy.

    PMI®, *The Standard for Program Management*, 2008, 236 and 238

143. c. Program C

    In using net present value (NPV) as a selection criterion, the time value of money is considered based on the fact that a dollar one year from now is worth less than a dollar today. The more the future is discounted (that is, the higher the discount rate), then the less the NPV of the program. If the NPV is higher, then the program is rated higher. In this situation, you would select Program C.

    Milosevic, *Project Management ToolBox: Tools and Techniques for the Practicing Project Manager*, 2003, 43–44

    PMI. *Program Management Professional* (PgMP)® *Examination Content Outline*, 2011, 6

144. a. Baseline budget

    The program financial management plan is an output of the Develop Program Financial Plan process, which documents the program's financial information, such as funding schedules and milestones, the baseline budget, contract payments and schedules, financial reporting processes and methods, and any financial metrics that are used.

    PMI®, *The Standard for Program Management*, 2008, 216

145. c. Checklists

    Checklists are a tool and technique in the Plan Program Quality process. These checklists can be very helpful in ensuring that items are not missed as well as in reducing the time it takes to develop quality management plans.

    PMI®, *The Standard for Program Management*, 2008, 256

146. a. Request for information (RFI)

    The request for information (RFI) is a tool and technique of the Conduct Program Procurements process. The purpose of the RFI is to help the organization to formulate its requirements and identify qualified sellers.

    PMI®, *The Standard for Program Management*, 2008, 195

147. d. Risk avoidance

    Benefits tend to be categorized as tangible and intangible. However risk avoidance should be considered as a further benefit as in many instances risk avoidance can be the main driver for a change.

    PMI. *Program Management Professional* (PgMP)® *Examination Content Outline*, 2011, 13

    Williams, D. and Parr, T. (2006) Enterprise Programme Management. New York: Palgrave Macmillan, p. 179

148. c. Ways to ensure all stages of the program are managed in a way to satisfy the use of the program's outputs

    The benefits realization plan identifies the business benefits and documents their realization. Among other items, it should ensure all stages of the program are managed in a way to satisfy the utilization of the program's outputs, since the objective of managing by programs is to ensure there are more benefits than if projects were managed in a standalone way.

    PMI®. *The Standard for Program Management*, 2008, 109

149. d. Business strategy

     Benefits management, as part of enterprise program management, directs business change toward valuable, desired results. To identify, measure, track, and communicate benefits effectively, one needs knowledge, skills, and competencies in business strategy. It is necessary to ensure the program is in alignment with the organization's strategic plan, objectives, priorities, vision, and mission statement.

     PMI®. *The Standard for Program Management*, 2008, 25

     PMI. *Program Management Professional* (PgMP)® *Examination Content Outline*, 2011, 6

     David Williams and Tim Parr, *Enterprise Program Management Delivering Value*, 2006, 169

150. b. Develop a qualified seller list

     The program manager negotiates and finalizes program-wide policies and agreements. Qualified seller lists are a tool and technique in the Conduct Program Procurements process. If available, these lists can facilitate the procurement process, as procurement documents can be sent to these prospective sellers to gauge interest and to see whether they want to present a proposal or quotation.

     PMI®, *The Standard for Program Management*, 2008, 195

151. d. Manage risk in accordance with the risk management plan

     Using contractors is a way to transfer risks. All risks, however, need to be managed in accordance with the risk management plan in order to ensure benefit realization.

     PMI. *Program Management Professional* (PgMP)® *Examination Content Outline*, 2011, 11

152. d. You realize project stakeholders are also program stakeholders

     The stakeholder inventory identifies stakeholders and their roles and responsibilities. Each component project also will have stakeholder management guidelines to be considered at the program level. The project stakeholders are also program stakeholders since dissatisfaction by project stakeholders can negatively impact stakeholder acceptance criteria of the whole program.

     PMI®, *The Standard for Program Management*, 2008, 238

153. c. Follow the Monitor and Control Program Changes process

    Gate review requests are formal in nature and contain supporting documentation to facilitate board decisions. However, program and component changes should follow the Monitor and Control Program Changes process before the governance board is approached for a final decision.

    PMI®, *The Standard for Program Management*, 2008, 261

154. b. Use audit reports

    The audit plan is part of the plan and establish governance process. Audit reports from both planned and unplanned audits are an example of external viewpoints to use as a check and balance opinion for governance decisions.

    PMI®, *The Standard for Program Management*, 2008, 261

155. b. A strong connection between execution output and strategic objectives

    Organizational culture is an important part of the success of program management. If executives view development efforts as strategic and linked to the success of the business rather than as tactical, program management is recommended.

    PMI®, *The Standard for Program Management*, 2008, 14–15 and 23

    PMI. *Program Management Professional* (PgMP)® *Examination Content Outline*, 2011, 6

    Milosevic, Martinelli, and Waddell, *Program Management for Improved Business Results*, 2007, 430–431

156. d. Financial reports

    The status report, financial report, and resource deviation report are examples of reports submitted to the governance board to assist the board members in its oversight and control role. They also may wish to review analysis results, recommendations, proposals, or alternatives made by team members and/or from subject matter experts.

    PMI®, *The Standard for Program Management*, 2008, 261

157. c. Communications

    Communications are the primary tool for managing stakeholders; negotiation, conflict management, and influencing are also important, but communications are the most important competency for program managers.

    PMI®, *The Standard for Program Management*, 2008, 12 and 241

158. b. Propose a solution to these risks escalated by the project managers

    As the program manager, you must resolve issues raised by your project managers. When risks remain unresolved, the program manager ensures that they are escalated progressively higher in the organization until they are resolved.

    PMI®, *The Standard for Program Management*, 2008, 158

159. b. Program B

    Programs should have a strategic fit with the organization's long-term goals. In this example, Program B fully supports four of the five goals.

    PMI®, *The Standard for Program Management*, 2008, 23

    Milosevic, Martinelli, and Waddell, *Program Management for Improved Business Results*, 2007, 286

160. b. Document the relevant parties' responsibilities regarding risk.

    At the program level, responsibility in the Conduct Program Procurements process is to negotiate and finalize various agreements that will support the project components and other ongoing work of the program. If these agreements involve insurance or services to protect the program, it is necessary to document the relative parties' responsibilities regarding potential risks and incorporate them into program files.

    PMI®, *The Standard for Program Management*, 2008, 192

161. c. Promote continuous improvement

    Project governance ensures governance is in place, and feedback is received to improve the components and the program; therefore, governance is internal-looking where continuous improvement of the governance process and its framework can be fostered.

    PMI®, *The Standard for Program Management*, 2008, 260

162. c. Determine how the program will help the organization meet its business and strategic goals

There are many reasons why a business case should be prepared, and its primary reason is to answer the following critical question: "How will this program help our company meet its business and strategic goals?" With a business case, all crucial information for the program is included. It then is used to assess the feasibility of investing in the program based on cost, benefit, and business risk and once prepared can provide the vision to guide program planning and execution.

PMI®. *The Standard for Program Management*, 2008, 23

Milosevic, Martinelli, and Waddell, *Program Management for Improved Business Results*, 2007, 284

163. c. Program budget allocations

The program budget allocations are an input to the Plan Program Procurements process. The program budget takes into account all individual component budgets. Where possible, costs can and should be shared across components. It is the responsibility of the program manager to determine the best use of funds when allocating the budget.

PMI®, *The Standard for Program Management*, 2008, 189

164. d. Review the benefits realization plan

The benefits realization plan, among other items, should ensure the planned program outcomes have been achieved prior to formal closure of the program. This is a key component of the plan, and it requires review by the program manager, sponsor, key stakeholders, and members of the Governance Board before official closure.

PMI®, *The Standard for Program Management*, 2008, 109

165. a. Market needs and expectations

Market knowledge is required to understand customer and end-user expectations. Such knowledge is helpful in making the business case for a program, because it provides information—such as market size, market segmentation, and sales potential—that will increase the probability of program and organizational success.

Milosevic, Martinelli, and Waddell, *Program Management for Improved Business Results*, 2007, 368

PMI. *Program Management Professional* (PgMP)® *Examination Content Outline*, 2011, 6

166. a. Review your program charter

In addition to linking the program to the ongoing operations of the organization, the program charter defines the program manager's level of authority and responsibility. Thus, it is an input to the Plan Program Procurements process.

PMI®, *The Standard for Program Management*, 2008, 189

167. c. Using mentoring

Mentoring can be used effectively in this scenario to model the appropriate behavior these two project managers should follow especially as they learn the various standard processes to use. As they gain confidence, the mentoring relationship then can change from one that is less formal and is more consultative as they will not need your active involvement as often.

PMI. *Program Management Professional* (PgMP)® *Examination Content Outline*, 2011, 10

168. c. Quality

Changes on programs should be managed in accordance with the change management plan in order to control scope, quality, schedule, cost, contacts, risks, and rewards.

PMI. *Program Management Professional* (PgMP)® *Examination Content Outline*, 2011, 11

169. b. Describe the business opportunity and product, service, or result that you are proposing

Before going into detail in the business case, first define the business opportunity. Then, relate it to the organization's strategic goals and show the benefits associated with this program. Later, describe the cost/benefit analysis and other financial benefits, intangible benefits, and the risk and complexity.

PMI®. *The Standard for Program Management*, 2008, 23

PMI. *Program Management Professional* (PgMP)® *Examination Content Outline*, 2011, 6

Milosevic, Martinelli, and Waddell, *Program Management for Improved Business Results*, 2007, 285

170. a. Who will ensure architectural principles are not violated?

     A number of questions should be answered to determine the roles and responsibilities for the governance board, one of which is ensuring architecture principles are not violated. This question is significant since the program architecture serves as the technical baseline for the program.

     PMI®. *The Standard for Program Management*, 2008, 249

Appendix: Study Matrix

Overview

In 2006, the Project Management Institute (PMI®) published the *Program Management Professional (PgMP®) Examination Specification*. PMI® also published the *Standard for Program Management* and began to offer the PgMP® credential. In 2011, PMI® released a new Examination Specification based on a new Role Delineation Study it conducted, titled as the *Program Management Professional (PgMP®) Examination Content Outline*. This *Examination Content Outline* and the *Standard for Program Management—Second Edition (2008)* serve as the foundation for the PgMP® certification exam.

The distribution of our two practice tests is as follows:

	I	Strategic Program Management	15% or 25 questions
	II	Initiating the Program	6% or 10 questions
	III	Planning the Program	11% or 19 questions
	IV	Executing the Program	14% or 17 questions
Performance Domain	V	Controlling the Program	10% or 17 questions
	VI	Closing the Program	3% or 5 questions
	VII	Benefits Management	11% or 19 questions
	VIII	Stakeholder Management	16% or 27 questions
	IX	Governance	14% or 24 questions

The matrixes for both practice tests are included following this Appendix and identify each practice test question according to its performance domain for the relevant practice test.

Each matrix is designed to help you to—

■ Assess your strengths and weaknesses in each of the performance domains
■ Identify those areas in which you need additional study before you take the PgMP® exam

Here is an easy way to use each matrix:

■ Step 1: Circle all the questions that you missed on the practice test in Column 1.
■ Step 2: For each circled question, note the corresponding performance domain in Column 2.
■ Step 3: To determine whether any patterns emerge indicating weak areas, tally the information that you obtained from the matrix.
■ Step 4: To ensure that you have a good understanding of the knowledge and skills required to perform the major tasks that are included in each of the domains, as well as the content of the program management processes described in PMI®'s *The Standard for Program Management*, we strongly suggest that you use *The Standard* as well as the *Program Management Professional (PgMP®) Examination Content Outline* for study purposes. The *Standard for Program Management – Second Edition* (2008) may be purchased directly from the PMI® Bookstore at www.PMI.org. The *Examination Content Outline* can be downloaded from the www.pmi.org web site.

The last column in the matrix is provided for your notes.

Study Matrix—Practice Test 1

Practice Test Question Number	Performance Domain	Study Notes
1	Strategic Program Management	
2	Executing	
3	Stakeholder Management	
4	Initiating	
5	Governance	
6	Strategic Program Management	
7	Benefits Management	
8	Benefits Management	
9	Planning	
10	Stakeholder Management	
11	Strategic Program Management	
12	Controlling	
13	Planning	
14	Planning	
15	Executing	
16	Benefits Management	
17	Governance	
18	Strategic Program Management	
19	Initiating	
20	Executing	

Practice Test Question Number	Performance Domain	Study Notes
21	Planning	
22	Planning	
23	Controlling	
24	Executing	
25	Stakeholder Management	
26	Strategic Program Management	
27	Benefits Management	
28	Initiating	
29	Executing	
30	Controlling	
31	Closing	
32	Executing	
33	Controlling	
34	Strategic Program Management	
35	Strategic Program Management	
36	Stakeholder Management	
37	Stakeholder Management	
38	Executing	
39	Governance	
40	Benefits Management	

Practice Test Question Number	Performance Domain	Study Notes
41	Controlling	
42	Stakeholder Management	
43	Strategic Program Management	
44	Governance	
45	Executing	
46	Closing	
47	Planning	
48	Stakeholder Management	
49	Strategic Program Management	
50	Planning	
51	Benefits Management	
52	Stakeholder Management	
53	Controlling	
54	Initiating	
55	Strategic Program Management	
56	Planning	
57	Stakeholder Management	
58	Stakeholder Management	
59	Governance	
60	Executing	

Practice Test Question Number	Performance Domain	Study Notes
61	Benefits Management	
62	Strategic Program Management	
63	Executing	
64	Stakeholder Management	
65	Initiating	
66	Governance	
67	Benefits Management	
68	Strategic Program Management	
69	Executing	
70	Stakeholder Management	
71	Governance	
72	Initiating	
73	Closing	
74	Governance	
75	Executing	
76	Stakeholder Management	
77	Controlling	
78	Stakeholder Management	
79	Governance	
80	Strategic Program Management	

Practice Test Question Number	Performance Domain	Study Notes
81	Controlling	
82	Benefits Management	
83	Executing	
84	Governance	
85	Planning	
86	Stakeholder Management	
87	Governance	
88	Strategic Program Management	
89	Planning	
90	Executing	
91	Governance	
92	Controlling	
93	Governance	
94	Strategic Program Management	
95	Planning	
96	Stakeholder Management	
97	Executing	
98	Controlling	
99	Strategic Program Management	
100	Initiating	

Practice Test Question Number	Performance Domain	Study Notes
101	Planning	
102	Benefits Management	
103	Controlling	
104	Stakeholder Management	
105	Planning	
106	Controlling	
107	Strategic Program Management	
108	Executing	
109	Closing	
110	Benefits Management	
111	Initiating	
112	Executing	
113	Controlling	
114	Controlling	
115	Strategic Program Management	
116	Planning	
117	Benefits Management	
118	Benefits Management	
119	Executing	
120	Executing	

Practice Test Question Number	Performance Domain	Study Notes
121	Governance	
122	Strategic Program Management	
123	Benefits Management	
124	Benefits Management	
125	Planning	
126	Governance	
127	Executing	
128	Executing	
129	Stakeholder Management	
130	Stakeholder Management	
131	Strategic Program Management	
132	Governance	
133	Stakeholder Management	
134	Controlling	
135	Governance	
136	Initiating	
137	Planning	
138	Executing	
139	Governance	
140	Stakeholder Management	

Practice Test Question Number	Performance Domain	Study Notes
141	Governance	
142	Strategic Program Management	
143	Executing	
144	Benefits Management	
145	Planning	
146	Stakeholder Management	
147	Planning	
148	Controlling	
149	Governance	
150	Stakeholder Management	
151	Strategic Program Management	
152	Governance	
153	Benefits Management	
154	Governance	
155	Stakeholder Management	
156	Strategic Program Management	
157	Closing	
158	Stakeholder Management	
159	Governance	
160	Benefits Management	

Practice Test Question Number	Performance Domain	Study Notes
161	Strategic Program Management	
162	Initiating	
163	Planning	
164	Executing	
165	Controlling	
166	Stakeholder Management	
167	Strategic Program Management	
168	Governance	
169	Stakeholder Management	
170	Benefits Management	

Study Matrix—Practice Test 2

Practice Test Question Number	Performance Domain	Study Notes
1	Benefits Management	
2	Strategic Program Management	
3	Executing	
4	Initiating	
5	Executing	
6	Controlling	
7	Strategic Program Management	
8	Planning	
9	Closing	
10	Executing	
11	Stakeholder Management	
12	Benefits Management	
13	Controlling	
14	Governance	
15	Initiating	
16	Strategic Program Management	
17	Executing	
18	Governance	
19	Planning	
20	Controlling	

Practice Test Question Number	Performance Domain	Study Notes
21	Governance	
22	Benefits Management	
23	Strategic Program Management	
24	Strategic Program Management	
25	Executing	
26	Governance	
27	Planning	
28	Controlling	
29	Closing	
30	Initiating	
31	Planning	
32	Benefits Management	
33	Strategic Program Management	
34	Executing	
35	Stakeholder Management	
36	Controlling	
37	Governance	
38	Planning	
39	Planning	
40	Controlling	

Practice Test Question Number	Performance Domain	Study Notes
41	Strategic Program Management	
42	Initiating	
43	Executing	
44	Benefits Management	
45	Stakeholder Management	
46	Stakeholder Management	
47	Executing	
48	Strategic Program Management	
49	Benefits Management	
50	Stakeholder Management	
51	Governance	
52	Controlling	
53	Benefits Management	
54	Benefits Management	
55	Strategic Program Management	
56	Governance	
57	Stakeholder Management	
58	Benefits Management	
59	Stakeholder Management	
60	Planning	

Practice Test Question Number	Performance Domain	Study Notes
61	Executing	
62	Controlling	
63	Stakeholder Management	
64	Stakeholder Management	
65	Benefits Management	
66	Governance	
67	Stakeholder Management	
68	Initiating	
69	Strategic Program Management	
70	Benefits Management	
71	Benefits Management	
72	Planning	
73	Controlling	
74	Executing	
75	Executing	
76	Executing	
77	Stakeholder Management	
78	Strategic Program Management	
79	Stakeholder Management	
80	Governance	

Practice Test Question Number	Performance Domain	Study Notes
81	Stakeholder Management	
82	Stakeholder Management	
83	Executing	
84	Controlling	
85	Governance	
86	Stakeholder Management	
87	Strategic Program Management	
88	Initiating	
89	Governance	
90	Stakeholder Management	
91	Planning	
92	Controlling	
93	Stakeholder Management	
94	Stakeholder Management	
95	Stakeholder Management	
96	Governance	
97	Benefits Management	
98	Strategic Program Management	
99	Executing	
100	Governance	

Practice Test Question Number	Performance Domain	Study Notes
101	Initiating	
102	Initiating	
103	Planning	
104	Governance	
105	Strategic Program Management	
106	Executing	
107	Governance	
108	Closing	
109	Benefits Management	
110	Stakeholder Management	
111	Stakeholder Management	
112	Governance	
113	Stakeholder Management	
114	Strategic Program Management	
115	Planning	
116	Planning	
117	Executing	
118	Executing	
119	Controlling	
120	Closing	

Practice Test Question Number	Performance Domain	Study Notes
121	Strategic Program Management	
122	Governance	
123	Executing	
124	Controlling	
125	Initiating	
126	Planning	
127	Benefits Management	
128	Benefits Management	
129	Governance	
130	Strategic Program Management	
131	Planning	
132	Governance	
133	Executing	
134	Controlling	
135	Stakeholder Management	
136	Stakeholder Management	
137	Strategic Program Management	
138	Controlling	
139	Initiating	
140	Closing	

Practice Test Question Number	Performance Domain	Study Notes
141	Executing	
142	Stakeholder Management	
143	Strategic Program Management	
144	Planning	
145	Planning	
146	Executing	
147	Benefits Management	
148	Benefits Management	
149	Strategic Program Management	
150	Executing	
151	Controlling	
152	Stakeholder Management	
153	Governance	
154	Governance	
155	Strategic Program Management	
156	Governance	
157	Stakeholder Management	
158	Planning	
159	Strategic Program Management	
160	Executing	

Practice Test Question Number	Performance Domain	Study Notes
161	Governance	
162	Strategic Program Management	
163	Planning	
164	Benefits Management	
165	Strategic Program Management	
166	Planning	
167	Executing	
168	Controlling	
169	Strategic Program Management	
170	Governance	

References

Levin, Ginger and Allen R. Green. *Implementing Program Management. Templates and Forms Aligned with the Standard for Program Management—Second Edition* (2008). Boca Raton, FL: CRC Press. 2010.

Levin, Ginger and J. LeRoy Ward. *Program Management Complexity: A Competency Model*. Boca Raton, FL: CRC Press, 2011.

Milosevic, Dragan Z. *Project Management Toolbox: Tools and Techniques for the Practicing Project Manager*. Hoboken, NJ: John Wiley & Sons, Inc., 2003.

Milosevic, Dragan Z., Russ J. Martinelli, and James M. Waddell. *Program Management for Improved Business Results*. Hoboken, NJ: John Wiley & Sons, Inc., 2007.

Pritchard, Carl L. *The Project Management Drill Book: A Self-Study Guide*. Arlington, VA: ESI International, 2003.

Project Management Institute. *Program Management Professional (PgMP®) Examination Content Outline*. Newtown Square, PA: Project Management Institute, 2011.

Project Management Institute. *A Guide to the Project Management Body of Knowledge (PMBOK® Guide), 4th ed*. Newtown Square, PA: Project Management Institute, 2008.

Project Management Institute. *The Standard for Program Management, 2nd ed*. Newtown Square, PA: Project Management Institute, 2008.

Ward, J. LeRoy. *Dictionary of Project Management Terms, 3rd ed*. Arlington, VA: ESI International, 2008.

Williams, David, and Tim Parr. *Enterprise Programme Management: Delivering Value*. New York: Palgrave Macmillan, 2006.